I'm a Park and You're a Deer

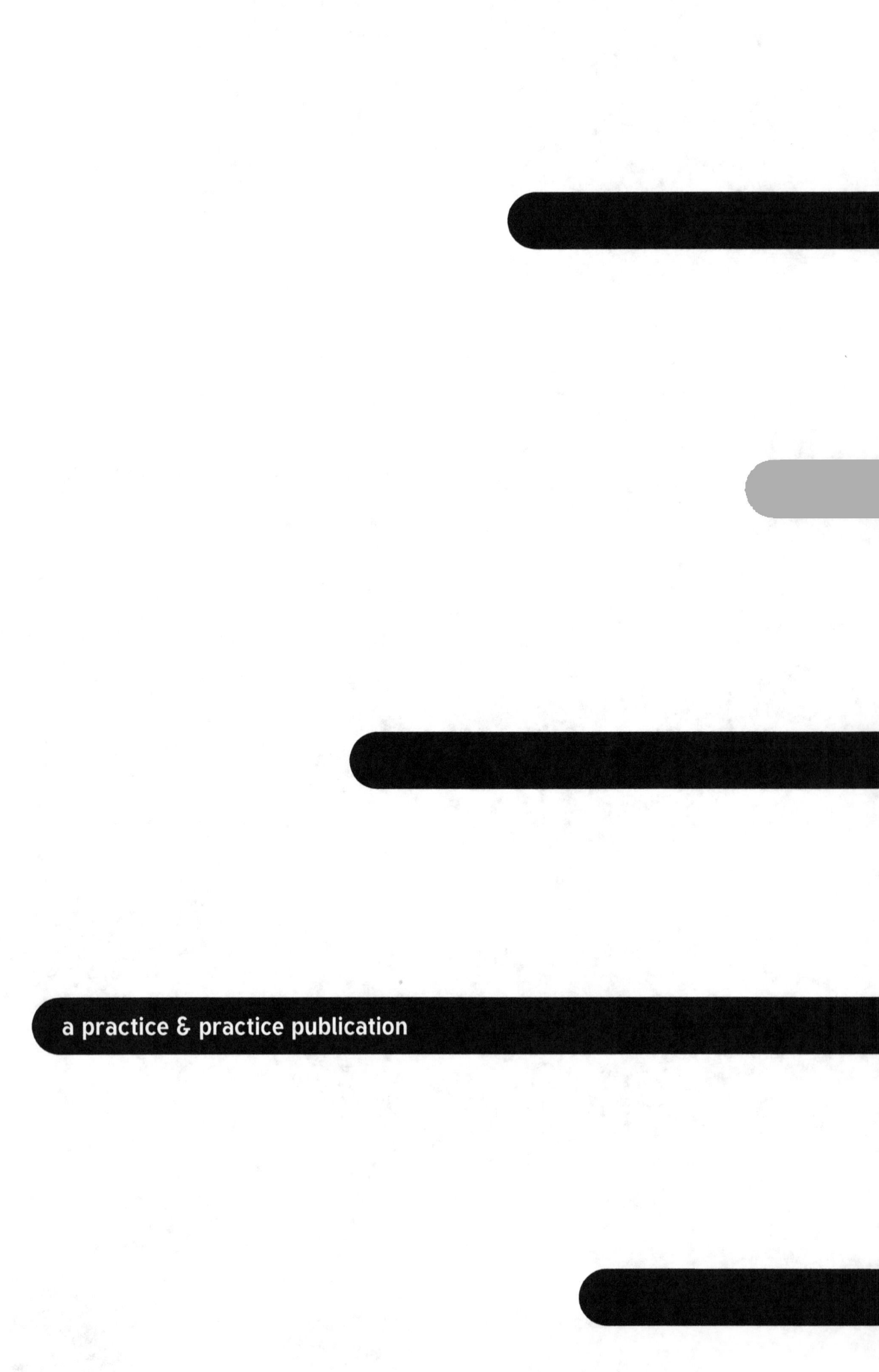

a practice & practice publication

I'm a Park and You're a Deer

First published 2009
by Practice and Practice
http://practiceandpractice.org

This book was produced through the generous support of the Alternative Exposure Grant from Southern Exposure and in collaboration with the Social Practices Area of Concentration at the California College of the Arts.

Editors: Malak Helmy, Forrest Lewinger, Anthony Marcellini, Lauren Marsden, Lynne McCabe, Rebecca Ora, Piero Passacantando, Matthew Rana, Ruth Robbins, Brindalyn Webster, Anna Whitehead, and Wafaa Yasin

Contributing Authors: Iain Boal, Amy Franceschini, Malak Helmy, Forrest Lewinger, Anthony Marcellini, marksearch, Lauren Marsden, Lynne McCabe, Myvillages, Oda Projesi, Rebecca Ora, Piero Passacantando, Ted Purves, Matthew Rana, Ruth Robbins, Michael Swaine, Nick Tobier, Brindalyn Webster, Anna Whitehead, Wafaa Yasin

Design and project direction: Sara Thacher

Special Thanks to: Wapke Feenstra, Fritz Haeg, Mika Hannula, Hope Hilton, Henrik Lebuhn, Marina McDougall, Oda Projesi, Antje Schiffers, Sara Thacher, Nick Tobier, Daniel Tucker, Rosten Woo, the wonderful staff at the San Francisco main public library, especially Wendy in the San Francisco history room, Dodie Bellamy and Dennis Maness

I'm a Park and You're a Deer

ISBN 978-0-578-02231-4

Contents

'Fondling,' she saith, 'since I have hemm'd thee here
Within the circuit of this ivory pale,
I'll be a park, and thou shalt be my deer;
Feed where thou wilt, on mountain or in dale:
Graze on my lips; and if those hills be dry,
Stray lower, where the pleasant fountains lie.

Within this limit is relief enough,
Sweet bottom-grass and high delightful plain,
Round rising hillocks, brakes obscure and rough,
To shelter thee from tempest and from rain
Then be my deer, since I am such a park;
No dog shall rouse thee, though a thousand bark.'

From the poem "Venus and Adonis" by William Shakespeare.

Reflections on a Title

Anthony Marcellini

This book began in the CCA Social Practice workshop as a discussion on public space with Golden Gate Park serving as a potential site of fieldwork. The park is in a perpetual state of mutation – it is complicated by each of us—and it stands unto itself as a site of pleasure and curiosity as much as it embodies the legal, social, material and symbolic desires that form the city. Battling historical and political narratives, the construction of publics and counter-publics, the condition of leisure space and forms of ecology all became part of our dialogue through a collective investigation. Our title, "I'm a Park and You're a Deer" connects us to this book's origin: a classroom, and a collective investigation of a vast public space, Golden Gate Park.

As the title for our book we chose a line paraphrased from "Venus and Adonis", a poem by William Shakespeare. This poem represents not simply a struggle between two fabled lovers but also a struggle between power/control and freedom. "Venus and Adonis" concerns the love of a god for a mortal who the god knows will eventually die as all mortals do. Adonis was a hunter and is eventually killed by an animal he hunts, a boar. Venus tries to save Adonis from certain death by containing him in a park (Venus) and transforming him into a deer (Adonis). Venus implores that within these confines Adonis will have everything he desires: sustenance, beauty and her. Likewise, she will have everything she desires: Adonis, contained and free from death but at the expense of his freedom. Adonis however, rejects this suggestion of containment, thereby rejecting Venus' love and is later killed.

In this poem the park represents a god, which could also stand for the state or the law. The deer represents a mortal, a human being, which could also symbolize choice and freedom.[1] The law gives us the park, as 'our park', and it represents a free space in which all our desires are fulfilled; we are given grass lawns, perambulating walkways, flowers, tennis courts, golf, science museums, children's playgrounds, et cetera. However, this park is not free. It is confined: there are invisible borders, rules, laws, order et cetera. We are supposed to be content with this free and public space, yet we are aware of the control that defines and governs it. We are aware of the limit, 'Within this limit.'[2] It is in our nature as human beings to resist limits, though we know there are repercussions: the law and death. It seems that this year's social practice class is interested in precisely this negotiation between the law or laws, and freedom. We are concerned with how freedom is played out in public space, whether in the home or homeland, in memory/history, in aesthetic expression, in our body, in our identity, and how it is defined by and for us and through our civic duty. All of the works in this publication illustrate and express this, whether conflicts, expressions or negotiations.

The park as public space, represents one site of limits that we are compelled to explore and test, examining how far can we push against it, how many steps forward we can take to expand the limit and how hard it pushes back. We, like Adonis, are compelled by our desire to explore beyond the ivory pale, to see what lies beyond in the shadow, in the uncertain spaces beyond the borders.

---

1 "Man is born free..." says Rousseau in the opening lines of the Social Contract.

2 "but everywhere is in chains." Rousseau's sentence concludes

Behind a Group of Trees
Piero Passacantando

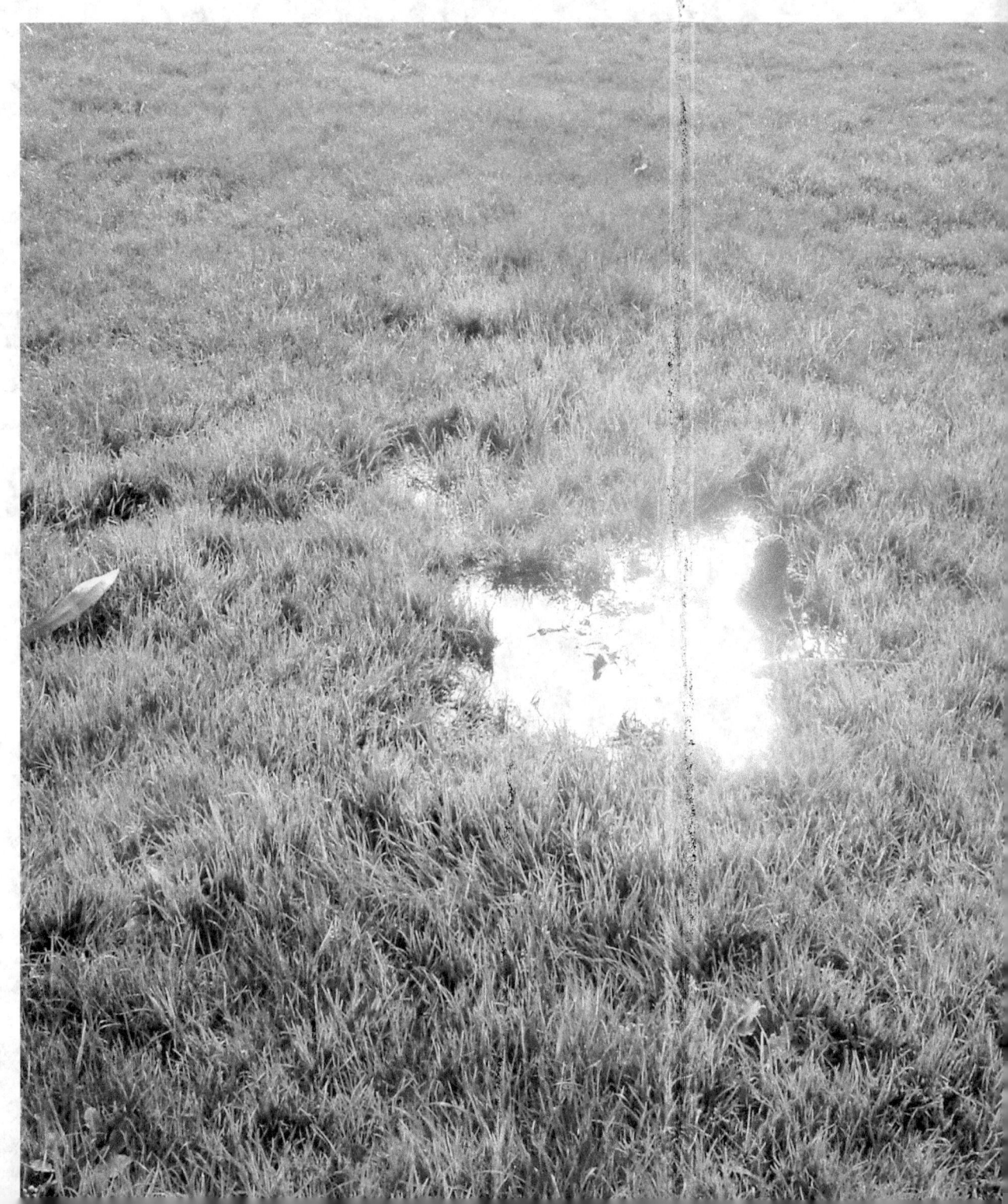

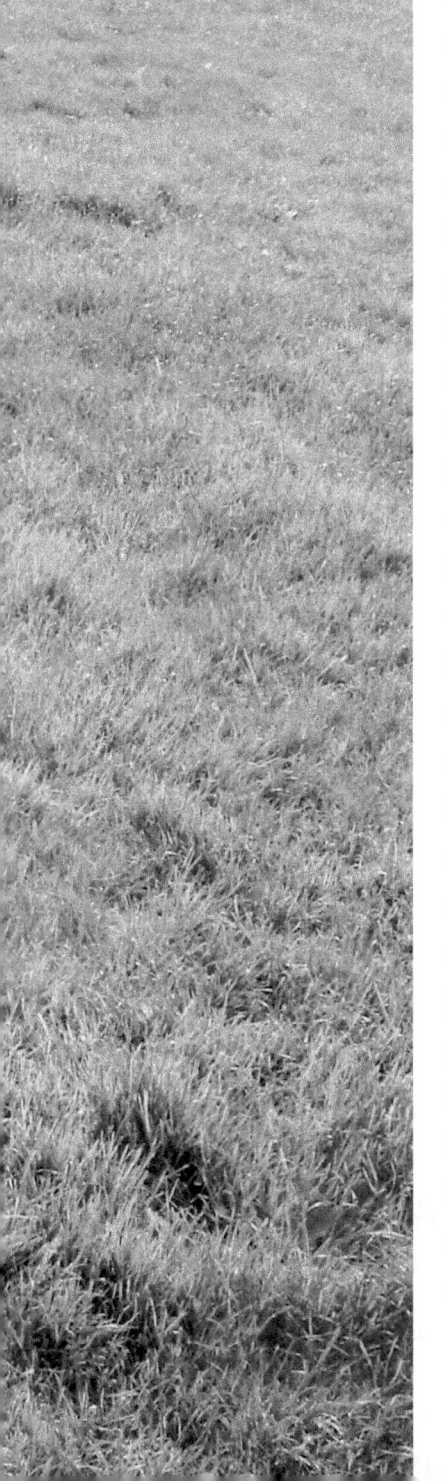

Behind a group of trees, a path. A man is walking alone through the woods. I guess he is not completely alone. I am there as well. He is a 100 feet from me, walking towards me. He stops, and observes as I walk towards him. His body is still. Only his head rotates as I walk by him. My heart beats fast. A pile of shredded documents, a large pool, a teddy bear, some police tape. A man stretches unbelievably. Do not cross. Everything here is not so real. I was here with my fiancé, her nephews and family. We went to the park playground. No adults allowed without children. Different kids are running around, playing. There is a mysterious structure on a slope. I can't tell if it is man-made or not. Green. A soccer ball props up a person like a pedestal holding a statue. I suspect many people live around here. At first I felt safe, but after walking through the woods... I am alone now. I pee on a tree. I find lots of shit and trash and toilet paper. Poor buffaloes. Floating circles. This looks like England on steroids with those flowers inside. People are living in abandoned police stables. I wish I were ballsier. I enter a path, chosen randomly. The path goes into the woods. I don't know where it is leading me. I follow my curiosity. I enter another path. This time it is because I have to go back in a certain direction. I can't change the world. You can't change the world. Motorboats versus sail boats. The noisy renegades against the silent prepsters. A battle of the remote control, a proxy of conflict. Where am I going. I feel my body. I am wearing an orange sweater. Who knows what she is doing. Brown and blue. I see a guy peeing near his car. Almost in his car. Some students are shooting a movie. One has on a giant panda head. I can change the world. Groups of people smoking pot and getting drunk. There is movement everywhere. Will I make something interesting. Things don't have an end. Goth, hippy, rave, dogs, bottles. What am I going to make. Fly fishing in the artificial blue. A grid of falsity. I feel my arms swinging at my sides. Green, green, green. I move the leaves apart with my hands. A spider-web on my face. My shoe sinks in the mud

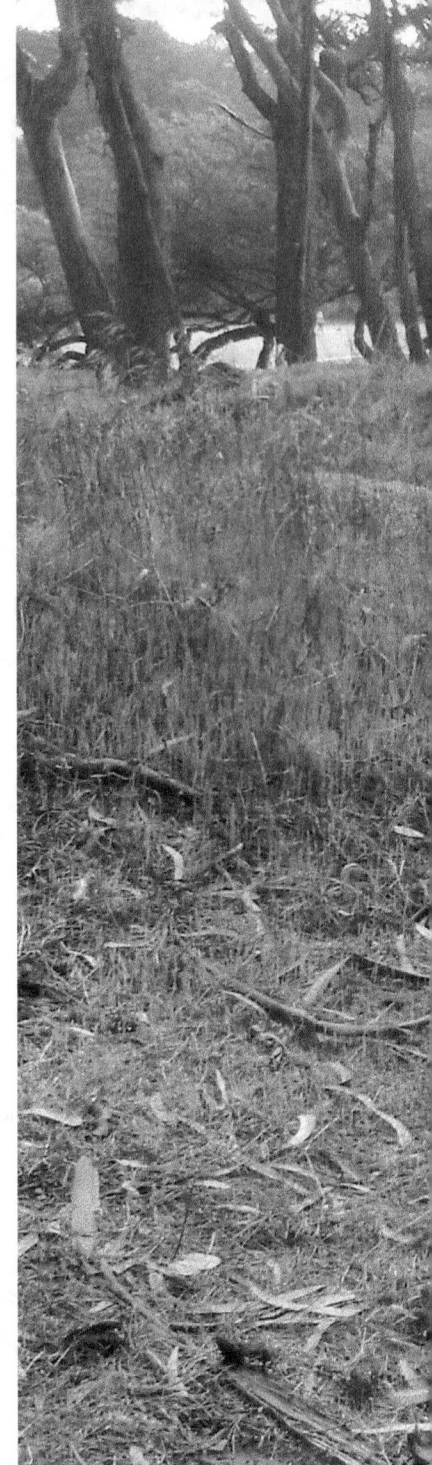

and the lake is only one foot wide. The wind swooshes through the leaves. Coots are swimming and a married couple heads for the future. They gave us cups, luckily. Strollers. Where is the dissent. The distance between abstraction and realism. High schoolers are racing around the polo field and proceed to run elsewhere through the woods up the hill. A dude plays with a stick. I hope to find someone fucking somewhere. I have never seen anyone else fucking in real life, I mean in front of me, and I want to. Death. They have BBQ pork sandwiches and Buddha dogs and tea gardens. There are paths for exercising, and sprouts come out of the ground. The sun joyfully lifts leaves of their matter. I observe vicariously, mischievously. Some trees form little spaces, either through defining ceilings or walls. These are magic spaces. You enter them. War. The sprinklers are also in the middle of the forest. Golf, Frisbee golf. Big redwoods darken the path. Their shadows glow like a flame of bark. A giant stone cross with moss growing on it, lets you know. These plants don't belong there or here, but they look okay. Yellow balls bounce back and forth. There was a bonfire here and there is a dude is in the bushes. We sat together on that lawn eating lunch. I ate a sandwich. People are playing music. A drum circle, someone has a guitar. I remember Washington, DC. Jogging, definitely jogging. Shaun wouldn't stop going down the slide on a McDonald's tray. I hope to find some hallucinogenic mushrooms. The Rose Garden, the de Young. What do you mean. Monuments for the dead in WWII. Grass and sand on top of each other. Fucking. The waterfall is in Disneyland. The cave is not a cave but a tunnel.

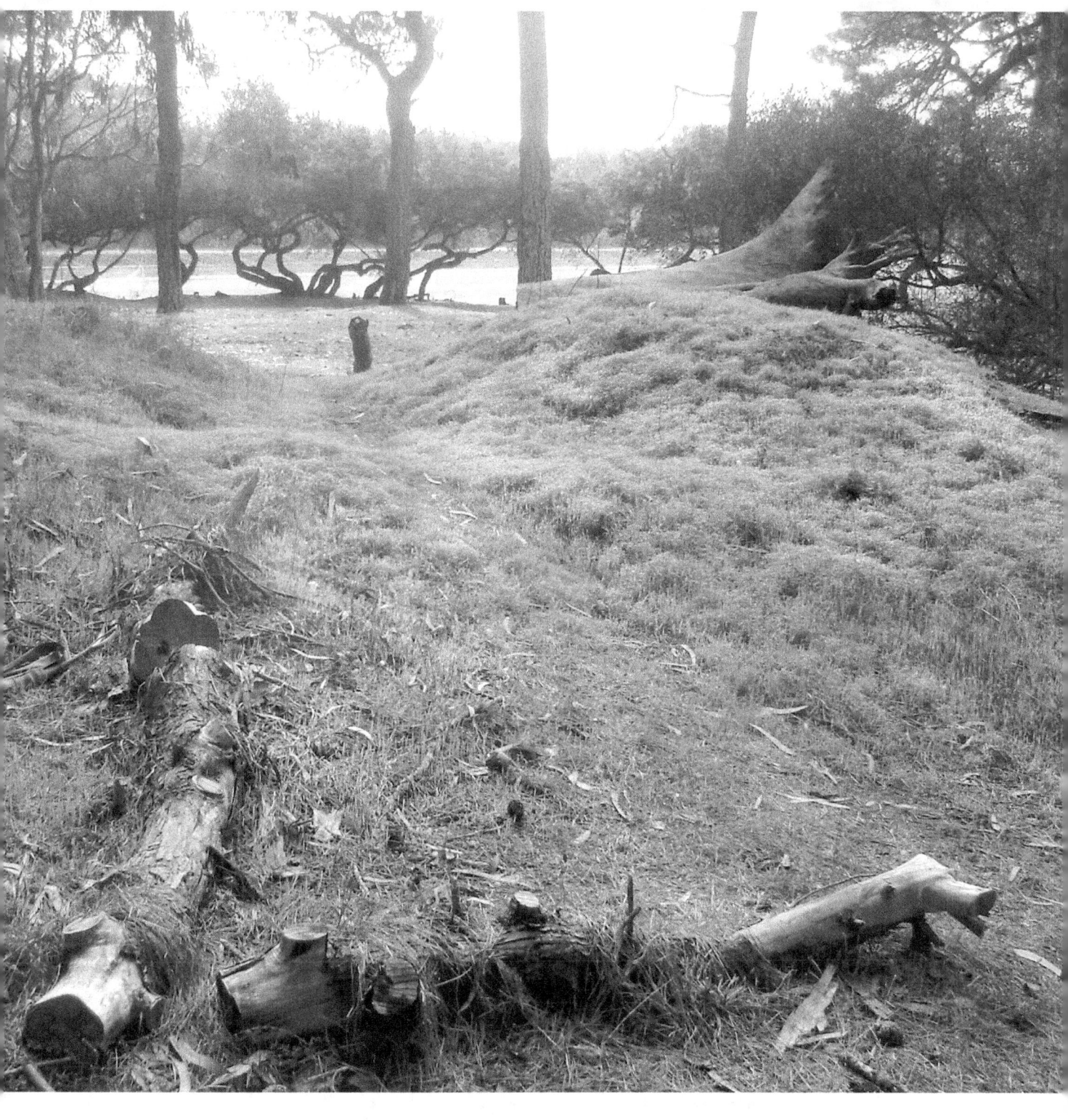

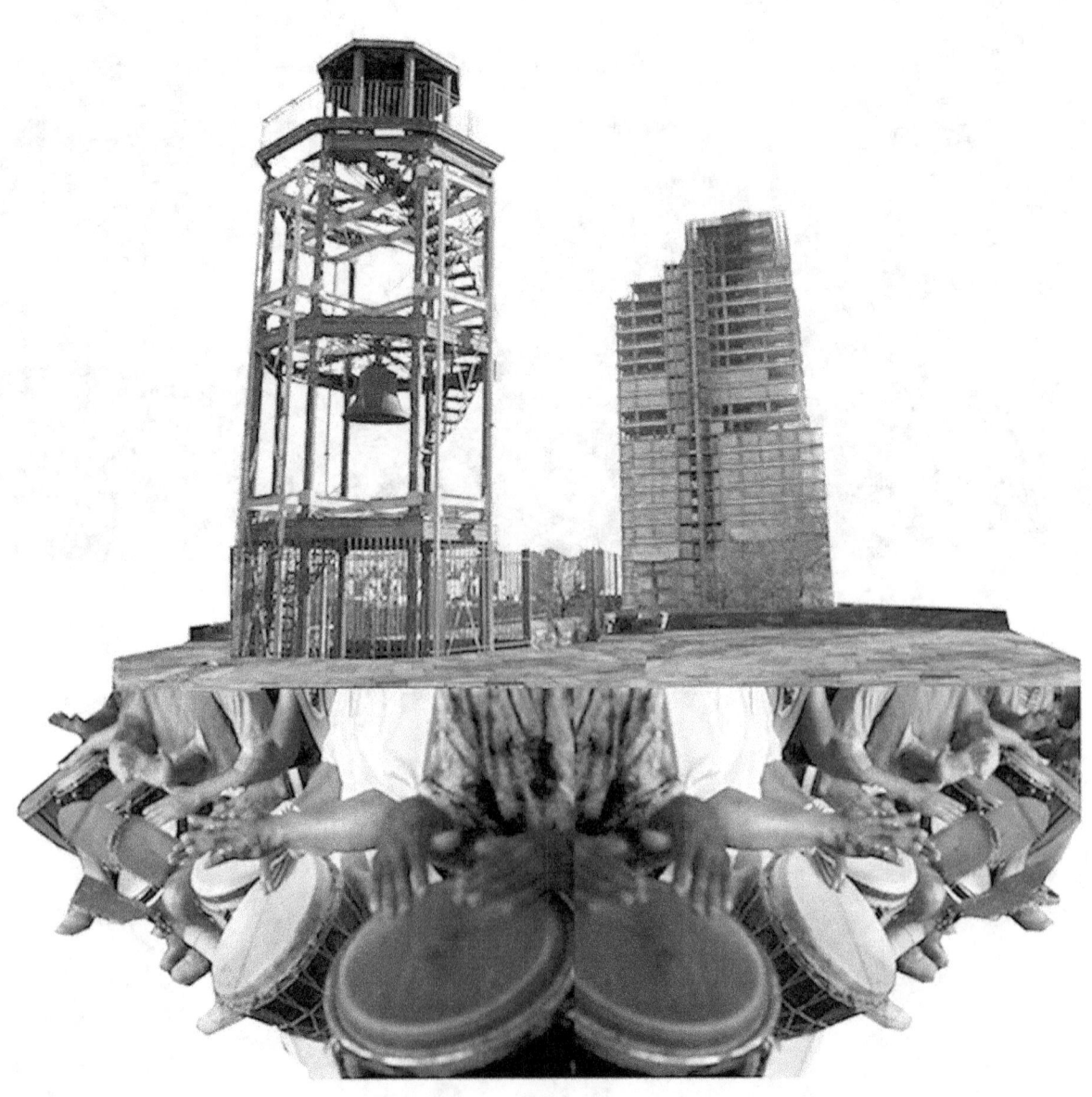

Nick Tobier

Drumming a Call for More Clamoring in Parks

There's a rumbling sound coming from Marcus Garvey Park. Like a gentle thunder as it comes closer, the sound is equal parts drum and rumbling social lives.

The Drumming Association in Harlem's Marcus Garvey Park has got itself a conflict with new arrivals to the area. The tensions around the drummers of Marcus Garvey Park—between what can be described as 'from here' and an influx of outside or invasive elements—are part of what I see as the necessarily messy role of city parks. Rumbling, social lives. How we contend with these tensions indicates our capacity to see parks as living systems—both ecologically and culturally.

Since 1969, the drummers have gathered every Saturday to play in the park—once known as Mount Morris Park, as the larger neighborhood is called. A core group of 30 men and women drum play spoons, cowbells, gourd rattles and tambourines. The group has no leader and no requirements to join. When a drummer feels a rhythm, he or she pounds out a beat. Others accept or reject it, adding their own beats. Today, across the street from the park, where there was once a vacant lot sits 2002 Fifth Avenue, a new seven-story cream and red brick luxury co-op with a doorman, one million dollar apartments and a lobby with a fireplace. The new tenants have complained about the noise the drummers make.

The drummers in the park are African-American, African and Afro-Caribbean. The circle they create has played in the park since the neighborhood was a more dangerous place. For years,

Marcus Garvey Park was a garbage-strewn home to squatters, muggers and drug dealers. On summer Saturdays, the musicians' drumming provided a window of time for the neighborhood's children to play in safety, residents said. The musicians are widely credited with helping to make the park safer over the years.

2002 Fifth Avenue is mostly occupied by young white professionals, who have a different perspective on the effect of the drums: residents say, they are unable to sleep, hear their television sets, or speak on the telephone. Some say they cannot even think straight.[1]

The conflict between the drummers and the new condo residents began when the Police, following up on noise complaints from the new residents, approached the group and asked them to stop playing as they did not have a permit. The new arrivals to Harlem, unused to the sounds of their new environment are part of a growing statistic taken from the City's Department of Environmental Protection: noise complaints have risen dramatically; there were 123 complaints in 2002, in 2008 there were 518. Agnes Johnson, a drummer, says that one of the first things slaves brought from Africa was told was to stop drumming.[2]

What to Do About New Arrivals: the roles of insiders and outsiders in parks:

> "The gardens...shall express a spirit of America, and therefore shall be free of foreign character as far as possible. The Latin and the Oriental...creep more and more over our land, coming from the South, which is settled by Latin people, and also from other centers of mixed masses of immigrants. The Germanic character of our race, of our cities and settlements, [has been] overgrown by foreign character. Latin spirit has spoiled a lot, and still spoils things every day."
>
> -Jens Jensen, designer of Chicago City parks, 1937

While the fight over the drumming association has become drawn out and racially incendiary this conflict is not without precedent in recent US park history. The drummers say we were here first, and have thrived in place in their naturalized location in the park (to continue the ecological metaphor, being native, is a function of two factors: location and time—native basically as belonging to a particular ecological region before either massive displacement or introduction of by non-native/immigrants.) The new residents have said, 'we have the right to live here too." And they do. The drummers see the new arrivals as akin to the foreign character Jensen writes of above. The new arrivals, like any invasive species, are wreaking havoc on an established cultural ecosystem as they contend for their share of the park.

At its best, the Marcus Garvey Park conflict reveals the vital role parks continue to play in our cities. At its base, is a longer history of the contentious roles planning has played in giving form to social and racial programs through parks. 19th century park reformers, notably Frederick Law Olmstead, saw parks as an antidote to the overwhelming congestion of the city. For Olmstead, parks with their emphasis on individual experience with nature served an anti-urban function, offering a retreat from the city, and regulating behavior through design that separated ages and activities from one another. What is brewing around Marcus Garvey Park is, in part, the inevitable entry of the city into the park and vice-versa, where the separation that kept contention at bay is no longer physically possible.

In *Against Nativism*,[3] author Michael Pollan pointed to a an outbreak of native-plant mania in Nazi Germany, which "saw the rise of a natural-gardening movement founded on nationalistic and racist ideas that were often cloaked in scientific jargon." Joachim Wolschke-Bulmahn, director of studies in landscape architecture at Dumbarton Oaks in Washington, DC noted that in Nazi Germany, the exclusive use of natives became the landscape architect's swastika. Some American natural landscaping pioneers who were contemporaries of Nazi landscape designers— Jens Jensen cited above—exhibited "similar tendencies toward racist argumentation."[4]

The Marcus Garvey park conflict took this type of argumentation when a racist e-mail message was circulated among residents of the new building, advocating violence against the musicians (The message read in part "Why don't we just get nooses for everyone of those lowlifes and hang them from a tree?

They're used to that kind of treatment anyway!" It added: "I hope you all agree that the best thing that has happened to Harlem is gentrification. Let's get rid of these 'people' and improve the neighborhood once and for all.") In response, The New Black Panther Party has marched in support of the drummers. The scenario has grown into a wider dispute about class, race and culture as well as a flash point in the debate over gentrification, echoing debates on either side of the anti-immigrant rhetoric that surrounded Jens Jensen's native plants cause in the 1930's.

The lines are being drawn on the wide paved sidewalks that border the park—each side insisting that they have a right to their point of view. James Goodridge, a paralegal, has volunteered his time and expertise should the dispute ever reach the courts. He believes that there is a culture clash afoot. "You have this undercurrent of trying to make New York into Omaha Nebraska and trying to get rid of certain cultures," he complains.[5]

Dufferin Grove Park/ An Open Circle

The view from the drum circle is quite different. The musicians emphasize the spiritual and cultural elements of African drumming, an activity that was banned during slavery. No one is excluded. Anyone can bring a drum and sit in or bring a blanket and watch.

It is a similar attitude of an open circle that inhabits Toronto's Dufferin Grove Park. Sitting at the center of demographically distinct neighborhoods on the city's west side, the center of Dufferin Grove Park was for years like Marcus Garvey Park—a dangerous place. A residents group saw the park as a potential hub for the different cultural contests and turned what had been a series of flash points of differing attitudes into an asset. The Friends of Dufferin Grove Park built a wood-burning oven in the center of the park. Where there is food, people gather, reasoned the Friends' Jutta Mason. Right next to the oven and the herb garden that the pizza-makers use are the basketball courts, and a series of tables where older Portuguese men play dominos and cards. Cheek by jowl, active and physical pursuits right next to herb gardens, weekly farmers' markets next to daily chats, this park is humming with action— the presence of others in public space is a source for stimulation according to Sociologist William H. Whyte.[6]

This mix of generations, activities, and ethnic demographics indicates robust social diversity, and appeals to most ecologists' bias where diversity equals health in an ecosystem. Diversity, while clearly not one of the Nazi's highest priorities, has been the history of a garden for millennia--based on the exchange and growth of plants. Likewise, dynamic urban societies have benefited greatly from this exchange, and in fact are unthinkable without it.

Imagine then, that nativeness is not an issue—that ideally we'll enter a new era of thinking about parks as something other than preserves of fragile or otherwise controlled idylls or ideals, that naturalized species and new arrivals mix freely.

While past and indeed many contemporary parks embolden the ideal park as a contention-free zone, consider that the non-human world is a continual battleground of interaction and we can envision the future of parks more as Petri dishes for more social collisions. In the 2008 film, The Visitor, the actor Richard Jenkins, plays Walter Vale, a professor whose interest in life is reignited through a chance meeting with a drummer who first teaches him to drum and then accompanies him to a fictionalized version of the Marcus Garvey circle.

Ideally the social tensions at the real Marcus Garvey Park provoke discussion, if not a condo-owning drumming set. In our parks, cultural ecologies can thrive on the creation of new communities, combining influences and contestations from around the world, where the open and complex habitats of parks add new forms to our cities. Hopefully things will get a little louder.

---

1 For further discussion, see Neanda Salvaterra, Blackstar News, Jan 11 08

2 The conflict reached beyond Harlem based media in an article by Timothy Williams, "'An Old Sound in Harlem Draws New Neighbors" Ire," New York Times, July 6, 2008

3 Michael Pollan's article appeared March 20, 1994, The New York Times Magazine

4 cited in, Marinelli, Janet, Natives Revival—Is Native-plant Gardening Linked to Fascism? , Brooklyn Botanical Gardens, Volume 15, Number 2 | Summer 2000

5 Williams, New York Times

6 for further discussion see Whyte's excellent book, The Social Life of Small Urban Spaces, 1980, and City, 1989

In visibility
Anna Whitehead

1. **borderization**: the annihilation of borders;
   the "mutual invasion" of cultures.[1]

2. **The Fillmore.** After San Francisco's 1906 earthquake and
   fire, the Fillmore was one of the only neighborhoods left
   more or less intact; it became the new downtown while the
   city scrambled to rebuild itself in time for the International
   Exposition held in the Marina just nine years later. The
   area developed sizeable Jewish, Irish, Filipino, and Chinese
   populations, and became the new site of Nihonmachi, or
   Japantown.[2] In 1942, all people of Japanese origin on the West
   Coast were forced into internment camps and their newly
   vacated homes in the Fillmore were the only housing options
   offered to African Americans relocating to the city to join the
   war industry. Through the forties and the fifties, even while
   the San Francisco Redevelopment Agency was beginning to
   develop and implement a project of cultural decimation in
   the district, the Fillmore grew into what many came to call
   "the Harlem of the West." Louis Armstrong, Ella Fitzgerald,
   Billie Holiday, and scores of other blues and jazz legends all
   came through the Fillmore; besides being a hub of black bars,
   nightclubs and small black owned businesses, it was often the
   only place black performers could get a room while on tour.

3. **racial melancholia:** a failed attempt at assimilation, whose
   failure is guaranteed and self-perpetuating.[3]

4. **Redevelopment.** In 1949, the US Senate Committee on Banking and Currency passed the American Housing Act, and redevelopment in the Western Addition began in 1966.[4] Within a decade the Fillmore was devastated as over 60 square blocks were targeted for evacuation, demolition, and redevelopment. The project dragged on into the 21st century, with large chunks of land remaining undeveloped, while homelessness— and thus crime and drug use— began to rise.[5] Visiting the Fillmore in 2009, I can find a few public art nods to the neighborhood's past: a bridge with the words "blues" and "jazz" etched on the side, a "cultural center" with a current show up of photos from mid-century Fillmore. The Korean-owned beauty salon sits in between the black barbershop and the Ethiopian blues club, while Yoshi's sushi and Japanese restaurant down the street books international jazz acts. It has become— or rather, is forever in the process of becoming— a hybrid place building on a memorialized past, cultural amnesia and invisibility.

5. **The Frontier.** The frontier officially closed at the end of the 19th century.[6] Just over forty years prior, the US obtained Texas, Nevada, Utah and California during the Mexican-American War.[7] In 1959, the United States acquired a small island in the middle of the Pacific, 2,000 miles off of the coast of mainland US. This space, Hawaii, was the final state admitted to the union. Shortly after its admittance, space in general was declared the Final Frontier.[8]

6. **spacetime:** Albert Einstein's theory of relativity; the movement of objects in space in relation to time.

7. **Miscegenation.** In 1967, Richard Loving and Mildred Jeter won their case against Virginia's Racial Integrity law in the US Supreme Court, striking down anti-miscegenation laws across the country.[9] Nine years after the *Loving v. Virginia* case, my parents were married in North Carolina, where their honeymoon was interrupted with death threats from the Ku Klux Klan. They had my brother and I and we eventually relocated to a predominantly white, Latino, and South Asian suburb in Virginia. In my Virginia high school, I was one of three students that I knew of with multiracial parentage. I did not have a class with another black girl until the 7th grade.[10]

8. **San Francisco.** The median home price in San Francisco is about three times the median home price of the Western United States.[11] In an urban city where land is in such high demand, nary a half a block sits undeveloped. Furthermore, this demand makes the city itself a grid of contested space: as soon as Japanese renters and homeowners were forced into internment, African Americans were there to fill their spots— and they themselves could not stay long before someone else was looking to reinvent the property that had only through forced removal become their own. So it is that San Francisco in 2009 is a labyrinth of ethnic and cultural pockets. Nowhere is this more obvious than in the Mission district, and, in particular, between the streets of Valencia and Mission. Just a block apart and parallel to one another, they are two distinct worlds without overlap. Mission Street is home to dollar stores, bodegas, burrito places and working class and unemployed people of color (mostly Latinos). Valencia Street, on the other hand, is a land of boutiques, expensive themed restaurants, and hipster bars. It is a place populated by the mostly white middle class and well-to-do. A denim-and-work boot-clad Chicano on Valencia Street is about as noticeable as a white hipster in tight pants on Mission. There is a frighteningly precarious socio-economic balance maintained between these two worlds that is predicated on the unspoken agreement that the border between them (the side streets of Lexington, San Carlos, and Bartlett) shall not be breached.[12]

9. **Border-crosser.** In Southampton County, Virginia— home of the Nat Turner rebellion, the largest US Naval port and the town my father grew up in— there was a family of lightskinned, longhaired black folk.[13] My dad spoke about them as part of the black community of Norfolk, but separate. They had their own compound of homes that were slightly better than the other black people's houses, worked higher-paying jobs and retained more wealth. Everybody knew they were black (except for maybe them), but whites didn't treat them the same way they treated all the other black folk. They were the result of rape and inbreeding: like-black but not black.[14] The part European multi-racial— the mestizaje,

the halfbreeds, the mixed— wear on their bodies the legacy of physical take-over. Frequently, as in the case of the family in my father's town, these legacy-bearers can also perform and reiterate a border class sensibility, the result of the psychological conquest of all people of color in order to turn them against one another and create a significant buffer between white white and black black. Thus, they are both representations of the collision of physical and social difference, as well as occupants of a different physical space: a border.

10. **New World Border.**[15] Where then, does the border belong? It is an imaginary frontier, which, frequently to our dismay, manifests itself physically as a boundary.[16] It is a thing to be policed, "kept in check," used as a tool of regulation but not as an end unto itself. My movement across the city of San Francisco as a lightskinned mixed-race black woman is thus marked with ambivalence. In the Fillmore, a place nostalgic for its own erased identity, I am not-white. In Bayview, a thoroughly black part of town settled by Fillmore transplants of the mid-20th century, I am not-black. In the Mission, where white people are common and black people are assumed to be transients looking for a way back to the Tenderloin or Oakland, I am almost invisible. Most likely these rules of hailing and passing would be flipped, reversed and inverted had I come along 20 years before. Perhaps 20 years from now the rules will yet be further rewritten, rules unimaginable from my current vantage of politics, space and time.

If the border is transmutable, if it is mobile, then it has the potential to be nowhere and everywhere. While it retells transgressions of the past (think of the Mexican-American War, or the family in my dad's town) it also points to future possibilities (like the somewhat transculturated hybridity of the Fillmore). It is the void, the space of mutual invasion between [multiple] worlds in which future culture is made: an absence that is both prescient and omnipresent. Where, then, does the border— or our comprehension of it— belong? Could it be that, at the close of the first decade of the 21st century, we no longer have any use for borders? The geographer

David Harvey posits that the postmodern lived reality of collapsed space encourages greater spatial differentiation; that true hybridity invites deeper lines drawn in the sand.[17] The claim, then, is that with the collapse of one border comes the delineation of another, and one could extend this to the identifiably mixed-race subject as an embodiment of that new space. But I do not want to embody a new border; I do not want to represent historical conquest. Is it possible to ever escape this, to expand the notion of "borderization" to the point that the "border" (but not its properties) is, in fact, no longer extant? And if the border disappears, do I disappear with it? Like that mythical meeting place in the Mission district between Lexington and San Carlos Streets, perhaps the boundary-less wonderland of extreme borderization is only made real when it can no longer be seen, when both borders and bodies become invisible.

---

1 Guillermo Gomez-Pena, *Warrior for Gringostroika: Essays, Performance Texts, and Poetry* (St Paul, MN: Graywolf Press, 1993).

2 Nihonmachi is one of three official J-towns in the US. The other two are both in California – San Jose and LA. There are several other neighborhoods with high Japanese and Japanese American concentration (including in Cambridge, Denver, Portland, OR, and New York City). The number of highly concentrated sites was much greater before World War II, when the 1942 internment of Japanese and Japanese Americans to US "War Relocation Camps" destroyed the localization of many of these communities. These camps were the most dramatic of a series of Asian-exclusion initiatives by the California and US Government since the turn of the century. These included prohibitions against naturalization and property ownership for any Asian-born person in the US, and the Immigration Exclusion Acts that aimed to prevent Japanese and other Asian citizens from coming to the US. The War Relocation Camps were not an eccentricity of the state.

3 David L. Eng and Shinhee Han, "A Dialogue on Racial Melancholia" in *Loss: The Politics of Mourning* (UC Berkeley Press, 2002).

4 The legacy of the 1949 Housing Act is twofold: it paved the way for massive housing projects like Chicago's notorious Cabrini-Green, and it gave legal footing to slum clearance.

5 The Redevelopment Agency's A-2 project officially closed on January 1, 2009.

6 This is to say that in 1890 the US Census announced that there was no longer any difference between the frontier and settlements – all potential frontier had been settled – and Frederick Jackson Turner corroborated this in *The Significance of the Frontier in American History* (paper presented at the meeting

of the American Historical Association in Chicago, July 12, 1893). For Teddy Roosevelt and others, this signaled a need to look elsewhere for new frontiers (in real space and elsewhere) in order to sustain what had become a uniquely American way of life.

7 The resulting Treaty of Guadalupe Hidalgo also guaranteed large parts of Colorado, New Mexico, Arizona and Wyoming to the United States. Around this same time, the US acquired a portion of the Oregon Country from the British. In light of all of this expansion, as well as the popularized notion of Manifest Destiny and the god-given perpetuity of US, the urgency and force with which the US government responded to the American South's attempt to at secession just a few years later is understandable. Two years after the United States Civil War, Alaska was purchased by the US from Russia.

8 "Space: the final frontier" is the opening line of the popular television series, *Star Trek*.

9 Virginia had been the first state to establish such a law in 1691. In 1924, the Virginia legislature strengthened this law with the Racial Integrity Act. Unlike other states' anti-miscegenation laws, which forbade marriage between whites and specific non-white racial groups, the Racial Integrity Act made marriage between a white person and any non-white person illegal. It also demanded that all citizens born in Virginia have their racial classification recorded at birth. This recording process ended up altering several generations of Indian ethnic identity, as all persons of indigenous ancestry were reclassified as 'colored.'

10 Alexis Vaughan and I met in the back of English class. We became best friends.

11 This is based on a comparison between what the National Association of Realtors lists as the median home price for the Western US in 2009— $213,100 —and what Onboard Informatics lists as San Francisco's median home price of $711,157.

12 But who lives in those alleys? Are these residents of the borderlands forced into marginality— belonging neither to the world of Valencia or Mission Streets? What happens between Lexington and San Carlos, and where do the *fronteristas* go at Cesar Chavez Street, when Mission subsumes Valencia?

13 In the summer of 1831, Nat Turner, a slave, gathered up a few other trusted rebels and went from house to house, methodically killing the white slave owners who lived inside. In two days the Turner militia killed 60 white people. No other slave uprising resulted in so many deaths. Eventually, Turner was caught, hanged, decapitated, and his body was quartered. See Stephen B. Oates, *The Fires of Jubilee: Nat Turner's Fierce Rebellion* (New York: Harper Perennial, 1975).

14 Homi Bhabha calls this "colonial mimicry ... a subject of a difference that is almost the same, but not quite ... Almost the same but not white." "Of Mimicry and Man: The Ambivalence of Colonial Discourse," *October* 28 (spring 1984).

15 Guillermo Gomez-Pena. *New World Border: Prophecies, Poems, and Loqueras for the End of the Century* (San Francisco: City Lights, 2001).

16 See Chantal Akerman, *From the Other Side*, 2002.

17 David Harvey, *The Condition of Postmodernity* (Oxford: Blackwell, 1990). 295

MASS

VENTRILOQUISM

BY BRINDALYN WEBSTER

AUTHOR'S NOTE

MASS VENTRILOQUISM was originally read on February 7, 2009 in San Francisco, California at Southern Exposure. The author approached newly acquired friends from Portland State University, Otis College of Art and Design, old friends from California College of the Arts and strangers hanging out after their participation in SFMOMA's "Social Practice West" panel discussion.

"Would you like to read a part in this play for the 2 Minute Presentation Series*? The part is less than a page and you don't have to act. Just read the words as you understand them to sound in your head."

The play was cast in under an hour.

MASS VENTRILOQUISM premiered when the panelists reconvened for the 2 Minute Presentation Series at Southern Exposure.

The script for MASS VENTRILOQUISM was handed out to one man and fourteen women. The parts were spot read in front of a small audience. The portraits of AUGUST WILHELM MALM and CAROLINA (as shown on last page of script) were projected on a wall. The readers stood in a semicircle in front of the projection, facing the audience. The play was read in roughly two minutes.

Brindalyn Webster

*Everyone who attended the 2 Minute Presentation Series was invited to put on a very brief presentation of one of their own projects, an idea, an activity, a thing they happen to have in their pocket, or something they were just not so sure about.

DIRECTION

The script for MASS VENTRILOQUISM should be handed out to people who are strangers or recently acquainted. Parts should be spot read, out loud, and never rehearsed. There should be no direction other than, read this out loud, un-theatrically, as words that you are first coming across.

COSTUME PLOT:
No costumes should be worn other than the clothes that the readers wear upon arrival.

CASTING:
Ideally, all parts but AUGUST WILHELM MALM should be read by female readers.

SETTING:
An additional audience is not required, but in the case that there is an additional audience the photos on the last page of the script should be projected on a wall behind the readers.

BLOCKING:
The readers should stand in a semicircle in front of the wall being projected on.

CHARACTERS

NARRATOR #1: The town adopts a whale
AUGUST WILHELM MALM: It is with great honor and pride
NARRATOR #2: The traveling host
NARRATOR #3: You give a centimeter they take a kilometer
NARRATOR #4: A much needed hiatus
NARRATOR #5: Some super-imposed character development
BARBARA JOHNSON: Thoughts on muteness envy
NARRATOR #6: Incredible shrinking women
NARRATOR #7: Speak when you are spoken through
FOOTNOTE #1: Homonyms
FOOTNOTE #2: One hundred thirty-two million, five hundred eighty thousand, ninety-six
FOOTNOTE #3: Role reversal
FOOTNOTE #4: Whales > dinos
FOOTNOTE #5: Long distance singers
FOOTNOTE #6: An ending

ORIGINAL CAST

NARRATOR #1: Sandy Sampson
AUGUST WILHELM MALM: Cyrus Smith
NARRATOR #2: Hannah Miami
NARRATOR #3: Laurel Kurtz
NARRATOR #4: Helen Reed
NARRATOR #5: Malak Helmy
BARBARA JOHNSON: Anna Whitehead
NARRATOR #6: Courtney Fink
NARRATOR #7: Ariana Jacobs
FOOTNOTE #1: Rio Robbins
FOOTNOTE #2: Lynne McCabe
FOOTNOTE #3: Katy Asher
FOOTNOTE #4: Lauren Marsden
FOOTNOTE #5: Jessica James Lansdon
FOOTNOTE #6: Georgia Carbone

MASS VENTRILOQUISM

NARRATOR #1: There is a quiet whale in Sweden.

They call her Carolina.

She was named after the wife of a wealthy quartermaster, August Wilhelm Malm.

At a young age, she was taken from her home at the Isthmus of Askim Bay and was brought to Gothenburg.

Two gentlemen, Carl Hansson and Olof Larsson escorted her with three steamboats.

In a trade magazine dated August 13, 1892, Malm was quoted as saying,

AUGUST WILHELM MALM: "Everything, everything I have thus put at stake... Everything has gone on my risk. But now, thanks to Providence!, I also arrived at the truly great goal. Victory is mine. I share the honor with all the arms, assist, and to repeat some of the words I spoke to thousands of spectators: this equally wonderful, colossal animal may not only be the single most precious adornment of our museum; it is, if all goes well, to be a pride for our town, not to say our whole nation, Whereas, if I know, no museum in the world can produce anything in the way, or value to compare with as this can to behold."

NARRATOR #2: Aware of the responsibility that came with her approval, Carolina did her best to serve her nation.

Made herself utterly available to her people. Went to lengths to see that they were comfortable. Furnished a salon with benches and tapestries for their visits.

In the summer of 1866, Carolina traveled to Stockholm. There she attended the Industrial Exposition, where she hosted over 36,000 visitors. Hamburg and Berlin followed.

In 1923, she moved into a new hall built specifically for her in Slottskogen.

She continued her role as a public host. Entertaining visitors; serving coffee. Punch.

NARRATOR #3: It was some time later that Carolina had to close down her doors and retreat to a more private life.

This was due to the indiscretion of some visitors who confused her hall for a hideout.

(Carolina's place was later referred to as "... a hideout for loving couples, and then a special couple were surprised in a too intimate situation.")

Carolina could no longer host. She became publicly inactive.

NARRATOR #4: The transition was a pleasant one. It provided her the quiet contemplative time that her youth was lacking.

She was no longer a public servant.

NARRATOR #5: In her seclusion, she became a bit of a mystery.

BARBARA JOHNSON: "Women with expensive and artsy tastes can, of course, be idealized, but probably only if they project an image of graceful muteness. One has only to think of the outpouring of feeling around the death of Jacqueline Kennedy Onassis to realize the genius of adoption of the role of silent image from the moment of the assassination onward. Prior to that time, the woman with a taste for French cooking, redecoration, and Oscar Wilde was a far less idealized figure in the American press. And the contrast between Jackie O's muteness and Hillary Clinton's outspokenness only served to give cultural reinforcement to the notion that grace, dignity, and class could only be embodied by a woman who remains silent."

NARRATOR #7: Carolina is silent and inaccessible for every day except election day. And on that day a small voting booth is erected inside of her and citizens come to cast their vote.

Sweden speaks through her.

NARRATOR #6: In the same camp as Jane Wyman, Holly Hunter, and Samantha Morton, Carolina's role as a mute should have brought her an Oscar.

But civic duty made her an exception.

And although she was only acting as a medium, the fact she is vocal at all disqualified her from the award.

FOOTNOTE #1: From Swedish, the word "valen" can be translated twice. It can be translated to mean 'whale' and it can be translated to mean 'election'. Both words speak of enormity.

FOOTNOTE #2: In the 2008 U.S. General Election, 132,580,096 voters left their house to voice their opinion in public.

FOOTNOTE #3: "In Book II, Chapter 2 of his book 'The Spirit of Laws', Montesquieu states that in the case of elections in either a republic or a democracy, voters alternate between being the rulers of the country and being the subjects of the government. By the act of voting, the people operate in a sovereign (or ruling) capacity, acting as 'masters' to select their government's 'servants.'"

FOOTNOTE #4: The blue whale is the largest creature that has ever existed on earth. It is bigger than 25 elephants; bigger than a Brontosaurus and a Tyrannosaurus rex combined. A blue whale calf is about 7 m (23') long at birth.

FOOTNOTE #5: The sounds a blue whale makes can travel thousands of miles in deep water, leading to speculation that the whales may be able to communicate across oceans.

FOOTNOTE #6: Whales have long been a source of food, oil, and crafts' material. A famous Japanese Proverb quotes: "There's nothing to throw away from a whale except its voice."

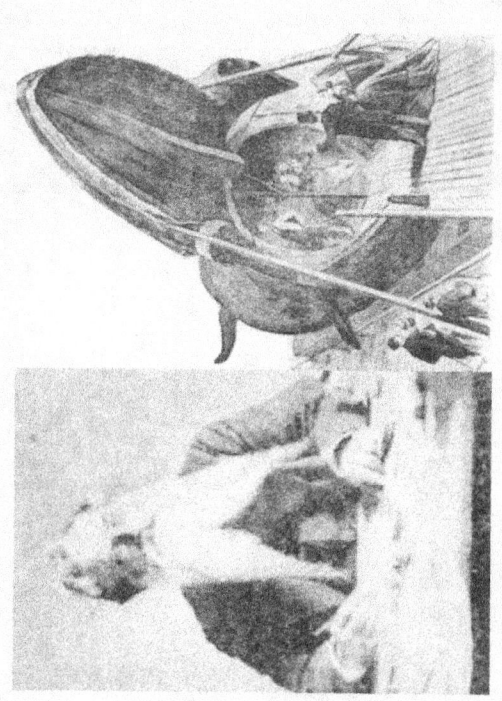

August Wilhelm Malm   **Carolina**

Conflicts on The Common:

An Interview with Iain Boal

Anthony Marcellini

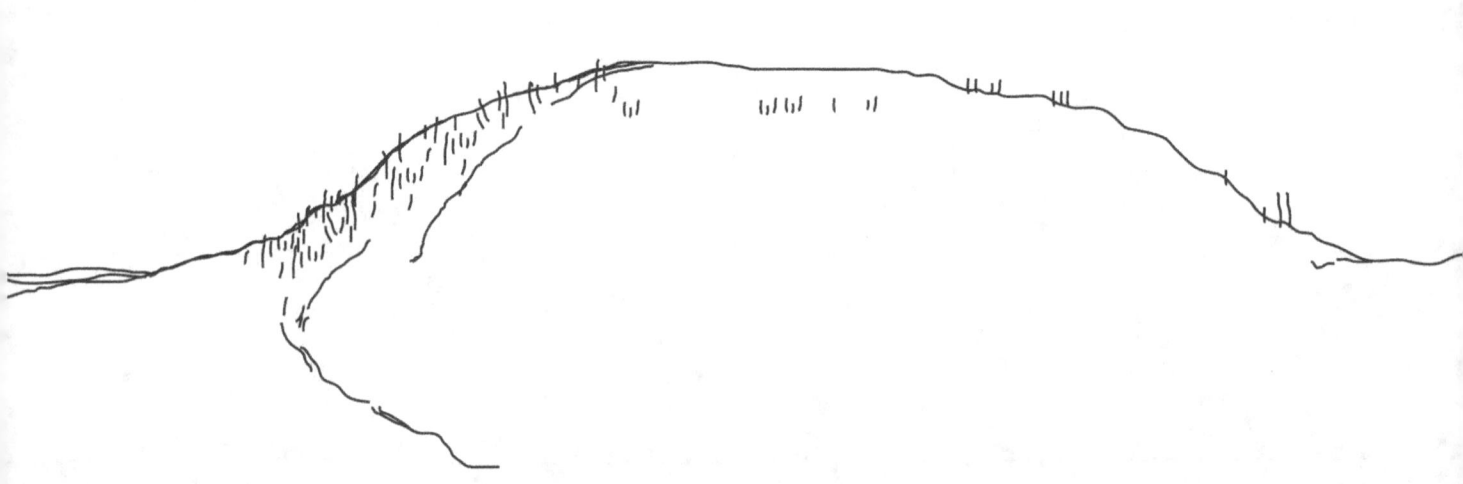

Dear Reader,

This interview between Iain Boal and myself took place on October 5, 2008, at the Café Roma in Berkeley, CA. It was conducted as a preamble of sorts, for a talk that Iain would present the following weekend as part of my project *A Grass Mound (With Kind Regards to Utopia)*. This project consisted of a sculpture of a small 7-foot wide natural grass knoll that I built for a group exhibition presented at the San Francisco Arts Commission Gallery. The mound—based on a larger form that I had found with Matthew David Rana, during a trip we took to investigate the site of a former social utopian commune called Alturia (1894-96)—served as a platform or stage for a series of six lectures and performances on utopian and aesthetic visions and the successes and failures in trying to achieve them. I had invited Iain to present because of his extensive knowledge, as a historian of the body and the commons and because of his interest in the role of the body to both perform and resist (or perform resistance) in public space. I decided to present this interview, in this publication because I found our conversation relevant to a number of other discussions and projects presented within. Furthermore, this interview in many ways helped to frame my current focus concerning the shifting boundaries of the space of performance when enacted in public space. To hear Iain and others lectures from the *A Grass Mound (With Kind Regards to Utopia)* project please visit blog.anthonymarcellini.info, search under the heading 'A Grass Mound'.

Best,
Anthony Marcellini

Anthony Marcellini: I thought we could begin to set the stage by having you describe your interest in the commons and the San Francisco Mime Troupe (SFMT) specifically their struggles for free expression and political protest in public space.

Iain Boal: Well I have two intersecting interests really, one as a historian of the commons and commoning, and the other as a historian of science and medicine. I am very interested in the history of the body and I did a very long project over several years focused in the 17th century when these two things came together. It was both a history of the enclosure of Ireland, of the Gaelic common land, following the invasion by Oliver Cromwell, and at the same time I became very involved in writing the biography of Ireland's most famous healer, who used the power of touch. And I did that in collaboration with somebody who had studied with the master of movement and mime Etienne Decroux in Paris, as Ron Davis of the San Francisco Mime Troupe (SFMT) did. So these wires were crossed for me long ago. I began seriously to investigate the history of the enclosure of the commons back in the 1980s, and that took me to the history of emparkment, the history of public space, and the history of the open air. If you look on the dustcover of Ron Davis's own history of the first ten years (R. G. Davis, *The San Francisco Mime Troupe: The First Ten Years* (Berkeley, Ramparts 1975)), you will notice the words "Engagement, Commitment and Fresh Air." Somewhere in there Davis mentions the flash of insight the troupe had about what the open air does to performance. It entails large gestures, and you are looking at the plebeian tradition of Commedia dell'arte, pantomime, and what a difference it makes to be out in the open. Next Saturday

Tecumseh is invited into the governor's mansion but refuses to enter. He replied: "Houses are built for you to hold council in; Indians hold theirs in the open air."

I should talk about a very haunting quote by chief Tecumseh when he meets the governor of Indiana, at the moment of the great enclosures of North America, two years before the war of 1812. Tecumseh is invited into the governor's mansion but refuses to enter. He replied: "Houses are built for you to hold council in; Indians hold theirs in the open air." He also refused to take a chair when offered one, saying that he would repose on the bosom of the earth, and he lies down on the grass. There is a resonance here with the barefoot spirit of the 60's and the movement into the parks and a literal reconnection with the earth. Of course one needs to take a dialectical view of this movement, and stay alert to the grisly record of the fetishizing of nature, "blood and soil" and all that.

AM: Do you think that an interest in earth has a relationship with Marxist ideology?

IB: No, I really don't think that Davis' interest in Marx motivated, for example, the move outdoors to natural settings qua nature. Marxian interest in nature is focused on nature as material substrate to be transformed by willed human effort, by the powers of the human brain and body enhanced by tools, the realm of technology. To the contrary, what Davis and the early Mime Troupe were doing was paring down, stripping away the apparatus, except for a prop or two, going back to basics, a certain kind of abstraction, an interest in the expressivity of the body, in order to critique bourgeois forms and alienated, exploited life under capitalism.

The big Marxist questions of alienation and class meant the occlusion of gender relations within the (SFMT, my emphasis) company itself and led to the split in 1970. (I'm happy to report that when I MC'ed the Mime Troupe's 40th anniversary event at Fort Mason in San Francisco things were amicable between Ron Davis and the old Troupers.)

After the founder took a "leave of absence", the Troupe as a collective went into another crisis because affirmative action melodrama makes for lousy theatre. The root of the problem had to do with the conservatism of traditional and popular cultural forms, despite the radical elements to be found in burlesque and knockabout theatre. Davis himself was certainly aware of this, and thought he saw a way out through Brechtian strategies. He went off to Europe to study the problem, and the Mime Troupe settled into its annual rituals of alfresco family entertainment.

Still, the "fresh air" question is actually very important. Why does popular protest take to the street? What is the history of art outside? Most of the major events in history have happened outside. I would even venture to claim that big-h-History will only be made in the open air. In the sense that the decisions taken inside, in the chancellories, boardrooms, smoke filled rooms etc, are ultimately conditioned by things that happen, or do not happen, in the open air. Of course this is an absurd thing to say but an interesting way to begin to think about it, no? And it is connected in my own mind to that haunting line of Tecumseh. I don't intend, in saying this, to romance the "red man", and they spent plenty of time in smoke-filled spaces (with eye and lung disease to show for it).

How, really, should we interpret Tecumseh's retort to Governor Harrison? Well, I take his remark not as a statement of "lifestyle" preference or personal comfort, but implying something profound about spatial and political form, about the different architectonics of propertarian and commoning societies. The spaces of modernity are shaped and dominated by private and state interests; under modernity public space is a subordinate category, residual even, and confined to what is left over once land has been seized, commodified and parcelled into private lots. What is left over is in the open air. Literally. Of course, the air is treated also by capitalists as a common, or an "externality", as they say in the business schools, which are commons of a peculiar capitalist kind, in this case used as a deadly sink for the waste produced during the manufacture of commodities. This amounts to the theft of a common, though it is sometimes hard to see since it doesn't happen all at once, nor everywhere. Like many other things, pollution is very uneven, and for sure it has a clear class geography, and is racialized too.

In general we can say that the condition of commons and the rights of common are even more degraded than public space, which is ultimately a state-derived form, and which therefore is afforded some protections – of speech, assembly etc – however vestigial. By the same token, "the public" as an imagined body has some political clout, at least formally, by virtue of the ballot etc. Clout, that is, compared with commoners whose use-rights have been either extinguished completely during the long theft called "modernity" or else massively eroded. The streets are just about the last public space, even though they have been for a long time given over to the demands of circulation and the movement of traffic. There is, therefore, good reason why there so much is at stake over "the streets", because they remain potentially a flashpoint.

AM: I am curious what your feelings are then about the "Grass Mound", something that was meant to be outside, grass, or a mound of grass, removed from the outside and placed in the well lit enclosed space of the gallery.

IB: Well, I take it to be some kind of poignant and dialectical comment on the pathos of human projects, and on the folly of utopian projects in particular. If you look at the history of utopias, not as a literary genre but as attempts to give material form to the longing for a better world, the record is of course depressing. In California if you ask what is left of them materially, it's hard to find even any ruins, although Mike Davis opens *City of Quartz* with a picture of the rubble of Llano del Rio, the socialist commune in Antelope County outside Los Angeles. I like very much your "Grass Mound", because although it is a metaphor for the absurdity of utopian dreams, it also speaks to the possibility of standing up and debating to the contours of another world built among the ruins of this civilization, which will not last and frankly does not deserve to. I take encouragement from the anarchist Durutti's line: "We are not in the least afraid of ruins."

After all, it is amid the ruins of the medieval commoning landscape that Thomas More begins his *Utopia*, the fountainhead of the whole genre. The entire first half of *Utopia* is a critique of the enclosures. It is their disappearance, the extinction of the commons in the early 16th century that prompts More to write *Utopia*. On Saturday I will be saying something about the paradox of utopias, about utopias that are dystopias, clearly. Say, Bellamy's *Looking Backward*, which projects a socialist utopia, yet from a contemporary ecological viewpoint its productivism is a kind of nightmare. Of course there is an egalitarian moment there, but the tone of it doesn't feel that much better to me then Dubai, which is now the iconic neo-liberal utopia, though of course a utopia of consumption. Dubai's Palm Jumeira Island, by the way, looks uncannily like More's island in form.

AM: The whole notion of a utopia being on an island indicates a fear of outsiders and a disinterest in communicating or exchange. It is a fortress.

IB: Yes, they do tend to be a kind of paranoid fortress, either islands or islands-in-the-land. On the other hand, given the ragged-arsed makeshift contingency of almost all countercultural utopias of the sixties, there is something fine about the scale and confidence of 19th century "blueprint utopias", as Russell Jacoby puts it.

That said, I think your "grassy mound" is a nice metaphor, or rather synecdoche. I like the non-specificity of it; it's a graveyard of buried dreams, and at the same time, as I said, a platform for discussion – "Fail again, fail better" in the great phrase of Sam Beckett. And also much more in the spirit of the utopias that I could stand with, as it were. In the 19th century it would be William Morris' *News from Nowhere*, which takes seriously the question of transformation, the getting there from here. In that sense, it's not a blueprint but in Jacoby's terms an "iconoclastic utopia". In the 20th century it would be Bolo Bolo, the Swiss anarchist utopia. And I should put in a word for *The Disposessed*, Ursula Le Guin's great imaginative projection that had its roots in 1930s Berkeley, just a few doors up from me on Arch Street, where Le Guin was born into the Kroeber household. She was surrounded by storytellers, ethnologists and anthropologists like the legendary Jaime De Angulo, contrarians and idealists, new world continuators of William Morris, makers and fakers who all the time were thinking in counter-narratives, imaginative counter-worlds. *The Dispossessed*, Le Guin's anarchist masterpiece messes with utopia as a genre in a wonderful way. I am convinced that Le Guin's genius was nurtured in the firelight of the arts and crafts drawing rooms and in the outdoor hillside theatres of her Berkeley childhood.

AM: In R. G. Davis's *The First Ten Years* he discusses how their initial performances in the parks were not being granted permits, but performing anyway because they felt their content was being censored and there was a real need to fight that. Though they begin to win these battles after a time and are allowed to perform, it seems that Davis' disillusionment with the Mime Troupe begins after these early successes, allowing for other events to take place in the parks that begin to overshadow theirs. So much so that by 1969, the music promoter Bill Graham and other SF music writers and promoters, proposed to present the west coast's answer to Woodstock, a "festival of life" in Golden Gate Park, but were opposed by all the art, political and protest groups in the Bay Area, from the Mime Troupe to the Panthers because they saw it as irrelevant, and a marketing ploy. Davis felt like the Mime troupe was trying to talk about real issues and trying to create community, not just entertainment. He says "Our passage in the park was no longer unique, rock bands were giving concerts to thousands." He also begins to get weary of fighting the state and remarks, "Fighting for the chance to present a radical show became a boring confrontation." Suggesting basically that he was more interested in the performance and not the fight. These are tensions, which I think are really interesting regarding public space or the commons. Is a concert enough as an act of engagement within the common space, or does the common space call for more?

IB: Actually I was thinking of these questions yesterday

Is a concert enough as an act of engagement within the common space, or does the common space call for more?

at the Hardly Strictly Bluegrass festival in Golden Gate Park. In some ways these events embody the spirit of those times. These are performances in the park, they are free, and there is a tremendously mellow spirit. Certainly too there was a political dimension to it. Listening to Steve Earle, and his great song about John Walker Lynd, I mean there is commentary in there. It is a kind of political theater. To be sure these tens of thousands of people are coming as spectators, to consume the music and the scene, but not just.

I think that Davis would be interested in how the seating arrangements are negotiated. In the tradition of bluegrass festivals, if anyone goes away for a break their area becomes squat-able until they come back. I was with a friend sitting in a couple of those folding seats, an hour an a half later the owners of the seats come back and they say 'thanks for keeping our seats'; they were complete strangers. In other words there is a kind of messing with the categories of a privatized world and a propertarian culture, which you might say are trivial but they are far from trivial actually. I would certainly agree with Ron and say that the Mime Troupe is stupendously boring now. Except in so far as it is a diminishment of alienation something that gets you away from the screen world and into an embodied face-to-faceness of a certain kind.

AM: Yes and that is something that the Mime Troupe has retained from earlier times, despite being boring. When I saw them two weeks ago there was still a feeling of relation between the actors and the audience.

IB: Yes, true, there is still a way in which certain kinds of spectacular distance and certain forms of bourgeois propriety have been dissolved. But the other kind of distancing, the Brechtian kind, is not there.

AM: I am curious about the Mime Troupe's interest in Brecht. Davis is supportive towards using Brecht's notion of breaking the fourth wall however he is also quite critical (or professes to be critical) of Brecht's pedanticism or didacticism. The SFMT's reaction to that didacticism seems to have been to use comedy, offence and provocation to break down the relationship between the audience and the actors, which is partially a way of creating a relation, of breaking the fourth wall. But I wonder: do these issues still make sense; was the Mime Troupe really moving beyond these notions?

IB: Breaking down the fourth wall and looking into a bourgeois drawing room was at a certain historical moment a radical move. The same goes for naturalistic "kitchen sink" drama in the class-bound Britain of the early sixties. However, breaking the wall doesn't on its own challenge the essentially passive relationship of the audience to the play or to the actors. And certainly Davis pushed against the separation early on, by having the actors constantly "break frame" in various ways. But I fear that this kind of debate – about theater and its conventions and Brecht – has been overtaken by historical developments. We have become so overwhelmed by the virtual life. There was a time when you had to go out and see drama; there was only live theater, which is no longer true now. It's not that drama is dead, far from it. When you reach the late 20th century people are watching more drama than at any time in human history. But people are watching it all on a screen, many people five, six, seven hours of it a day. How is Brecht able to help us on this? How do you get an alienation effect with television and film? It can be done in the limit case, as Guy Debord did, by making unwatchable films. I'm not saying these are not good questions, but I fear that they have been rendered for the most part irrelevant.

AM: Because the stage has changed so to speak?

IB: Yes the stage has changed in a qualitative way. It is still a question of form. But it is not about tearing down the fourth wall, or breaking frame out of a dramatic persona, or actors changing in full view and mingling with the audience. We have

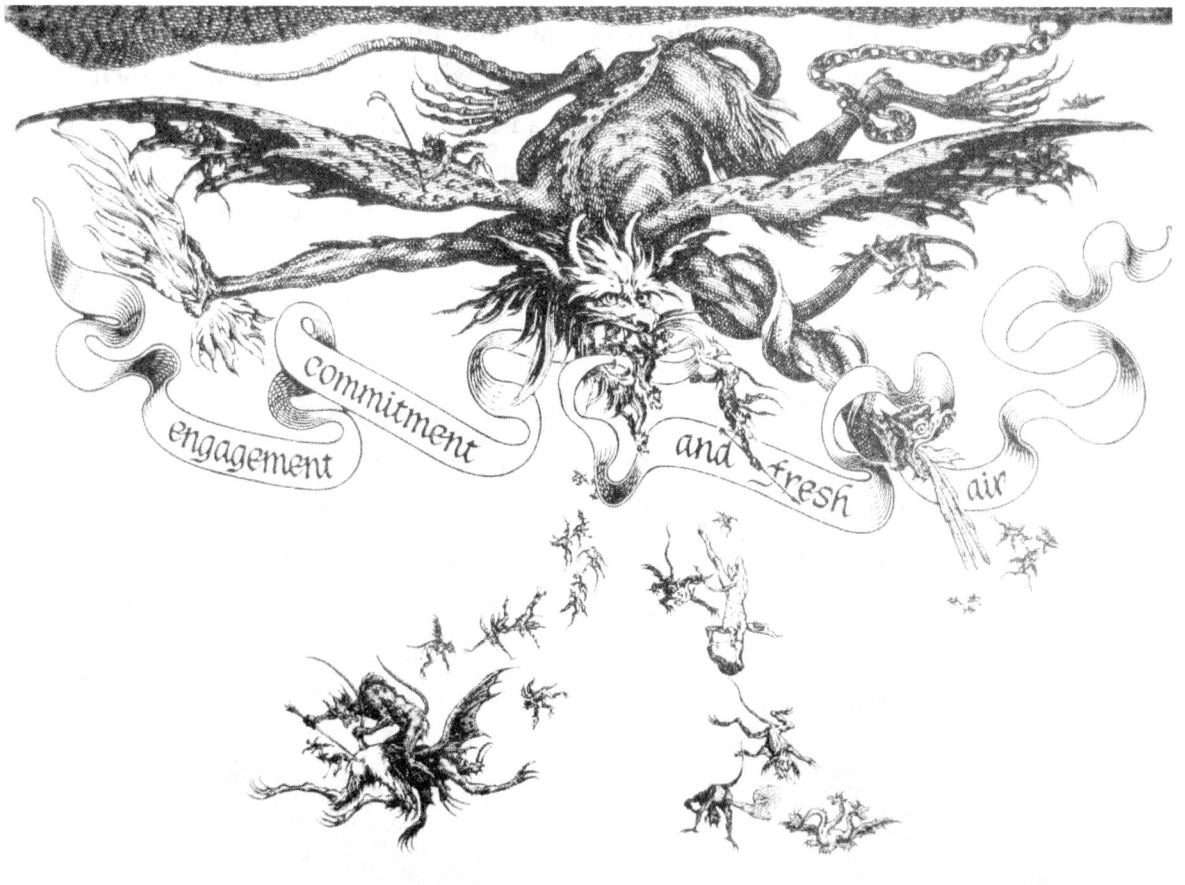

moved into a world of hyper-proliferating image machines that swamps all those brave gestures. That is what Retort's *Afflicted Powers* was trying to get at – the consequences, both for politics and for the human imagination, of the commodity penetrating into spaces previously untouched. We argue that the colonization of everyday life is a kind of globalization turned inwards. In this context all efforts at de-commodified sociability must be welcomed, including the tired old free concert in the park, even if it's only a parody of a false memory. And don't forget the open air and Tecumseh's retort. Here's a thought-experiment - what if all portentous decisions by bigwigs had to be made in parks, in the open air, with children playing around them.

Here's a thought-experiment - what if all portentous decisions by bigwigs had to be made in parks, in the open air, with children playing around them.

AM: That reminds me of the redesign of the Reichstag by Norman Foster. After reunification of east and west Germany, the German government relocated back to Berlin, and after a huge architectural renovation by Foster, back into the Reichstag. They ripped out the impenetrable doors, walls and roofs, and installed huge glass windows and a dome so that everyone could see all the way into the interior. This act was aimed at rendering German politics more visibility, so that the things that happened before, in the past, in the enclosed spaces will not happen again. Which is of course actually really beautiful. But I just wonder does it mean anything, really? Or is it simply an image, a façade, a hollow representation of the idea?

IB: Ultimately I would say it is a distraction because our problems are deeper than that. I'm not saying that the architects of the new Reichstag designed in bad faith, just that it's a move within the horizon of representational politics, and has little to do with direct horizontalist democracy, except maybe in order to dissimulate it. So what I like about your green podium is that, however fleetingly, it takes life off the screen, quiets the phone, unplugs the ipod, and allows us a face-to-face discussion of the news from nowhere.

AM: Is this kind of practice (more generally than the SFMT and ignoring all the problematics of the theatrical structures of Artaud, or Brecht) of performing art in public space and on the street, still relevant? Does it change people's relationships to have this happen in public or are they overly familiar with it?

IB: I think, for the reasons I have just mentioned, it has never been more important. It is not for nothing that we began *Afflicted Powers* by invoking those two extraordinary days of the Iraq war demonstrations in 2003. The problem is that the "community", the utopia if you like, conjured up during these brief reappearances of bodies-in-motion, given the de-realization of human collectivity under the conditions of spectacle, these moments produce only fleeting and often toxic manifestations of community. They were nevertheless extraordinary. You could feel it in something as banal as the free concerts yesterday in the open air. Why do people still hunger for it? Well, this brings me to a key theoretical point. Life under conditions of spectacle, under the reign of the commodity cannot deliver on its promises. At least that's the wager that those of us who are declared enemies of the present have made. In other words, a view of human powers and capacities from which it follows that the virtual life is a travesty. Similarly with the notion that the pinnacle of political participation is the vote; as if periodic ratification of our masters by ballot is anything other than an embarrassment. It is bad enough to have masters, but to choose them is simply embarrassing. The wager further implies – and here we have come full circle in our conversation – that there is an awful lot riding on the "commonist" strategy. That is, on claiming back the commons. And I am not talking about the denatured capitalist commons, which are entirely congenial to realtors and developers – you know what I mean, green parks, open spaces, well-maintained roads, clean beaches, etc. Fair enough, as far as they go. But I'm talking about rights of common that have use-value, in the traditional sense of providing livelihood and sustenance - food, energy, building materials, fodder, unpolluted water, all of nature's bounty. At the level of political spaces it is also important. Increasingly so. As the neo-liberal world order goes into profound crisis, it will be these other forms of commoning that will matter, mainly on the side of production. We will have to work together to produce our own lives. We are just in the dawn of a time when we must reinvent a whole range of extinct commoning practices. Meeting in the open air to deliberate over this would be a good start.

So my conclusion is, I suppose, somewhat paradoxical. Those intense struggles in 1950s San Francisco, to abolish censorship, to speak freely, to perform without license – Ginsberg and Ferlinghetti at City Lights, the syndicalists who founded Pacifica radio, the Mime Troupe in the city parks – seem to many just cold-war tales of long ago. The antics of some uppity theater folk, anarchists and longhairs irrelevant now. And in some ways, it's true, the powers accommodated to their demands. What performance now in Golden Gate Park would get you arrested? And surely any serious discussion of utopia has been utterly discredited, if you are to believe George Orwell or Isaiah Berlin or Karl Popper. Even Marx himself, for completely different reasons, snorted "I do not write cookbooks for the kitchens of the future." And yet, and yet. First, an obvious point, we may well be entering a new dark night of censorship – not much of a stretch, given the gulag of liberal state terror that has emerged with Guantanamo as its public face, all brought to us by disciples of Orwell and Berlin. So what price a conversation about utopia? Shall we shut up because Popper called them blueprints for fascism? Not as long as Wallace Stevens is somewhere in the park to remind us: "The imperfect is our paradise".

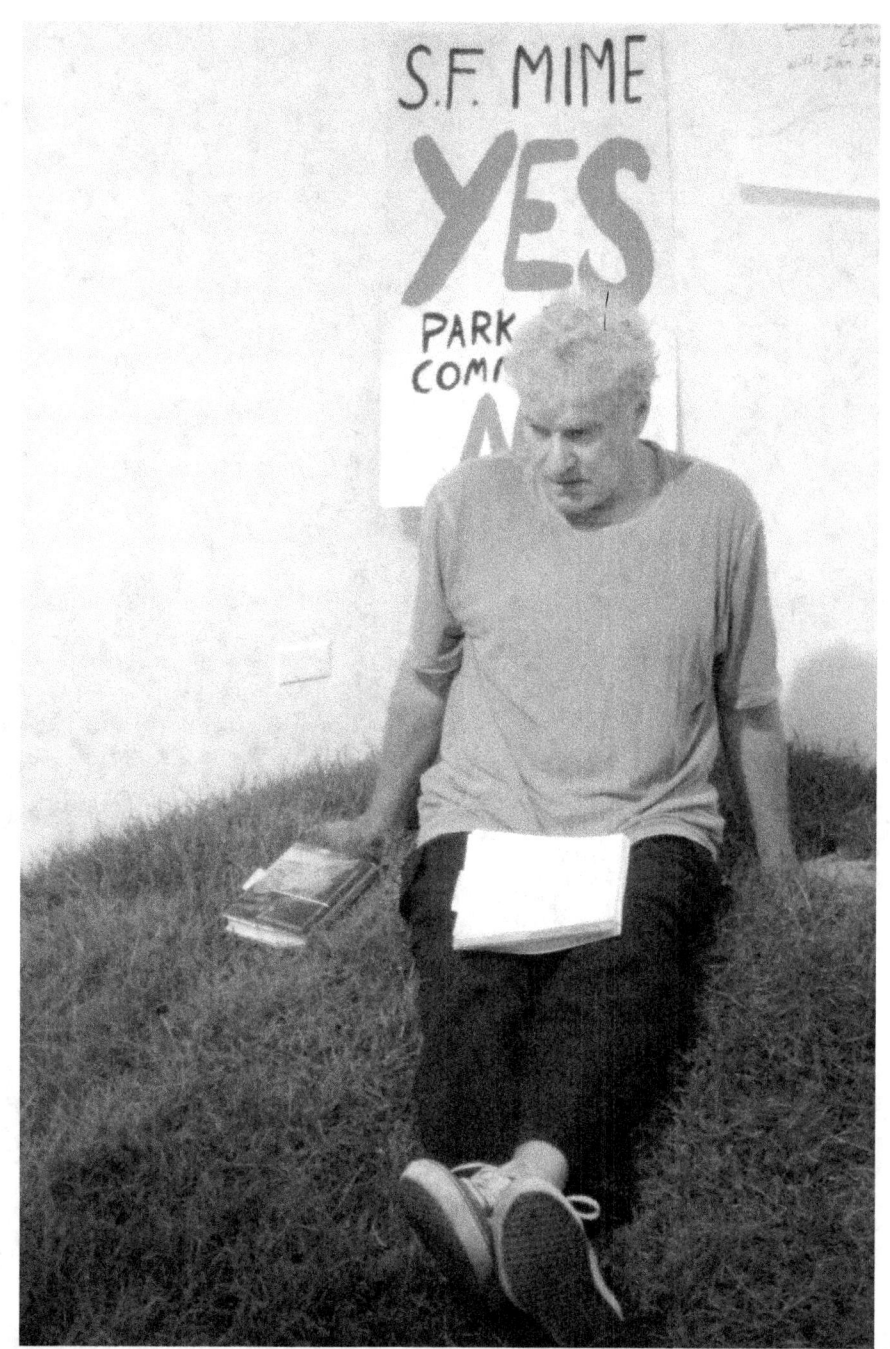

The Dream As Public Space

Wafaa Yasin

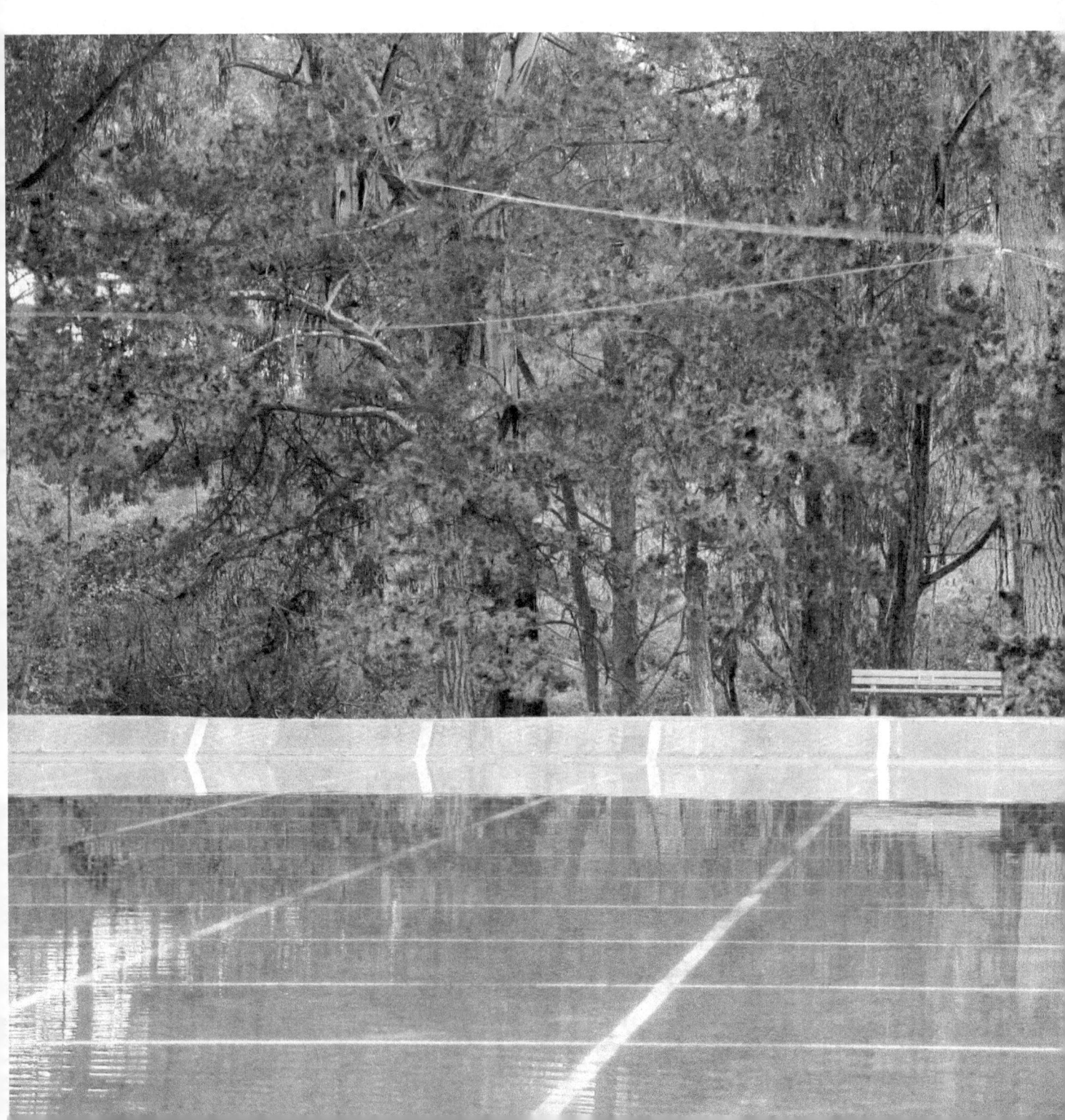

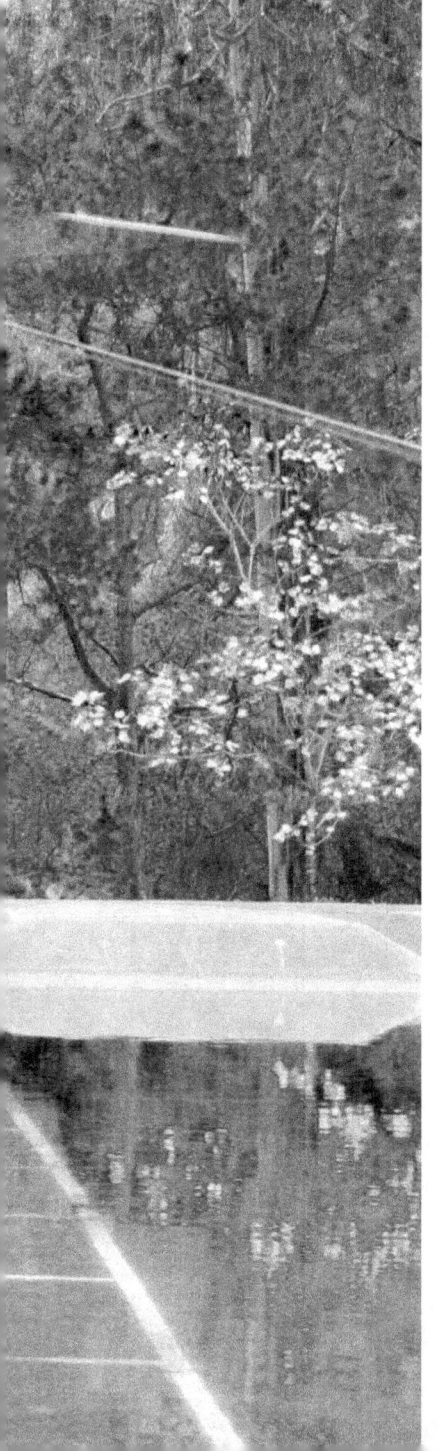

It was a very large pool, separated by three cement borders. I was swimming and yet, could not feel the water surround my body. In order to cross these borders, I had to fly. I was struggling between these two actions: of swimming in water I could not feel and defying the gravity of the pool to fly in the air. As I swam, each stroke of my arms brought me closer to the border between the first and second pools but the challenge was to avoid a confrontation with the borders, the water, the gravity and my own sense of wanting to float suspended between them. When I awoke, I realized it had all been a dream. As I moved between a dream state and being awake, it was as if I was in a mental fog, unable to see any details clearly, yet the feeling of the dream remained real and unmistakable.

The following day I was walking in a park and was drawn to a serene area with a grove of towering trees and a curved pathway. While walking down the path that wound through a small garden, I looked up and saw before me an enormous pool divided into three casting ponds. I felt a strange sense of déjà vu. It was the pool in my dream from the night before. My first impression of the space was how peaceful it appeared and I was enchanted. I was completely entranced by the ambience of the space and wondered if the dream gave birth to the space or did the space that is always in our subconscious mind and body give birth to this conscious reality?

The thought came to me that here I am, a body within a public space . When I'm thinking of a public space I tend to think of my body. Making an effort (trying) to investigate the public space through my body. As a stranger in a strange space, all that I know is my body.

A performance art project took shape in my mind. I imagined myself being filmed in the casting ponds in three distinct scenes. In the first I am in a one-piece turquoise swim suit covered by a nude overtop of sheer material with a black scull cap and water goggles. A single fisherman is practicing casting a fishing line. I swim past him until I reach the cement border and then I hoist my body onto the border and walk to the next pond, repeating this for the third pond and then back again over all three ponds. Afterwards, the fisherman's line becomes entangled in the sheer overtop and tears it from my body. As the fisherman repeatedly lashes out at my body I raise my hands around my head in a gesture of defense. In the second scene, I am wearing a black wet suit with black skull cap and goggles, only this time, I wear a mid-thigh overtop that clasps in the front made of a jersey knit material. After randomly tossing fifty bobbers with attached fishhooks into the three casting ponds, I swim under the bobbers until the hooks catch in the jersey material and the bobbers hang from my outer garment. In the final scene, I document a fishing tournament at the casting ponds, emphasizing how the fishing lines hit the water.

The elements of space deceive me. The coldness of the water eradicates my senses and puts me outside of my body. I gaze at this body as if it was only remnants. The water affects me in this way, and my movements as I swim affect the water, causing ripples and concentric waves. I know fully the temperament of the water as it also knows the mood of my intent. We are at odds with each other, observers of each other's reality, yet, participants in each other's illusion. We are not the same, but we encounter one another in a shared experience. The limitation of the imagination is the body, and limitation of the body is that of other bodies, and the shared limitation of the other bodies is the space. Crossing these limitations is the only way to merge and unite with the space.

"NO SWIMMING" - a statement of control. It is my conviction that this sign is placed in the space only for the sake of control and oppression which radicalizes my natural inclination, my convention to create contact with the space. Leading my body into the peacefulness of the ponds was jeopardization itself. There is nothing colder or more alienating than the sense of peaceful resistance. A police officer that wasn't a part of the performance, mounts a horse, rides up to me and begins to interrogate me about whether

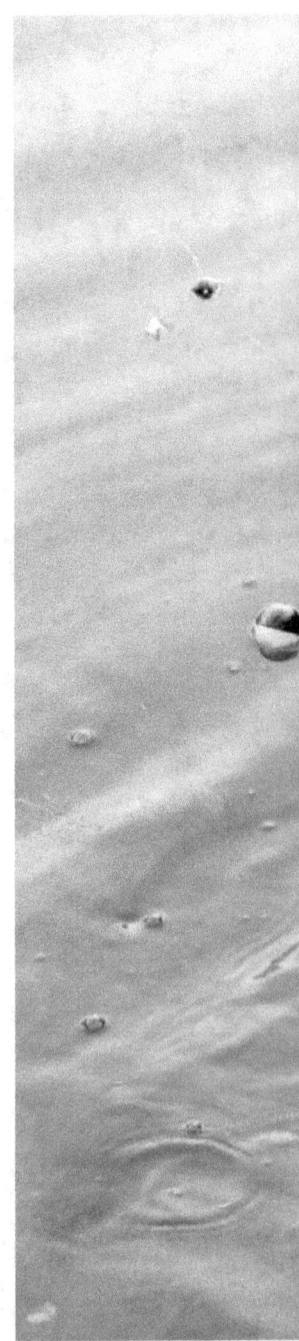

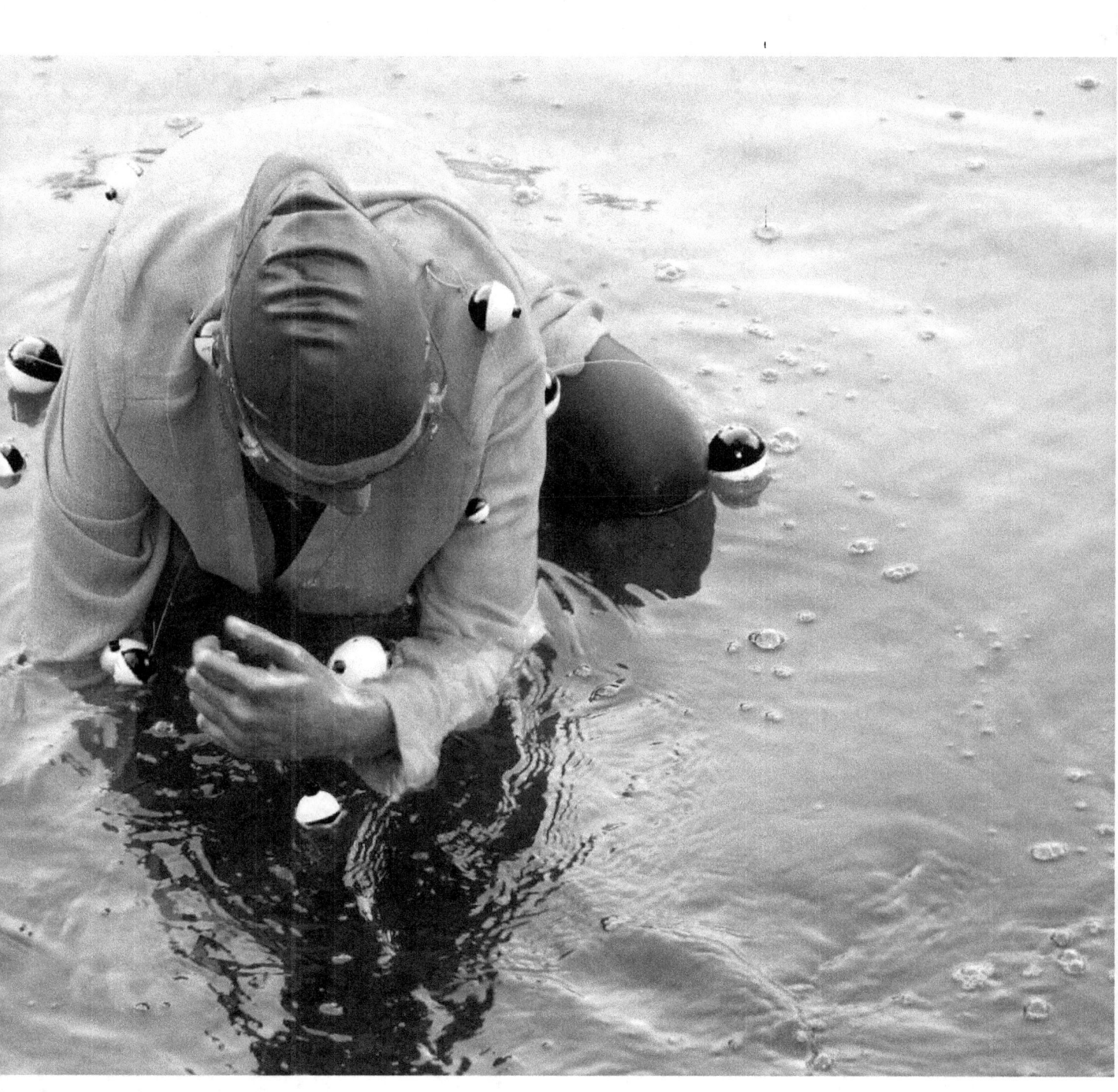

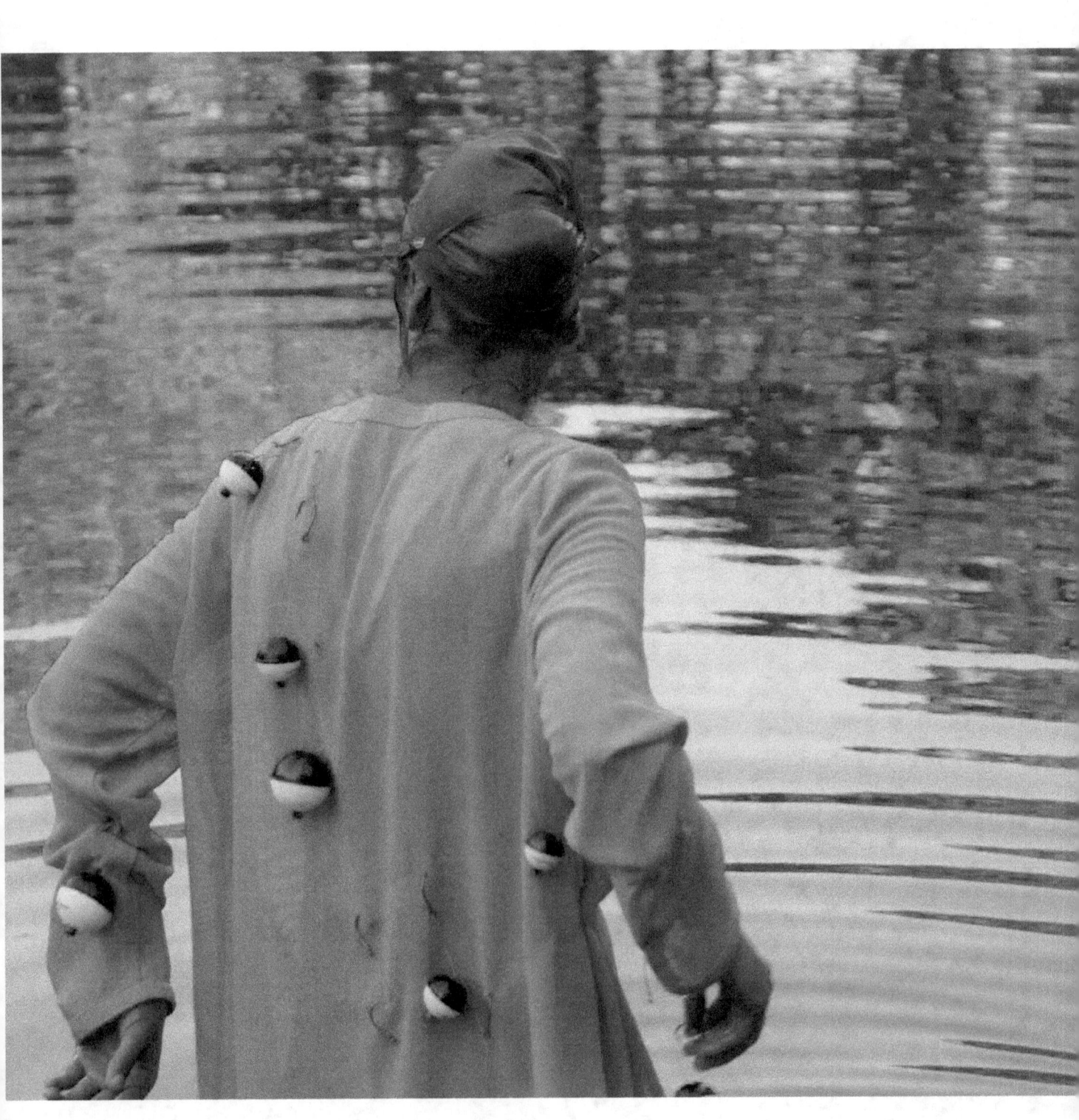

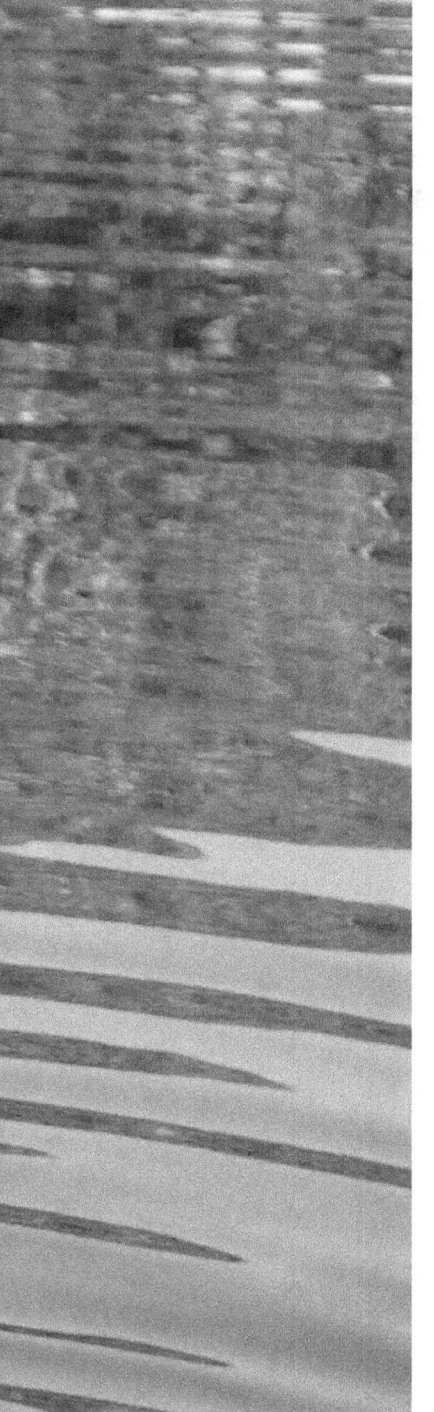

I have a permit to be here. He tells me that I am violating the rules. He claims that I am menacing and threatening and causing damage to the space, which is an opinion that comes out of his ignorance (and جهل) of the space. If he knew what I went through inside these ponds, how merciless and cruel the ponds were to me, he would punish the space instead of punishing me. I was peace within the war (of the space) . But what could I expect from him? In essence, the policeman is only a body and the limitation of his thoughts are my body, and we are both distinct from the space.

This confrontation with the casting ponds made me realize the concept of war as a public space. Within the war zone exists bodies of people, bodies of buildings and bodies of water. They are all at the mercy of the destructive power of the war. I keep searching my body to find out how the sounds and sights of war affect a body's reactions to war.

It made me wonder how similar or even identical the sound of thunder cracking is to the sound of a bomb. How can there be a bomb inside the rain? What limited the wide sky in order to build fury from one place to another, where the sky transformed from being a collective desire to touch and reach, to become a nightmare that we want to escape to the extent of seeking refuge under the ground? How does air turn into phosphor ? How is it acceptable that tanks are characterized as vehicles, driven in the streets with or without excuse/reason, at times simply for creating a noise that enforces its reason to exist.

The video project began to take on a life of its own. Within three simple scenes, it reflected a poetic sense of conflict and chaos within peaceful existence. In essence, this confrontation mirrors a body reacting to the ravages of war and sounds, far from the safety of a dream and caught in the harsh reality that we are all fish lured by bait in a casting pond.

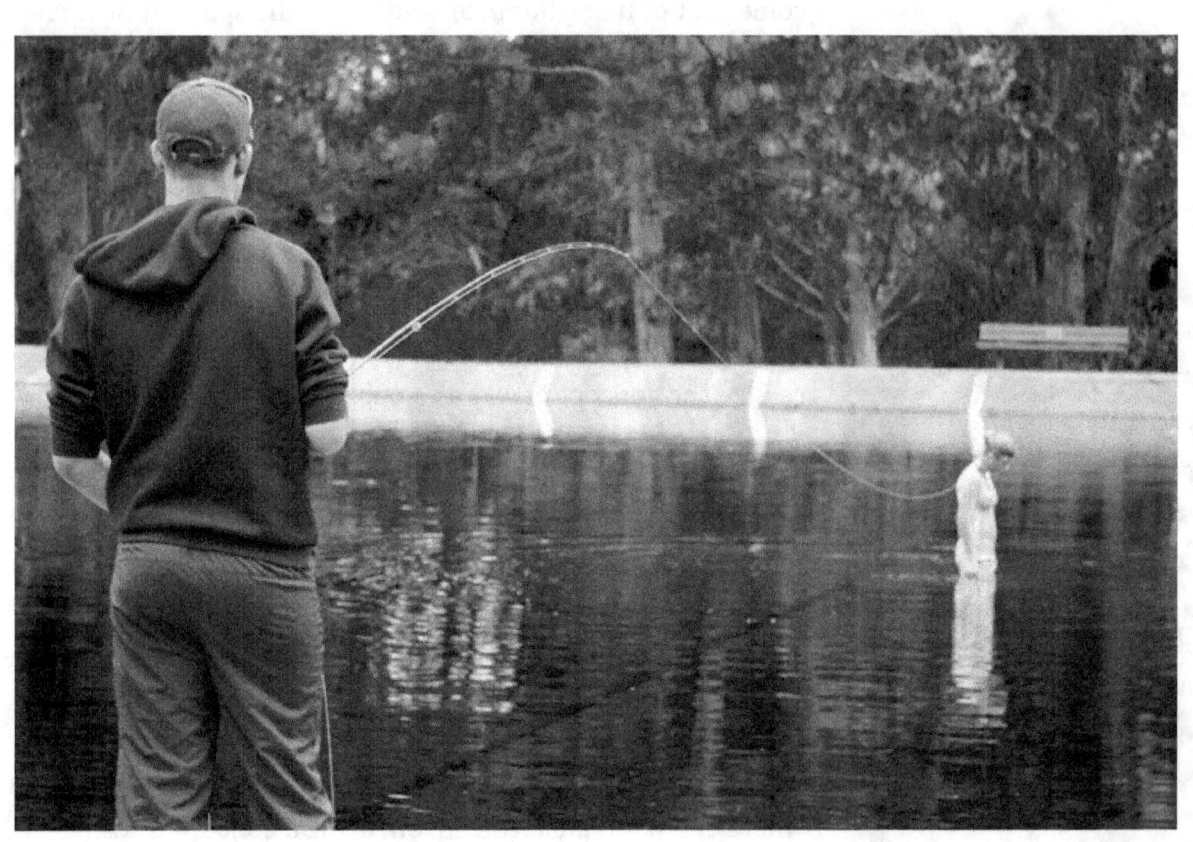

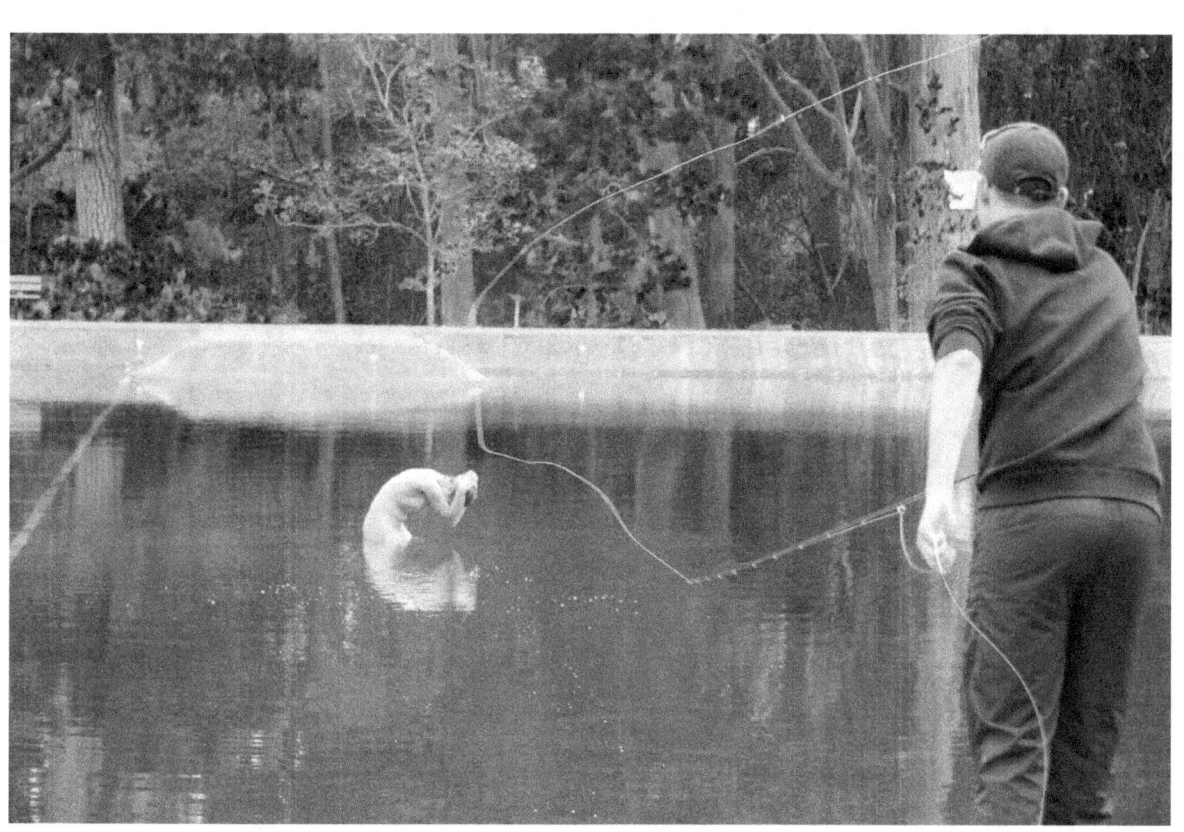

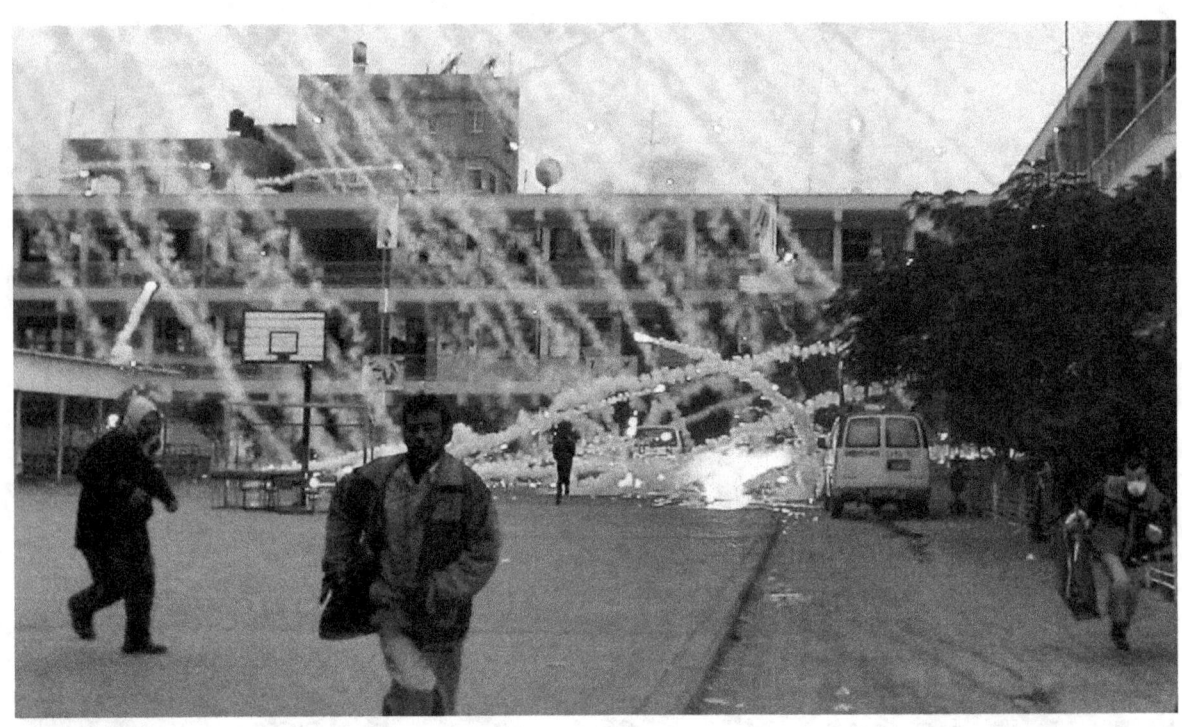

before/after before/after

والعدو من أمامكم " ـ طارق بن زياد

(People, the sea is behind you and

What is the limit of authority over my body? Can I cross the border
The papers are in order

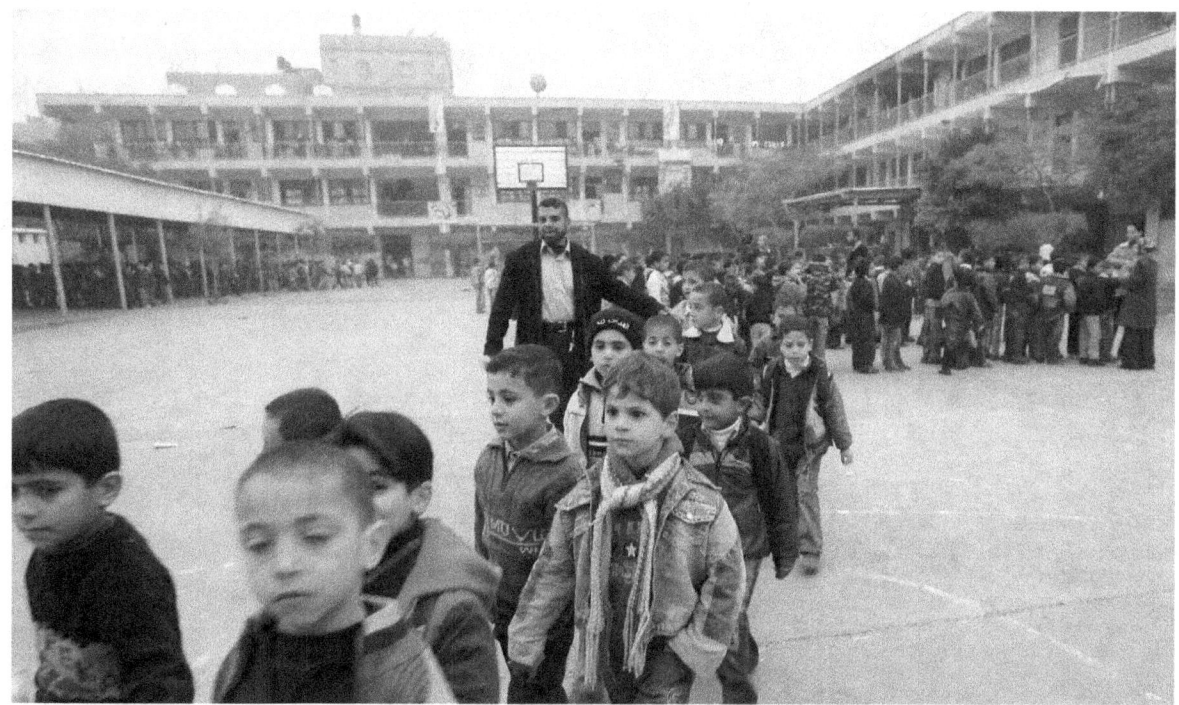

before/after before/after

"ياقوم البحر من خلفكم

the enemy is in front -Tariq ibn Ziyad)

with my body lying prone?
but my body is not.

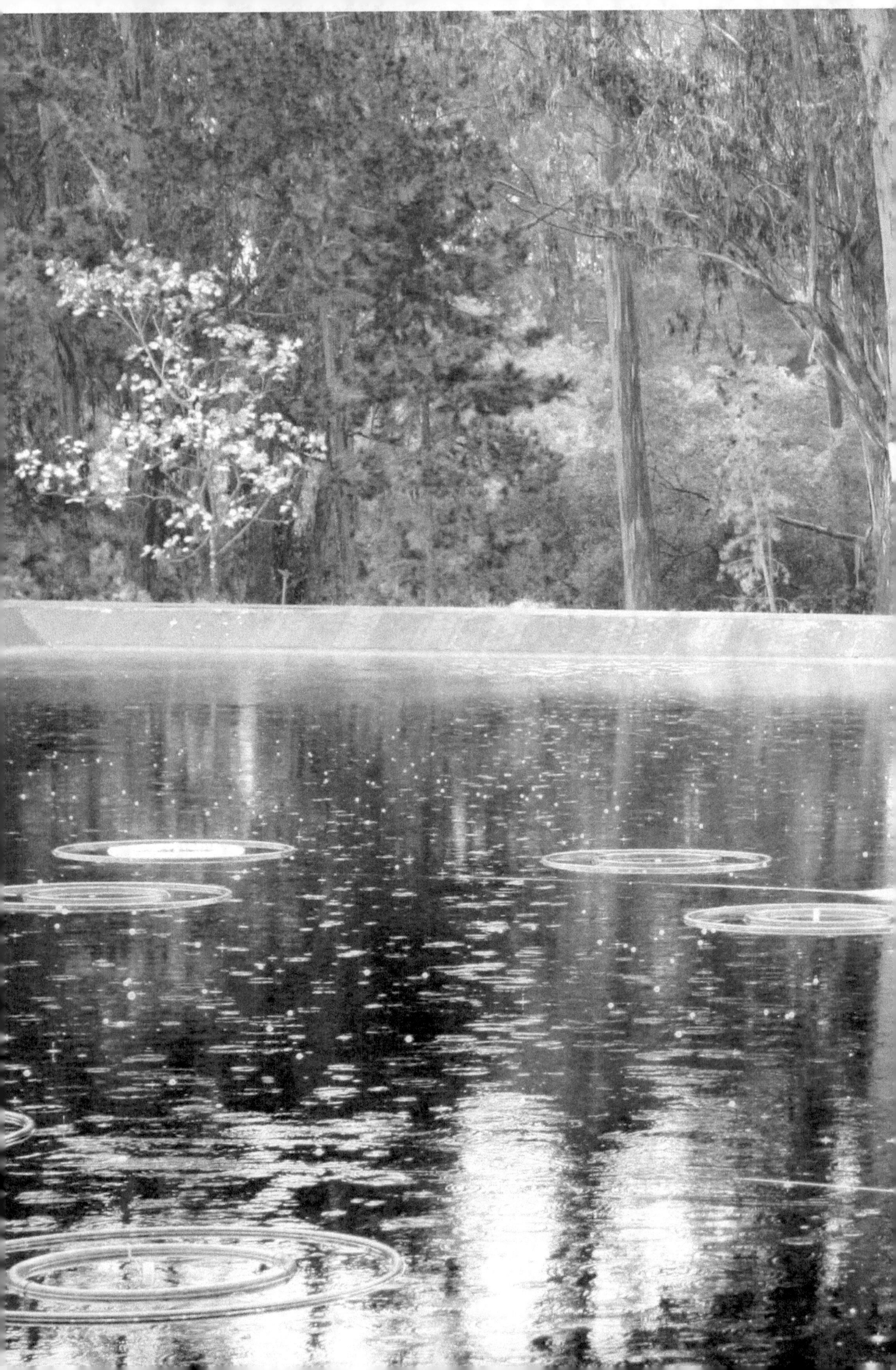

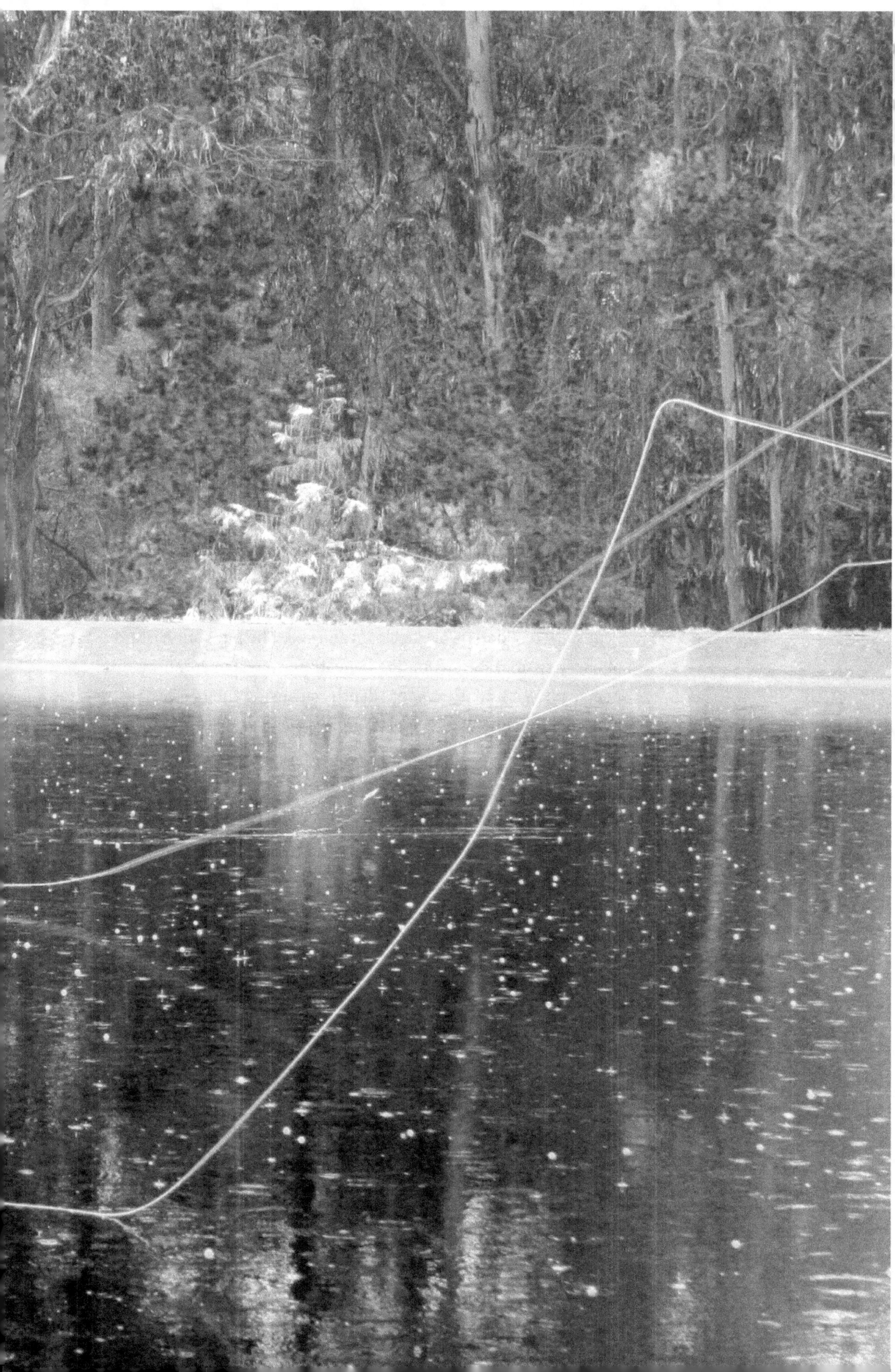

On Cannibalism
Lynne McCabe

I eat moist crumbling cakes soaked in heavy sweet milk,
with names I cannot pronounce. Cultures my being in
Europe has consumed.

Tres leche

I eat salty trodden meat, its bleat removed. The pungent irritant
of curry swimming, swimming beneath me. I watch cumin colored
people plunge into the waters depths cleansing themselves,
the Ganges holy. Hot and satisfying, my naan sops it up.

Lamb Bhuna

I eat sugar. It stains my teeth, it rots me. The land is so scorched
it smells like toffee. Sickly, sweet ruinous and sticky.

Sugar Cane

I eat pig and rice, I eat, I eat, I eat. The dumpling coddled and
holding skin, the red sea in my mouth sweet. The rice glutinous,
my eyes glaze. I don't recognize how perilous those chopsticks is.

Sweet and sour pork

I eat wombat it tastes like chicken. I grind its toughness between
my molars fingering the gristle as it gets stuck. Pulling at it.
Making an ugly face as I do it. Squeezing it between my fingers
and wondering why I didn't choose the crocodile, it taste like
chicken too.

Australia

I eat men. They taste like black olives. Sometimes I won't
feel hungry but they force myself all the same. Pink
ones, purple ones, sliver brown and cloaked, I choke.

Men

I eat my fathers history. It comes in the form of stewed cheap
meat. It makes a bed in my mouth. The folds of the meat
are to be tough to chew or change or swallow. I drink my
fathers history. My fathers history makes me drunk. I lose
focus, I feel sick. The barley sways and covers my mouth,
I cannot breath. I feel the drink drumming in my ears, if
only I could eat a potato, the flowery starch might help.

Ireland

My child eats me. First my blood, the calcium in my bones, the
nitrogen in my hair, the fibers in my muscles, the air in my lungs,
he couldn't get enough. He ate his way out of my cunt. Slurping
blood and shit. He ate my breasts, my milk, my want, my need.
He eats my time, my brain, and my patience. He ate my heart.

Gabriel

The Look of Being (especially in parks) and the Human Stand-In

Lauren Marsden

The Crowd, what is the code of its behaviour?
How is it recoded through an unauthorized congregation? How
long does it take for a chief to emerge?

In social space, even if a slight deviance from established norms
offers an initial moment of confrontation, disobedience behaves
as a dynamic image construction. Waywardness becomes
convention. Like swarm intelligence, individuals adjust their
actions by mimicking others as a way of achieving a collective
goal. We watch, we repeat. If a conflict is sustained, it ceases to
be anomalous to the established order and therefore contributes
to the picturesque or the ideal-normal. Only temporary
disruptions resist the embrace of the spectacle.

What if the conflict is not one of clear and stated
protest but one of leisured occupation? What if your leader
is Timothy Leary?
A miraculous meeting, a human forest.

(In)action.
The park cradles the interaction of idleness-sport in the spectrum
of leisure. Can idleness be perfected? The park is a repository
for passivity, as long as it falls into appropriate categories. The
picnicker, the jobless occupant, the spectator, even the wanderer
shall not stray far from the path. Here, labour is camouflaged.

For being to confront this order it must surprise
and rename itself.
This meeting was a baptism not a birthday party.

The Postcard is a way to figure the performance of pictures.
Picturesque behaviour requires that, at all times, a postcard
is being made. Recreational, moral, and dissident codes can
be distilled into their most basic forms, essentially into their
pictures or models. In the park, bodies move through the
"architecture" of fields and meadows, which become theatrical
stages. In this built idyllic space, the precariousness of the
actualized ideal, presupposes disorder. Restricted use code
which translates as regulated behaviour, allows for only one
notional picture to be made in a given space and anything else is
deviant. In our minds, we carry these postcards around with us.
Nearly everyone with something in their hands.

The Photographer must come to terms with the double role
as viewer-viewed.

The picture of the Human Stand-In (see back cover image)
is an implosion of the traditional methods of the touristic
appropriation of the landscape through its photographic capture
of the photographic capture. It is a colonization of pictorial
memory. It stems from the currently ubiquitous fashion of auto-
surveillance in the form of a staged self-reflection on history and
its documents. It is a re-imagining of self as posed against the
threshold of the photograph.
The paradox of a culture reincarnated by itself.

Recreation has the double meaning of pleasure and
rebirth. At the fair, the bohemian class can replenish
itself while publicly demonstrating its status.
Small groupings, arms linked moving gently from side to side.

The Photographic Imagination of one's position in the scene can be more readily determined by the casting of oneself into a pre-made tableau. Whether by cinema, photograph, webpage, there is always room for this imagined placement of self. Can I project my personal memory upon the historicized layers of this park? Perhaps it's too disappointing to actually be there now. *Be somewhere else now.* *

The Human Stand-In takes the now conventional representation of then deviant congregation, counterculture gatherings of the late 60s in Golden Gate Park and inscribes it on the current use of the site by staging a picture. It is a picture of layers constructed, briefly adjusting the postcard and its behavioural space. Provoked by the confused identity of the Christian White/Indigenous/Indian that was the American hippie, which adopted the pow-wow and the mela as its expression, it holds up history for examination. It attempts to create an almost now/almost then as a suspended moment. Then, by revealing a layer of pictorial memory, another layer is simultaneously obscured. Obscura meets lucida. It participates in the coming together through commemoration while it transforms to iconography and mythology. *The only way out is in.*

Italics are quoted from the underground newsprint publication, The Oracle (February 1967, San Francisco), "Human Be-In" article written by Steve Levine.

*Lawrence Ferlinghetti

Dear _____,

We were _____ in the park.

We came across a _____ and thought about _____. _____.

Yours truly,

_____

The Human Stand-In (after Dennis Maness) San Francisco 1967/2009

What is a Farm
Myvillages

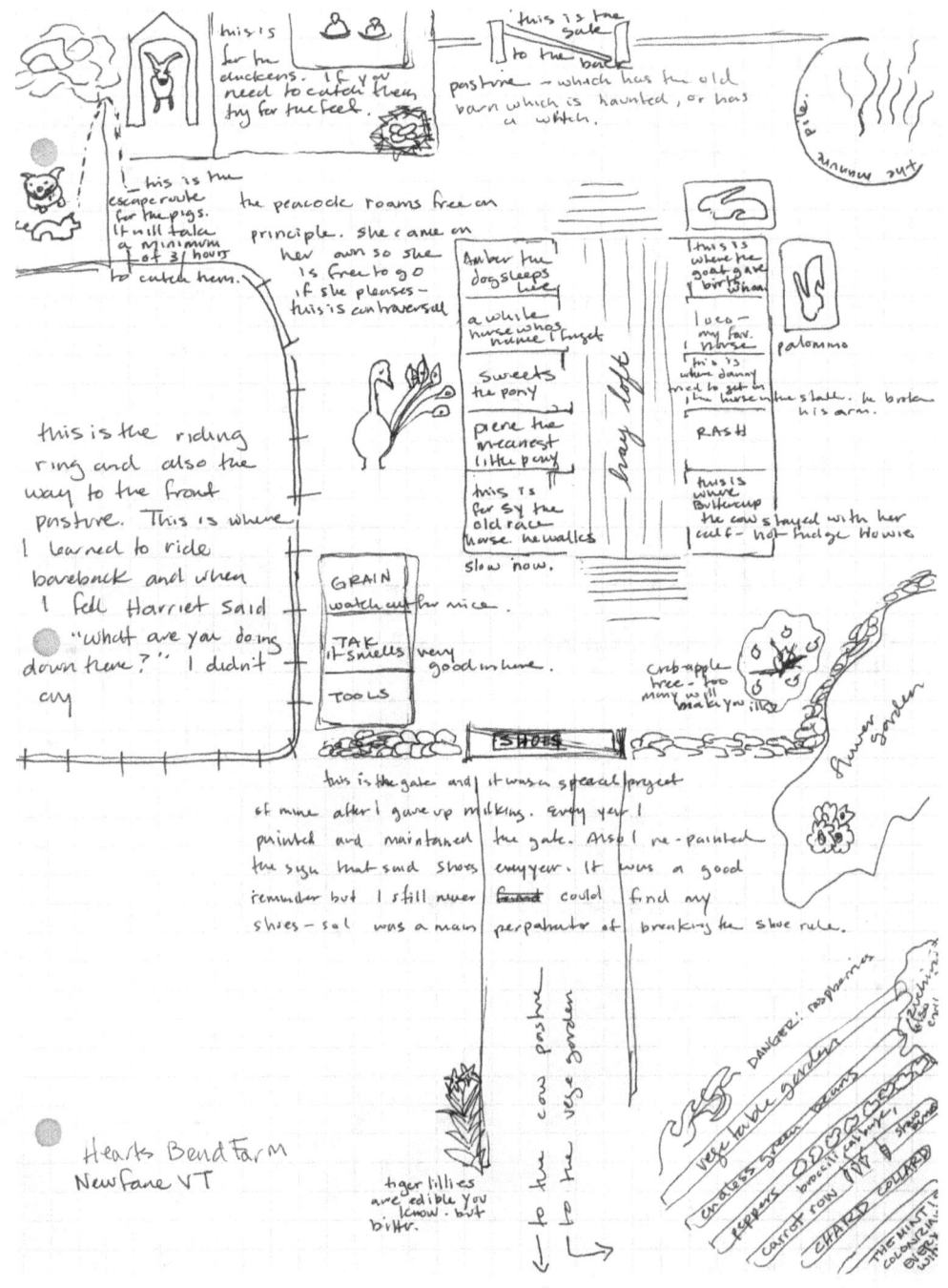

FIRST ACT

First scene

Social Practice Studio, California College of the Arts, San Francisco; many tables, dark carpeting; two guests from Europe are invited to teach for two weeks.

Wapke, Antje, Loudspeaker

Wapke. (farmer's daughter) I am educated but when you ask me for my first association with the word farm, animals pop up in my mind. They are animals that you tend and use for the production of milk, cheese and meat. Also pets belong to a farm. Animals lend their smell to the stables and the family. On the farm there are endless fields with a view so far that you can see the clouds driven by the wind. The farmer knows how to read the shape, colour and speed of the clouds. He acts as if he knows the weather forecast. I am standing next to my grandfather and we stare at the sky. His back is not good anymore, but despite this, he comes with us to help everyday.

Antje. We grew wheat and rye, barley and sugar-beet. We had cows, pigs and chickens. I do not remember that we ever went anywhere: we stayed on the farm with uncles and grandparents, occasional co-operators and frequent guests. Guests would just come in and step directly into the kitchen without ringing or knocking. There were all kinds of spaces: for us, for the animals, for the hay, for the tools, for the machines, and several dark ones with the smell of lubricants and grist containing long-term collections of things no one needed but that could be of use one day. Later, I lived in a Mexican village for two years. People were economically self-sufficient and lived from growing corn, beans and pumpkins on a very small scale. I must admit, I never saw them as farmers. For my internal definition of 'farm,' proper buildings, sheds, barns and stables are as integral as crops and livestock.

Speaker. (Wapke switches on the speaker.) The Dutch word for farmer is also used to indicate an uneducated person with rude behaviour. Wapke did not know this as long as she lived on the farm in the North of the Netherlands. Antje grew up close to the Iron Curtain. When visitors from far away came to that area, the frontier protection of the german-german border was the only interesting thing to show to them. To meet with aunts and cousins living fifteen kilometers away on the other side of the border, they had to drive all day and make a U-turn in Berlin to meet before sharing two hours in a motorway service area.

Second scene

After the lunch break. Cups of soup and a Brussels sprout salad on a studio table. The students are asked to each make a drawingof the first farm that comes to their mind, either an existing or a fictional one. Seemingly some do not like the idea, but they do not object. Some draw a map. Some go more and more into detail once they have started activating their memory. Piero takes the drawing seriously and goes to his desk to do it calmly.

Brin, Piero, Forest, Malak, Wafaa, Rio, Matthew, Anthony, Georgia, Anna, Rebecca, Lauren, Amy, Wapke, Antje, Ted

Forest. What is this good for?

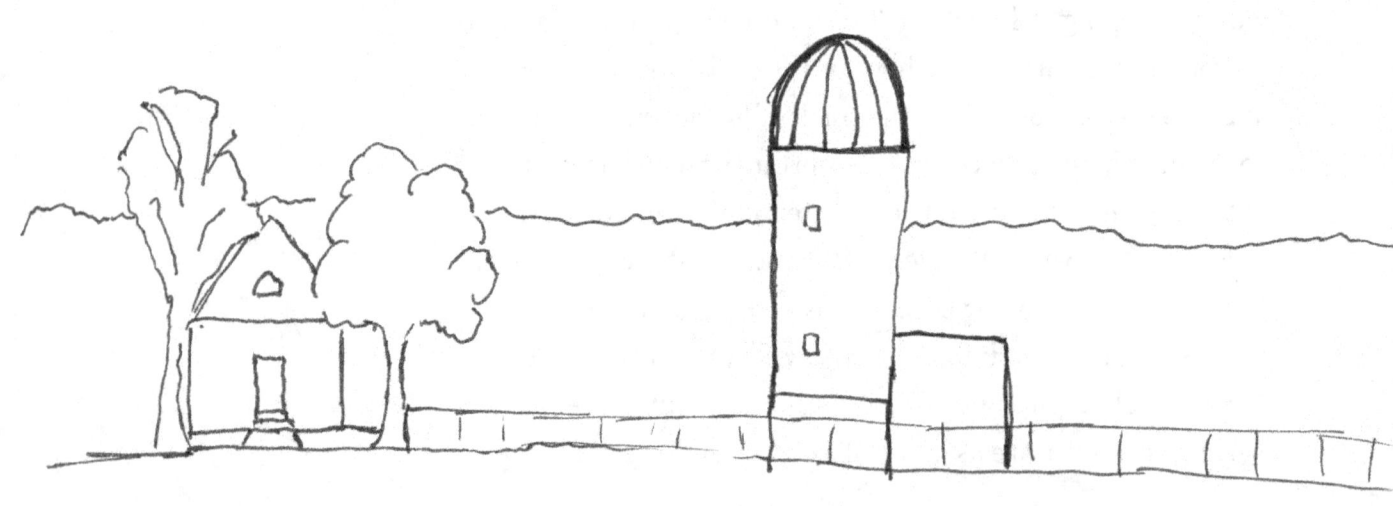

Innisfil, Ontario, Canada

SECOND ACT

First scene

The drawings hang on the white wall in the collective studio space.
Later in the evening the drawings are re-hung on a black wall with some
colourful graffiti that says "100 greatest hits". This wall was part of a
set made by Forest Lewinger in which amateur musicians played 100 greatest
hits in a day.

Second scene

Next day. Wapke comes in and passes by the new spot of the
drawings – not seeing them – than she looks at the white wall
were they were hanging yesterday.

Brin, Wapke, Loudspeaker

Wapke. Heh!! Where are the farm-drawings?

Brin. Last night we needed this wall for a filmscreening, so we
put them all on that wall. *(She points at the 100 greatest hits wall and
walks in that direction. Wapke follows her.)*

Wapke. Oh thanks, I did not see them. Are they all there?

Brin. Yes, I think so.
(Wapke points at the drawings and nods her head).

Speaker. When navigating the public space, expectations are
often stronger than the eye. In traffic this is dangerous! And
then, of course, it is also a gift, as without the expectation
that other will obey the rules nothing would work, in traffic
or business or friendship. Art shown in a public space deals
with this as well. It needs performance or narrative to catch
the eye. Size also matters wouldn't you say? Do not take the
size battle too seriously, because there is always a way to
communicate the quality of an encounter, or to make a good
registration of a moment.

Third scene

The day before Wapke and Antje leave San Francisco. They take all drawings from the 100 greatest hits wall in the Social Art Practise Studio. Some tape they remove, most tape they fold back. Wapke puts them in her suitcase and carefully folds the two big drawings to fit them in a A4 map.

THIRD ACT

First scene

Back at home. Emails between Berlin and Rotterdam.

Antje, Wapke

Antje. Do you have the drawings we made with the students? I don't know why, but suddenly I felt unsure and was afraid that they were left in our San Francisco apartment.

Wapke. Hi, I have them here, although I haven't scanned them yet.

Second scene

Piero pops up, multitasking. Emails between San Francisco and Europe.

Piero, Antje, Wapke, Loudspeaker

Piero. We are currently in the planning stages of a publication and were wondering if you are interested in contributing something for inclusion in the book. *(Fast answer required.)*

W & A. You probably remember that as part of our workshop we asked you for a drawing of a farm. Now we would like to take these drawings as a starting point for our contribution. What do they tell us about farms and what about cultural difference?

Piero. We would like to have a more specific idea of what you plan to do. Some people were "shy" about including their drawings directly in the book, since they didn't compose them for the publication.

W & A. That some of your drawings look like they were made by an amateur is not a big deal for us. We are very interested in art and non-art spaces and in interweaving amateurism. Using the drawings is more about location and activating memory by a real thing that is crosses through space and time.

Speaker. Wapke and Antje forgot something. How to define public space? Sounds like a bureaucratic question, doesn't it? Anyhow, we might agree that it includes shared mental images of common clichés like "what is a farm?" Maybe there are symbols that don't resonate with everybody everywhere and have their cultural limits. From now on, we should also keep in mind that, while working as an artist in public space, the line between you and me and between art and non-art is not clear anymore. Being interactive means putting parts of yourself in the hands of others and vice versa. How does a project participant feel when his contribution is not handled in the way he expected? Or: How does the initiator of an art project deal with his aesthetic pretensions or with the demands of the art world when all participators produce boring kitsch? In the field of art in public space and social practice you probably have to embrace these questions, you have to feel challenged.

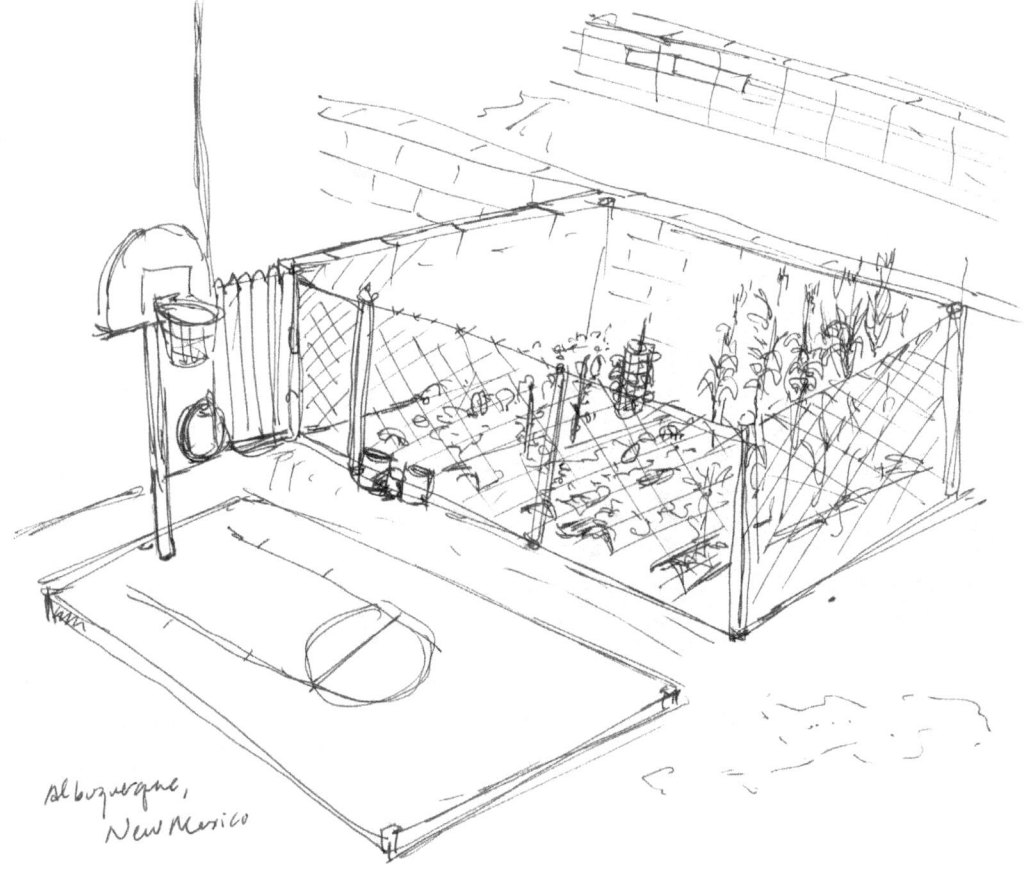

Albuquerque,
New Mexico

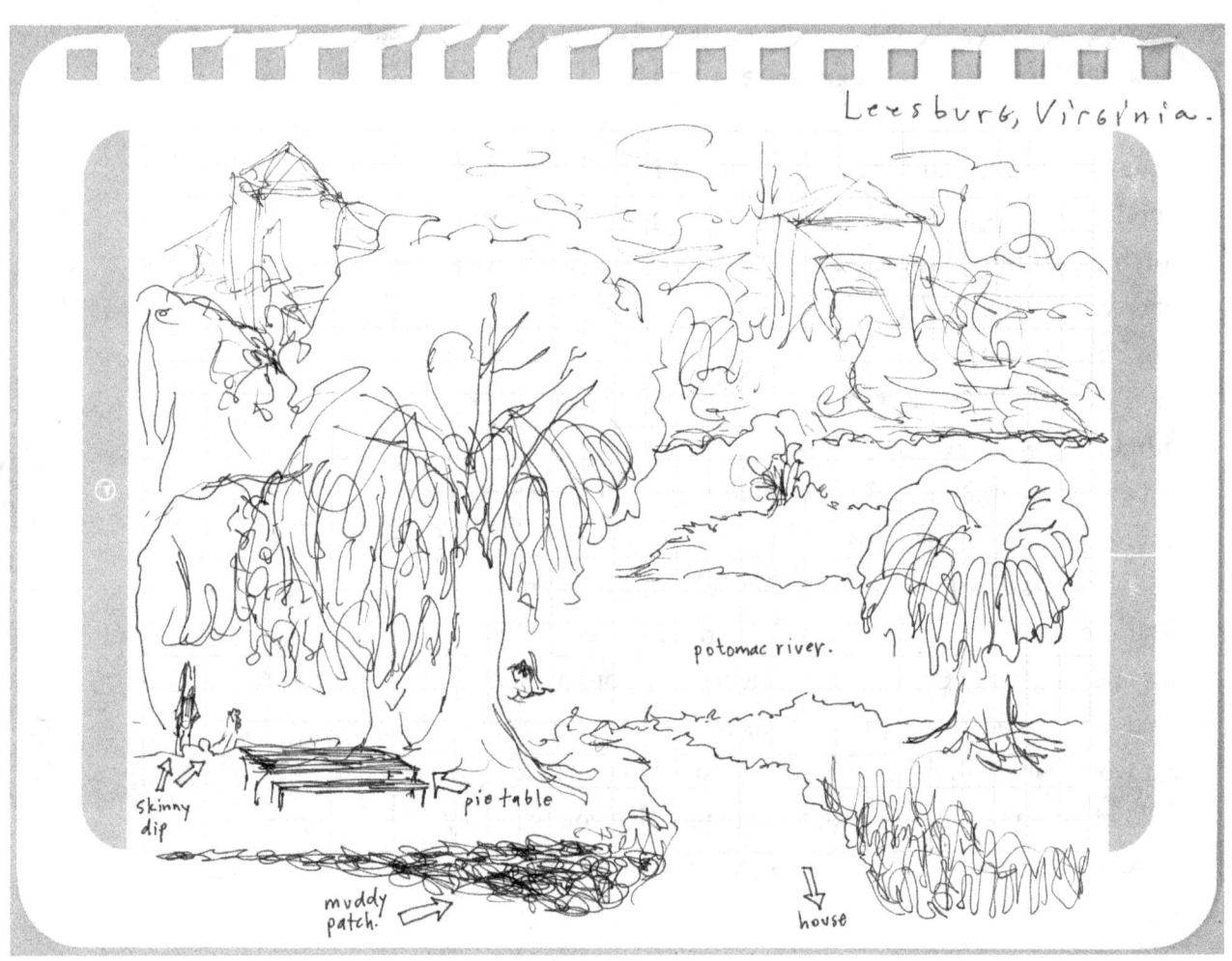

FORTH ACT

First scene

Two locations. Antje looks at the drawings on her screen. Wapke sits in her studio in Rotterdam. Drawings lay on the table.

Antje, Wapke, Piero, Loudspeaker

Antje. I am attracted by maps and the names of places, rivers and mountains. When I studied linguistics, we were told that the names of rivers were the oldest of all names. The history of American naming is probably different from European. Anyhow, Potomac River sounds promising and mysterious, and that's what the drawing looks like too. It has wild lines, so it probably has wild vegetation. There are weeping willows along the river. Some buildings in the background could be houses or old two-storeyed barns. If they are barns, they look old-fashioned, built generations ago. They do not look like ones that are very popular these days among farmers, but perhaps like ones favoured among people converting them for country living. Are they overgrown by nettles and thistles, ivy-covered, hidden under young birches, creeper, parasitical plants or all the secrets of the forests and swamps of Virginia? I have never been to Virginia. I have no idea of how remote or populated a place like this at the Potomac River really is. What is for sure: The drawing shows a place for pleasure, for picnics and naked swimming behind the muddy patch. If it is a farm, it seems to be a guest remembering it, a child maybe, no need to focus on production.

Wapke. We arrive by donkey quite late at the yard of the Eldefrawi-Farm in Egypt. The dog is scared by our appearance and makes sounds you cannot define as either barking or screaming; it is just a strange mix. The sun sets. The next morning the same dog sounds as we cross the citrus yard. I am glad we did not eat pigeon last night: their houses are full of shit and they look stressed. We walk on. Our sight is limited by all of the full-grown cornfields, we see no horizon anymore when we arrive in Vermont. This farmhouse has two porches, but most windows are blinded with paper, one is broken. A horned goat pops up in front of the shed. Is this a Billy goat? "Not a clue!" the food containers say aloud. They tell us about strong winters when all the corn in the containers is eaten by goats and cows that prefer to live indoors.

In South Lanarkshire sheep can collect their own food again, once the snow has melted. They graze high fields where just one tree and an old black road can be seen. These sheep are left to their own devices. In Tamra, Palestine, a flock of white sheep has year-round access to feed and is therefore also fenced off. A skinny farmer fills the manger with a number of trips carrying three buckets. Filling mangers by hand is a sporty occupation. Also, grandma doesn't need city sports, she is weeding or busy watering the vegetables in her garden. But next to her garden in Albuquerque young Mexican men manically play baseball. Grandma has to protect her garden, which is surrounded by high metal fences and two walls. We also see high fences around an apple orchard in Fithian Illinois; do they protect their apples from wild animals? In Italy instead we see a more symbolic fence, low and fragile protecting an olive tree, a slightly hilly landscape, with a food container and a shed.

Piero. Not sure if it is Italy, it could also be somewhere in California...

Speaker. Wapke and Antje are keenly aware that they lack the knowledge to read these farm-drawings; they have to dig up their own memories, all they have seen and heard before, to fill in their stories. They do not understand how algae can grow in water pipes in the kibbutz. All of the farm-drawings have told them that food production is still an idea commonly associated with farms. The subject seems to be one that everybody links to memory and personal experience, even if the personal experience is an urban backyard garden. Nobody drew a farm as they had seen on TV or taken from another non-personal source.

FIFTH ACT

First scene

Several small couches. Everyone is there, some people just over Skype. Antje wears glasses, Wapke takes notes.

Everyone

Antje. In our investigations on the subject we often observed that the idea of farming is linked to innocence, just as childhood memories are – and we suspect that the resistance to doing these drawings is also one to this idyllic and naïve connotation. (Wapke hands over a note with a deadline. Note flutters away.)

The End.

(Student choir sings in canon: Surprise us!)

EPILOGUE

The farm drawings will be part of a symposium on the image of farming taking place in Nordhorn on the dutch-german border in January 2010. It will be the third symposium organised by myvillages. Myvillages is an international artists initiative founded by Kathrin Böhm, Wapke Feenstra and Antje Schiffers (www.myvillages.org).

Some Parks That Rhyme and Don't [1]
Malak Helmy

1. Al-Messilah: Eastern Park - also known as Sunset Park. 1987.
Doha, Qatar. The compound is ten and quite new. There are
five parks in the compound, two on Mecca Street, one on
Casablanca, one on Western and one on Eastern. They all have
a hexagonal structure at their center nested in white sand. It
is circumscribed by a sharp-edged hedge that runs around the
periphery of every house. They all look the same. The hexagon
is guarded by a single tree that stands upright to its side.

I exit the house and walk to the left, not knowing if it is
towards Western or Eastern but it leads to the park five
minutes away. The street reflects bright light. It is smooth
and glossy. The walk there is silent save for the hum of
air conditioner's fans and the buzz of the security guard
on his bike circulating the compound again and again.

To the right of the hexagon, observing the park stands a
lone fitness-training board. An army green sign encased in
glass pressed between two thick pieces of dark, withered
oak. There are no oak trees there. On the board, mold
slowly spreads on a stick figure of a man leaning sideways
under instructions that say, "Exercise Number Five: Stretch
your right arm over your body and lean to the left. Repeat
on the other side." It is forgotten here from somewhere
else. We are young. The place is young. The sign is old.

2. Sporting Club. 2005.

Alexandria. There are security guards to whom to show
membership cards and tall gates from which to pass. There
is a road down which to proceed through a sporting club.[2]
The road leads towards a cottage-like structure at its center.
There is a short, green, wrought iron gate to be pushed open
– it is heavy and cold. Through it you walk down a small
hall, and climb up dark, musky stairs. The sound of children
running and cars trying to park are not heard here. On the
balcony upstairs four generations sit together, observing
each other. They do this every day. They order lunch from
an eighty-year-old waiter who has been serving at the club
through a revolution. There is competition between the
oldest men over familiarity with the waiter. The more inside
the joke with him the greater the testament to old family
glory. They refer to the good old days in French. Over lunch,
as they sit on the balcony, they observe the green golf field
circumscribed by apartment blocks that bow towards it.
Colored plastic bags float out of the apartment windows.
They sail in the air like balloons then eventually land on
the course. They finish their lunch. The grandfathers
collect their clubs and go to play with husbands and pre-
pregnancy wives. The mothers sit together and exchange
stories about motherhood and trouble with maids.

3. The Department of Special Gardens. March 2000.

Cairo, Egypt. The Governor of Cairo, Abdel Rehim Shehata,
an agriculturalist, establishes a department of "Special
Gardens" in the governorate of Cairo. Previously, these
gardens were under the jurisdiction of the *Ministry of
Beautification and Cleanliness* along with public spaces
and pavements. The new department identifies gardens
that will receive extra funding for maintenance and
administration, staff salaries and historical preservation.
They select twenty-three gardens, based, they describe,
on their national heritage or esteemed artistic value.

Several of the *Special Gardens* are public parks and gardens developed in the mid 1800s. Many were designed within the new European expatriates or bourgeois neighborhoods for, "healthy leisure activity that was both moral and modern."[3] *Special Gardens* are to look at from the outside, for exhibition, their landscaping ornate, their plant variety vast.

The *Department of Special Gardens* employs up to 1100 employees over 852,000 square meters of garden to maintain the parks- that is one person per 774 square meters. The gardens are protected by gates. There is a special fee for entry, varying from one to five EGP. The fee is generally too high for the current residents of the neighborhoods to pay. The fee is too low to buy other resident's interest. "A number of restrictions are in force - no sitting on the grass, no food admitted, no peddlers inside."[4]

4. Mohandiseen. May 2005.

Cairo, Egypt. There is a fine line separating the two ways of traffic, in it is a lick of grass coddled by knee-high fences. Six well-built men climb over the fence for their lunch break. They sit on the grass in a row, with backs leaning on fence behind and toes touching fence in front. Their heads are adjacent to cars moving past their view from right to left. One on the end is older and a little withered. They all squat with grey galabiya, white, salmon pink, draped around an arm flopping over knee. They fumble in their squat to get a good position to eat their lunch.

5. Department of Distinguished Gardens. 2001.

Cairo, Egypt. Since the secession of the twenty-three special gardens the Ministry of Beautification and Cleanliness has been monitoring pavements and public green squares under one budget. In 2001, the Ministry of Beautification and Cleanliness establishes The Department of Distinguished Gardens. Ten gardens are selected into the department; they are mostly in low-income neighborhoods. They are

gated too. They do not receive a special fund. One of the
gardens initially placed in this department, Al-Fustat
Garden, is one of the largest and most popular parks in the
city of Cairo. It was developed on a dumping ground for
refuse in 1989. It accommodates a large number of visitors
on flat grass. Its grounds cannot accommodate trees
since the treatment of the soil placed on the grounds has
been limited and cannot hold tree roots. Absence of tree
shade is compensated by placement of shading kiosks.

6. *The Garden of Waterfalls, (Geneinet El Chalalat). September 2007.*
Alexandria, Egypt. Sitting close to downtown is *The Garden
of Waterfalls* (Geneinit il Chalalat). I saw no waterfall, and so
did not know why it bore that name. It was dry and bore
some gentle hills that hinted at yellowed brittle grass.
There were stones and bricks that cave into a hovel.

In recent years Alexandria has been said to be 'brought
back': some said it was the new governor, some claimed it
was the French Archeologist Jean Yves L'Empreur and others
the increase in international funding from Mediterranean
cultural exchange. In that period of being 'brought back'
waterfalls appear in the park, with blue, red, orange
dramatic lighting. Flanking the blossoming gardens edges
is a gathering of sculpted trees and animated bushes: pram-
shaped, jester-shaped, two Pacman-like blobs - one smiling
one frowning, the name of God, the cosmos, twists, arrows.
The bushes are carved with precision. I try to find the man
responsible. The topiarist. I find an arborist instead- an
older man observing the gate to the protected corner of
the park; he is its self-proclaimed historian. He has been
standing there for thirty-five years. He tells me the gardener
has no idea what he was doing and is a mute, then proceeds
to tell me the history of the gnarled trees. With pride he
points to one of the trees to my right and his left, "this
was planted here in 1902, its one hundred and five years
old, it was planted by the British. Its a Sycamore tree."

7. www.oxfordplanters.co.uk. March 2009.

Topiary is the art and practice of clipping trees and
shrubs into ornamental shapes. The word has both
Latin and Greek roots, the Latin being topia; mural
decorations depicting landscapes, and topiarus,
more appropriately, a landscape gardener. [5]

The Greek *topis* is simply a place.

The hedge is a simple form of topiary to create a boundary.

The art of topiary traveled from one place to another in
the minds of slave workers. They applied their skills in the
different empires into which they had been annexed.

8. Dallas, Texas. August 2008.

Driving somewhere around the UNT campus between
large red brick mansions with pointed roofs and red
shingles. I see two, six-foot dog-shaped shrubs, Terriers
to be precise. They remind me of Jeff Koons' fourty-three-
foot Puppy that stood once at the Rockefeller Plaza. I saw
it in a book once. It now stands in Bilbao Guggenheim.
One version of it was auctioned for 23.6 million dollars.

9. Golden Gate Park. November 2008.

San Francisco. On the review website, Yelp, two hundred and
twenty five people confirm that there is a lovely Tea Garden
with Japanese topiary. On a weekend afternoon I go to the
park with a friend. Walking between a polo field and the car
park I find a sign, army green encased in dark, withered Oak-
the fitness-training board. This one is number seven and it
says "Step Up: Choose Stump of challenging height. Place left
foot on stump. Step up; step down with right leg. Then step up
with right leg, step down with left. Continue by alternating
legs." A stick-figured man demonstrates on the board. I stop.
In this park they extend into an extensive circuit of fitness
training numbered one to twelve. They decorate the path that
leads into a forest of Oak trees where spritely young people
jog by and someone else's memory of a *be-in* sits to the left.

10. *Horreya Garden. March 29th 2007.*

Cairo, Egypt. Horreya Garden "accepts only two hundred visitors at a time, commensurate with the number of seats available in the garden." I recall that on days past while walking I had peered at fast edits of green spliced between the bars of its gates. A distant snipping of bushes was cut in rhythm and a hum of leaves was swept in between. I paid five EGP for entry and fifteen for my camera. There were six people inside. Four of them were cleaning.

11. *Downtown. January 2009.*

Cairo, Egypt. 180 people sit in a factory-space-turned-lecture-hall in Downtown Cairo. Between them and a large projection screen sits the urban planner of one the major real-estate companies developing two of the new housing and commercial districts on the desert outskirts of the city. He speaks of his firm's attempts to improve housing rights, economic, environmental and social conditions through their new designs and mixed land use initiatives. During the Q and A a woman in the audience asks why the developments on the desert outskirts are all built around golf courses. He responds by explaining that the operating zoning law specifies that 76% of a Cairene plot of land must be left un-built- a zoning law prioritizing agricultural development. He says it is poor land-use policy. He follows by elucidating that real-estate companies build golf courses to abide by these laws while keeping land value high and getting a return on their investment.

12. *Channel One, May 1997.*

Cairo, Egypt. President Hosni Mubarak inaugurates a private golf course on the outskirts of the city on live television. He says that he sees there a green lung for the Cairene people.[6]

13. *Las Vegas, 2008.*

A writer from In Business Las Vegas, interviews a Las Vegas-based landscaper about the upsurge in sustainable and native landscaping in the desert city. The landscaper says that the landscaping modifications are mostly motivated by requests made by the very businesses that were deemed "water guzzlers" in the past. He follows to say that it is not awareness, environmental conservation or a shift in aesthetics that motivates this desire for a natural look, but rather an interest in budget cuts.

"Native" desert plants can largely survive on their own; they do not require mowing, pruning fertilizing and watering as would a non-native landscape of grass fields and show-stopping ornamental plants and flowers that had grown to become the norm in Vegas landscaping. Natives such as Apache plumes, mesquites, yuccas can get by almost entirely on rainfall, they occasionally require a watering during dry years.

He says, "Its an approach that isn't for everyone but people have to be willing to let the desert win. 'The natives' and the 'Introduced Natives' create more of a natural desert design and look. Either you love it or you hate it here in the desert."

14. Corniche. 2001.

Doha, Qatar. On Fridays everyone flocks East towards the Sea, at 5 pm, close to Sunset, they take walks on the corniche. The 10-minute lateral auto migration is of the weekend; the 10-minute longitudinal auto migration is of the weekday.

The corniche was made up of a long stretch of sea and cacti, prickly garden bushes and adapted shrubbery of dark greens. Qatar receives an average of 3.5mm of annual precipitation and its native plants are few.[7] It had embraced an 'introduced native' landscape that was well maintained. Around 2001 the plants are uprooted and a carpet of golf grass green is laid down in their place that extends as far as the eye can see. It is streamlined to complement the sharp lines of the blue glass towers that begin to pierce like crystals into the sky. On occasion the green landscape reflects on the glass buildings and suddenly the horizon shoots green bars into vertical space. Ribbons of water pump into the air forming arcs in between. We are encircled by a matrix of green.

15. *Al-Messilah, Facebook. 2006*

There is a group on Facebook called Al-Messilah Mafia. It has
three hundred and twenty seven members, none of whom
live in Al-Messilah anymore. The Al-Messilah Diaspora.
One of them uploaded images of the compound, one of
which is an image of this house. Six claimed the picture as
a photograph of their house, two of them were right. This
is 138 Sunset. Another two were living two houses away,
three years apart. The smoothness of the image promotes
amnesia. Or the smoothness of the place promotes amnesia.
But its all the same, we all share the same flat recollection
of this place and begin to revel in that flatness. 138 Sunset
is Extra Large. Other houses also come in Large and
Medium. That is as far as the variation in memory goes.

All the houses had red painted tiles around the garage,
one thin palm tree, red shingles on pointed roofs
that protect us from imaginary rainy weather and
cardboard walls that are dented by sibling brawls.

On Facebook people who lived in Al-Messilah from 1987 to
2009 now suffer from nostalgia. When they were living there
they had not heard of nostalgia. They had been trained not
to attach sentiment to place by an educational dislocation of
text from image, emotion from subject, self from structure.
They all left at the age of eighteen. Outside, people learned of
the concept of nostalgia. And when they did they found that
they became nostalgic for amnesia, the silence save for the
hum of fans on air conditioners and nondescript roads. The
glossy smoothness. The absence of before or after. Sitting on a
hexagon in a park with a security guard circling around them
hourly observing them on his bike. And so Facebook became
a respite for eyes and memory. They began to live through
the Al-Messilah Mafia, with all 350 of the people they did not
know but who had once lived in the same misremembered
houses. They photograph themselves voraciously. Upload
images daily. Comment on them daily. Re-script them daily.

1. After Jordan Wolfson's, "Some Words that Rhyme and Don't," a solo exhibition and artist talk delivered on Tuesday, February 3rd 2009 for The Exhibition Formerly Known as Passengers 2.6 at the CCA Wattis Institute for Contemporary Arts. The Exhibition Formerly Known as Passengers is a constantly transforming exhibition, combining solo and group presentations. In his solo show Jordan Wolfson presented a half-rolled, patterned green carpet that revealed its rubber underlining. Beneath it lay a printed image of a Diet coke can in a cosy. On the other side of the room two foldable black metal chairs hung on one of the gallery walls and a printed image of a puddle in muddy grass on a wall opposite. The carpet-area of the installation was flanked by two large black speakers propped on stands that would alternately say "things that rhyme, and don't" - in a dead pan voice, then "things that rhyme, and don't" - in a theatrical voice. The statement was orated by the voice of one woman, and repeated.

2. The Sporting Club was established in 1898; it was frequented by British Officers during their occupation of Egypt.

3. Behrens-Abouseif, Doris. 1985. Azbakiya and Its Environs: From Azbak to Ismail, 1487 – 1879. Cairo: Institut Francais d'archeologie orientale. As quoted in Vincent Battesti, "The Giza Zoo: Re-appropriating Public Spaces, Reimagining Urban Beauty" in Cairo Cosmopolitan Eds. Diana Singerman and Paul Ammar, 489 – 512. Cairo: The American University in Cairo Press, 2006.

4. El Messiri, Nawal. "A Changing Perception of Public Gardens" in Cairo: Revitalising a Historic Metropolis. Stefano Bianca and Philip Jodidio, eds. Turin: Umberto Allemandi & C. for Aga Khan Trust for Culture, 2004. 221-233.

5. http://www.oxfordplanter.co.uk.

6. This is elaborated on in Eric Denis's, "Cairo as Neo-Liberal Capital? From Walled City to Gated Communities" in Cairo Cosmopolitan: Politics, Culture and Urban Space in the New Globalized Middle East Singerman, Diana and Paul Ammar, eds. Cairo: American University in Cairo Press, 2006.

7. Al-Mohammadi, A.Rahman, Qatar: Country Report to the FAO International Technical Conference on Plant Genetic Resources. Doha, 1995; Leipzig, 1996.

8. "There is a conflict between the unprecedented penetration of the new methods of power and the need to make them more acceptable, more unnoticed, more effective against diseases like 'nostalgia' and thereby more efficient."..."The regimentation of the 'productive powers' of the country had made cultivation and forced labour a duty almost as oppressive as conscription into the army." (71) Timothy Mitchell, Colonizing Egypt. Cambridge: Cambridge University, 1991.

Bibliography

Augé, Marc, <u>Non-Places: Introduction to An Anthropology of Supermodernity</u> John Howe, trans. London: Verso, 1995.

Davis, Mike, <u>City of Quartz: Excavating the Future in Los Angeles</u> London: Verso, 1990; New York: Vintage, 1990.

El Messiri, Nawal. "A Changing Perception of Public Gardens", 2004 in <u>Cairo: Revitalising a Historic Metropolis</u> Stefano Bianca and Philip Jodidio, eds. Turin: Umberto Allemandi & C. for Aga Khan Trust for Culture, 221-233.

Glass, Charlotte Schoell "Serious Issues": the last plates of Warburg's picture atlas mnemosyne" in <u>Art History as Cultural History: Warburg's Project</u> ed. Richard Woodfield Amsterdam: OPA, 2001.

Kolbert, Elizabeth, "Turf Wars", <u>NewYorker</u>, July 21, 2008.

Mitchell, Timothy, <u>Rule of Experts: Egypt, Techno-Politics, Modernity</u> Berkeley: University of California Press, 2002.

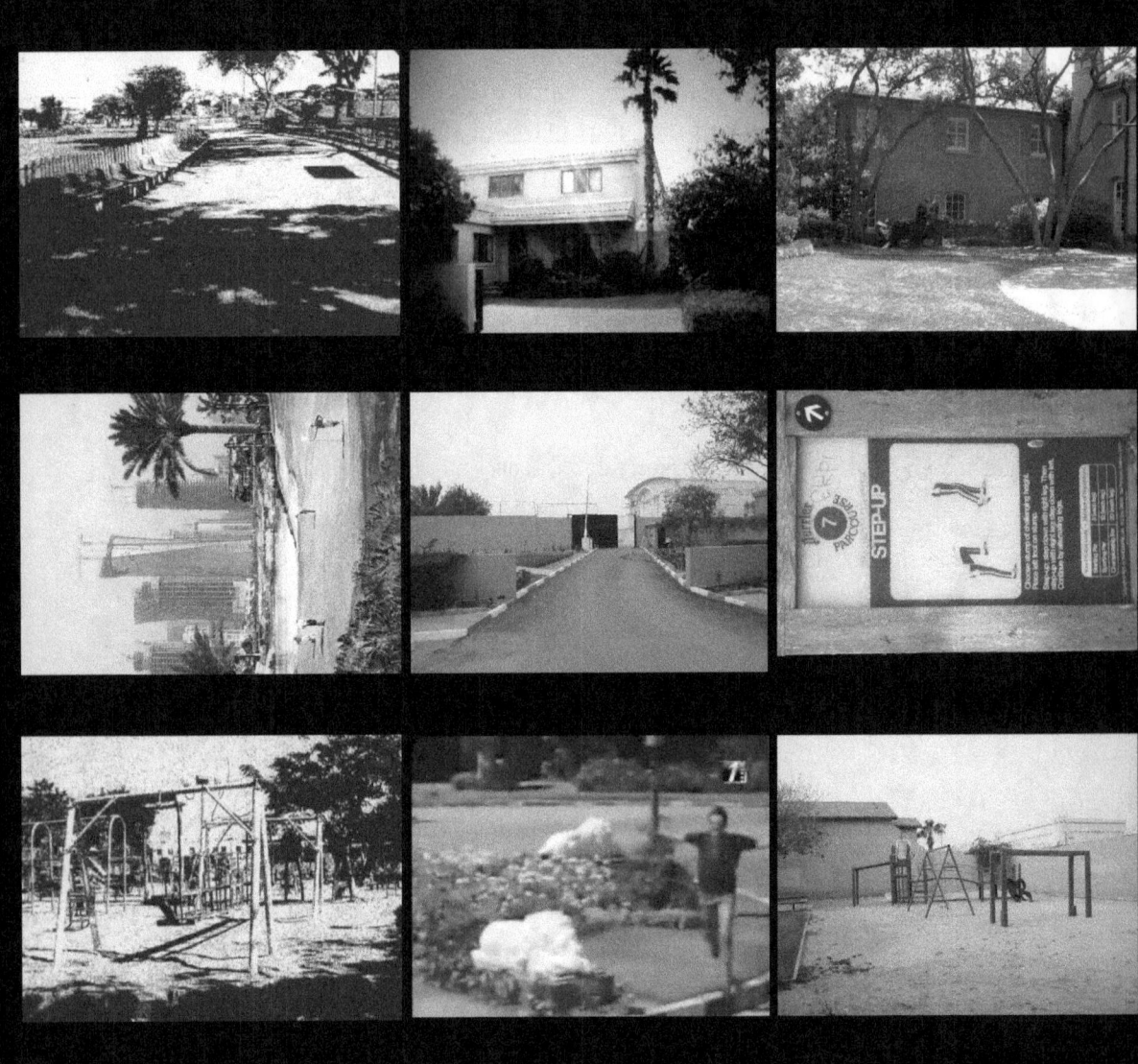

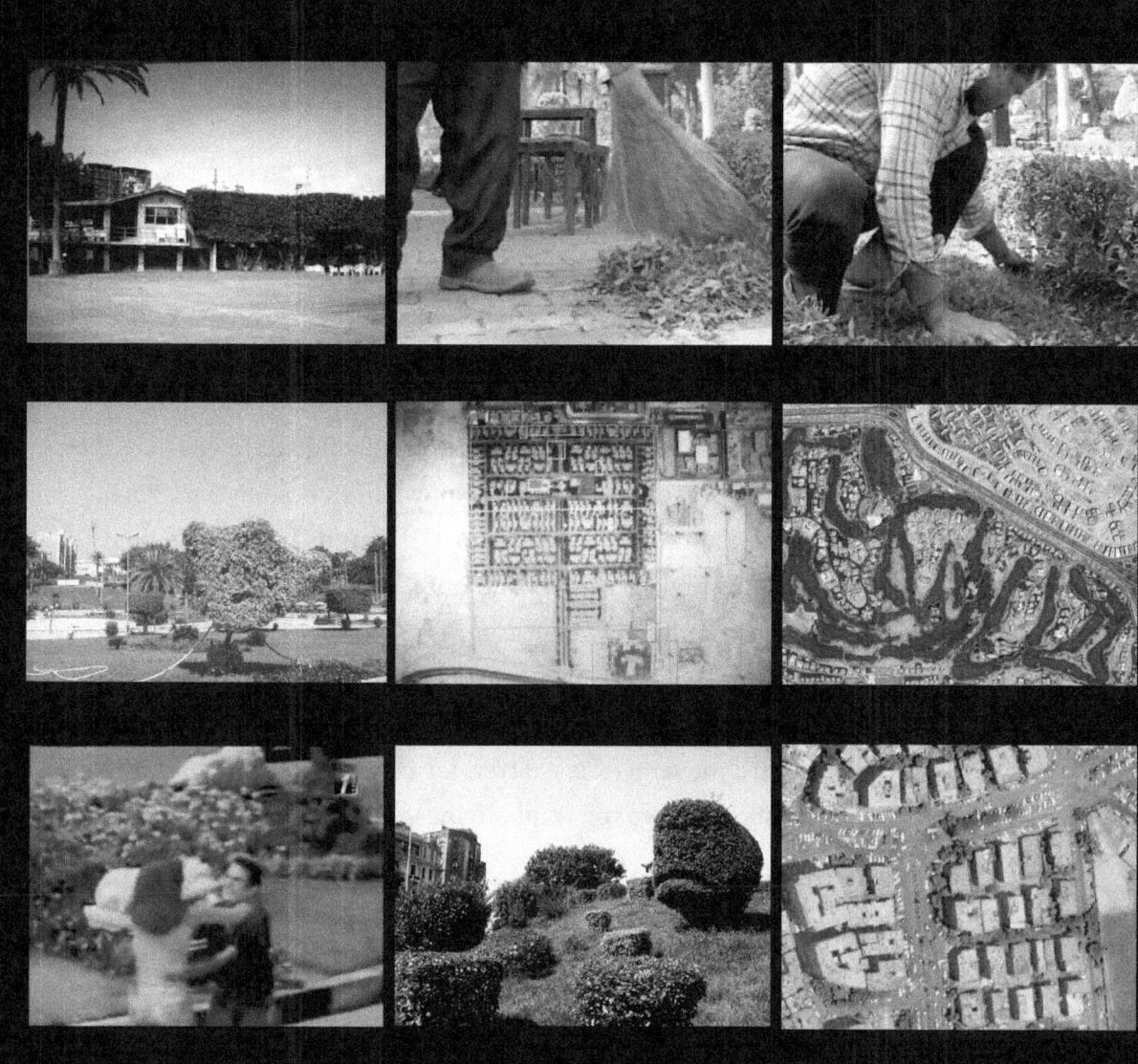

Two Drum Circles Surround an Accordion Player at Stowe Lake

Forrest Lewinger

The musical score, *Two Drum Circles Surround An Accordion Player at Stowe Lake*, was created out of the field recordings of different groups of musicians found playing at Stowe Lake, the Conservatory of Flowers, and Hippy Hill in Golden Gate Park on a particular day in February. The sounds from these field recordings were arranged and notated so that they may be played again. The first movement is for two conga, three bongo, two djembe, one shaker, one lead vocalist, and an indefinite amount of back up vocalists. The Interlude is written for one accordion. The third movement is written for two djembe, one humming vocalists, and two toy tambourines.

map of notes on a
drum head

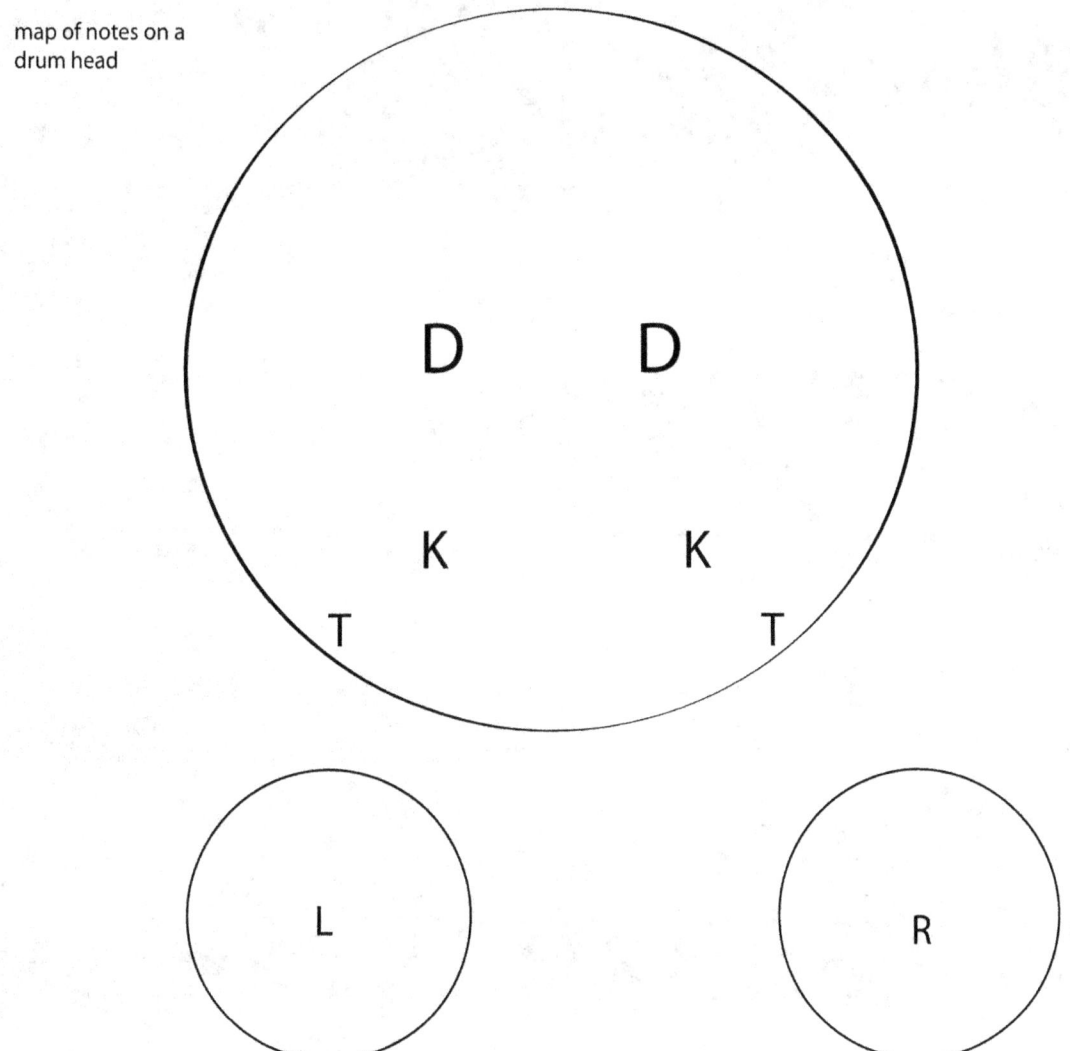

Key:

D	REFERS TO THE AREA OF THE DRUM HEAD (SOUNDS: DUM)	Λ	ACCENT
K	REFERS TO THE AREA OF THE DRUM HEAD (SOUNDS: KA)	∠	GRADUALLY INCREASE VOLUME
T	REFERS TO THE AREA OF THE DRUM HEAD (SOUNDS: TE)		
L+R	LEFT AND RIGHT DRUM ON THE BONGOS		

FIRST MOVEMENT: ON HIPPY HILL

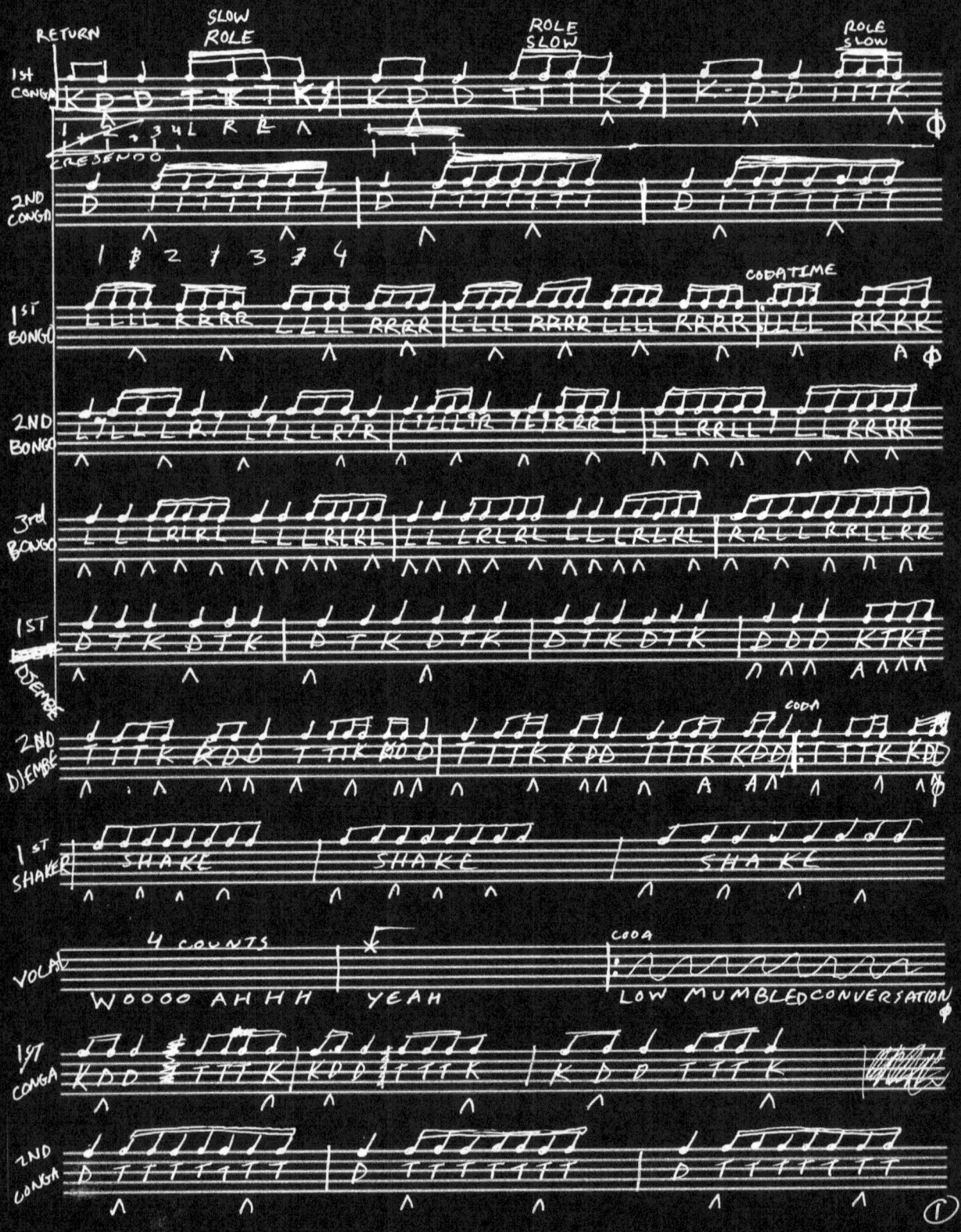

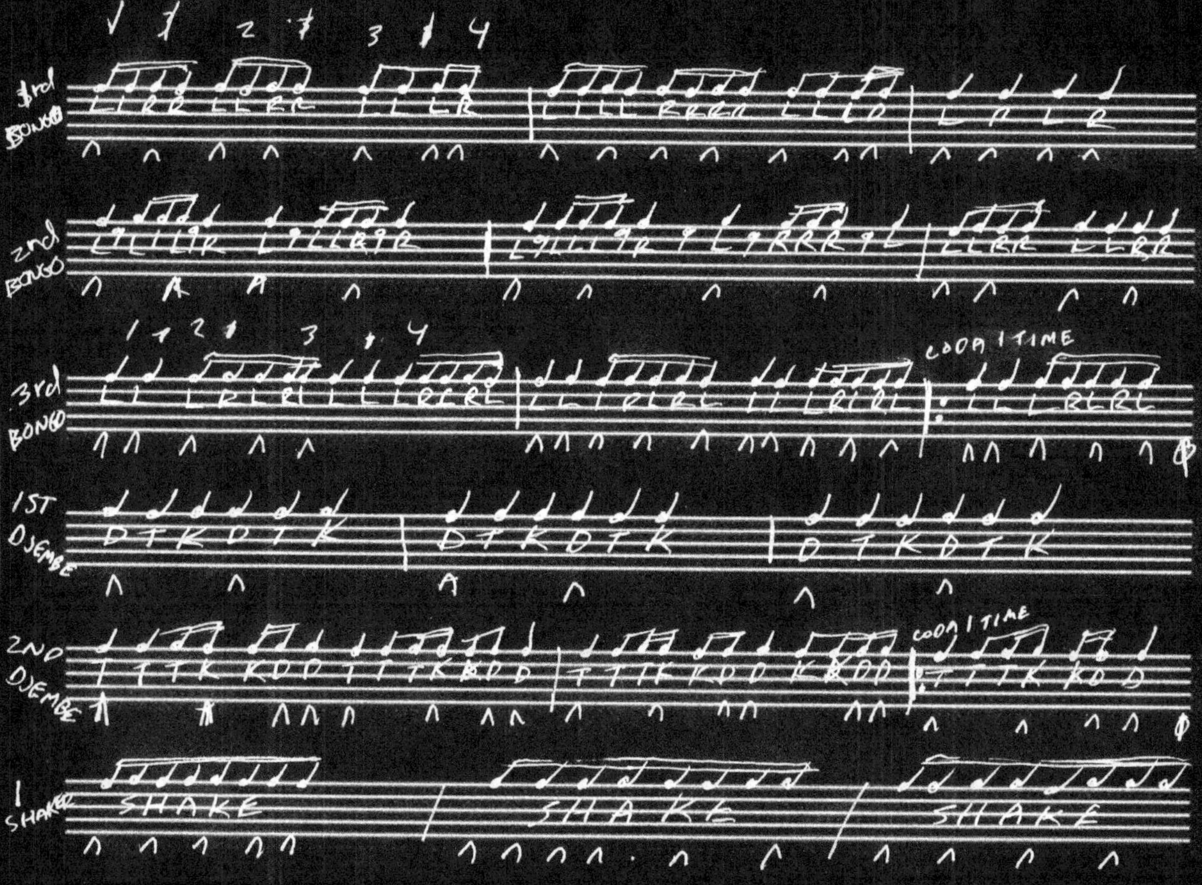
3rd BONGO
2nd BONGO
3rd BONGO
CODA 1 TIME
1ST DJEMBE
2ND DJEMBE
CODA 1 TIME
1 SHAKER
SHAKE
SHAKE
SHAKE
VOCAL
LYRKS: LOW MUMBLED CONV.
WHOOOOOOO WHOOP WHOOP
CRESENDO
LOW MUMBLE
1ST CONGA
2ND CONGA
1ST BONGO
2ND BONGO

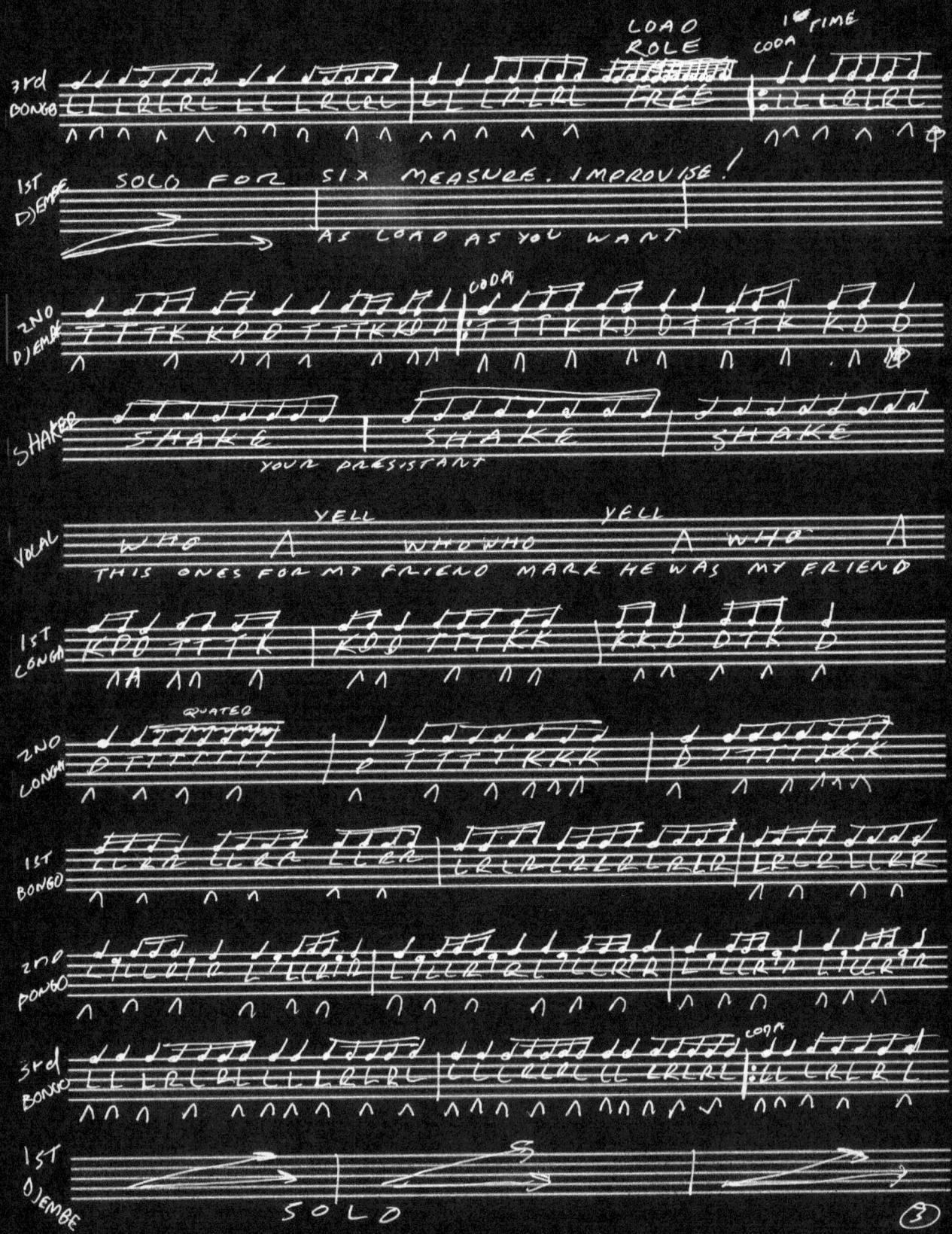

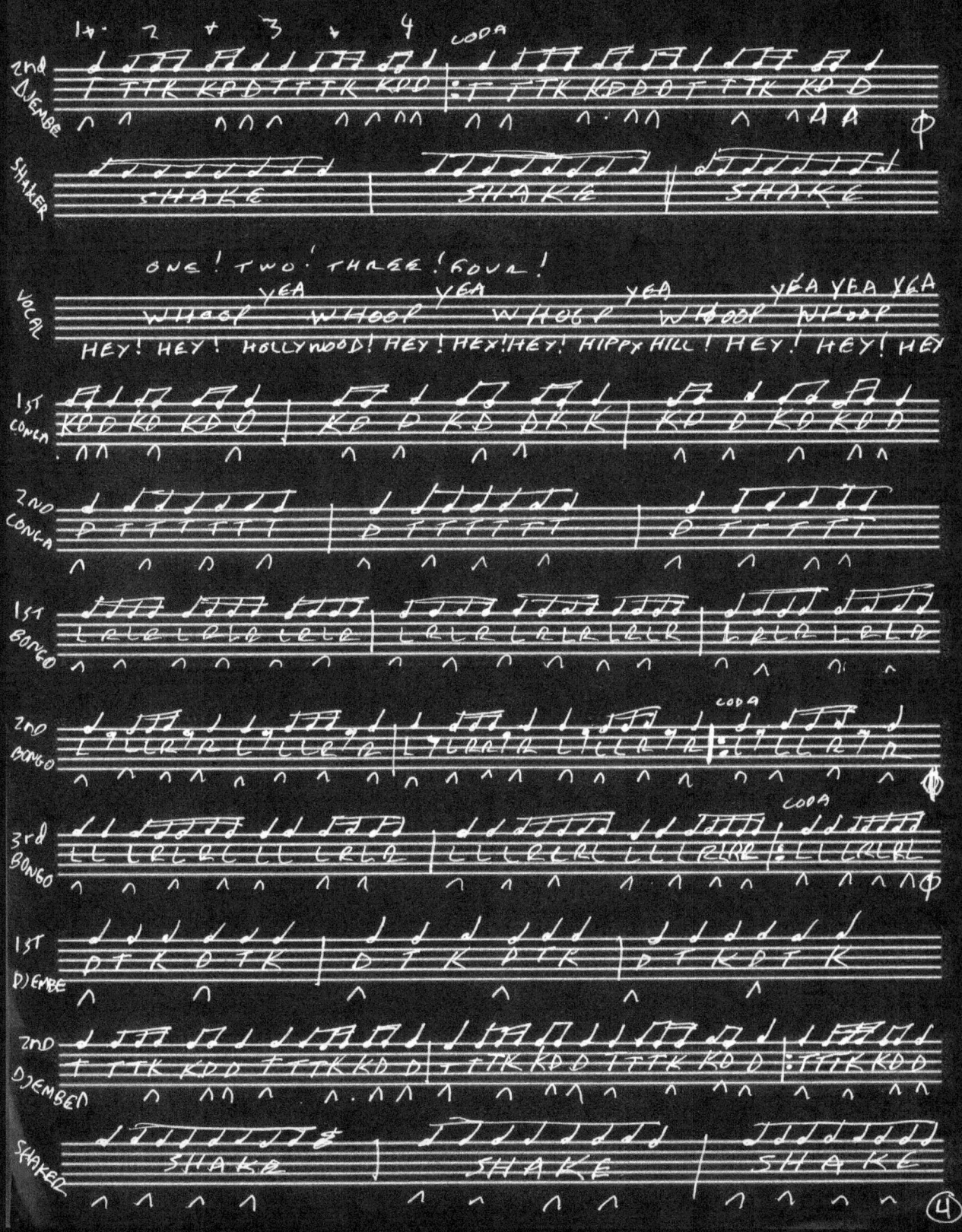

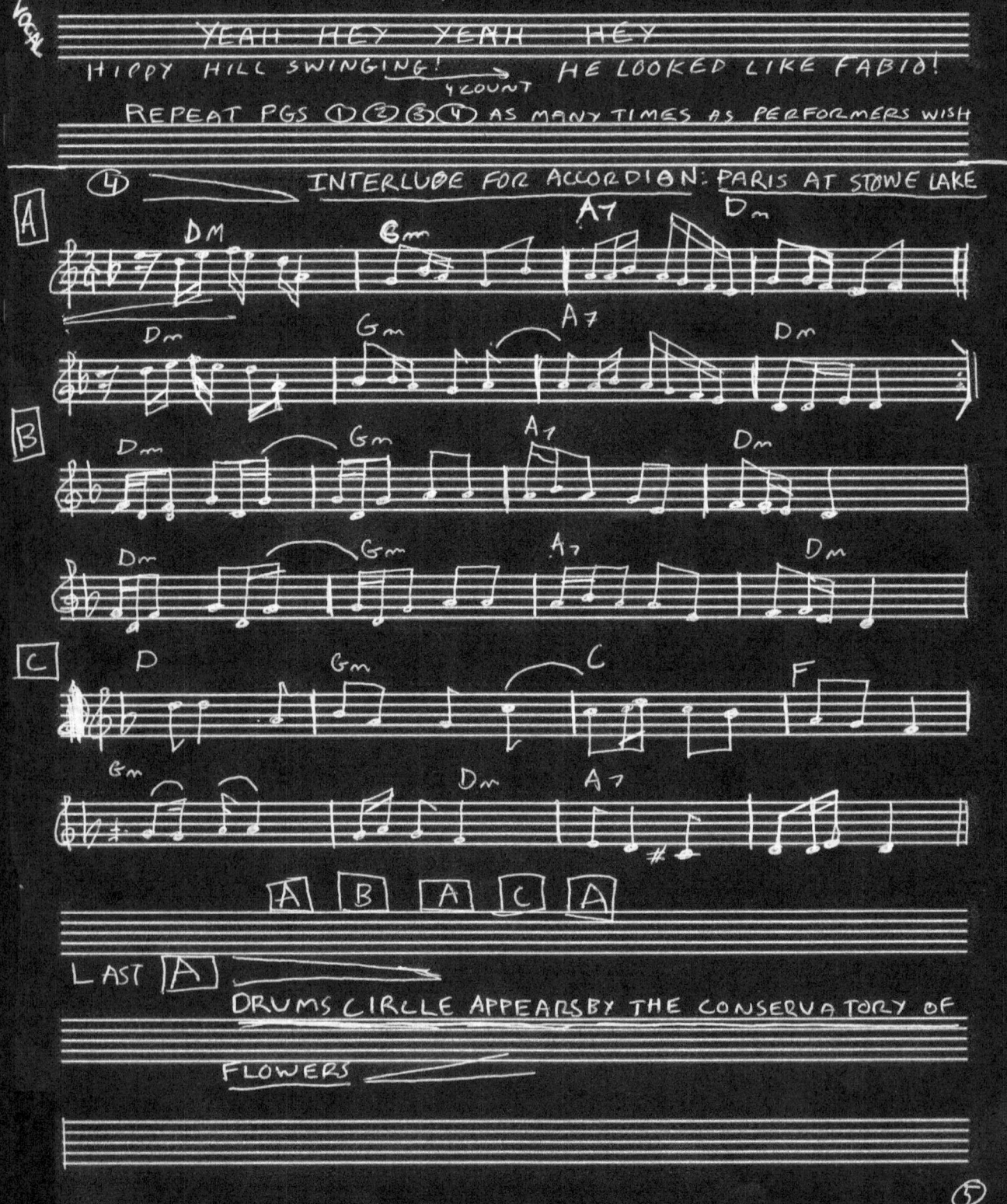

1 + 2 + 3 + 4

VOCAL

YEAH HEY YEAH HEY

HIPPY HILL SWINGING! 4 COUNT HE LOOKED LIKE FABIO!

REPEAT PGS ① ③ ③ ④ AS MANY TIMES AS PERFORMERS WISH

④ INTERLUDE FOR ACCORDION: PARIS AT STOWE LAKE

A B A C A

LAST A

DRUMS CIRCLE APPEARS BY THE CONSERVATORY OF

FLOWERS

⑤

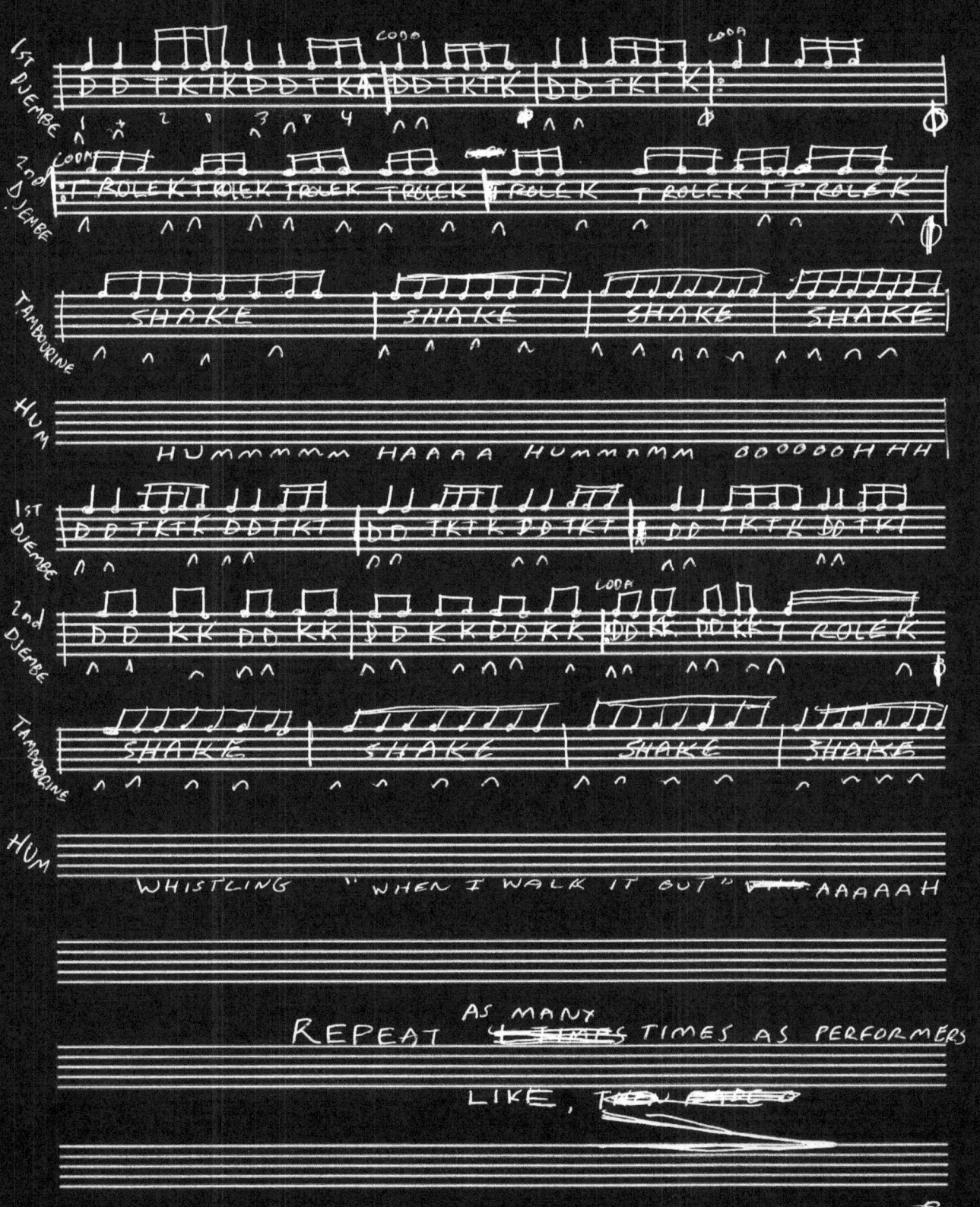

After a Project

Oda Projesi

Keep your eye on the wall!

There is a wall in Wilhemsburg- Hamburg that struck the attention of an artist collective from Istanbul and an artist from Berlin. This is a wall that stands near the U-bahn very close to the shopping mall next door. "The wall" is too big to be out of sight but strangely the group recognizes that it is invisible for most of the residents in the neighbourhood. So, they start to ask questions and search for answers and more questions about "the wall."

The project, *15x75m Hingucken-Weggucken*, started on the 17th of August 2007 with the collaboration of artists and neighbours from the region. The usage and the meaning of the wall was first examined by free climbers. Then, a minibus employed for the project meandered through Hamburg to search for possible meanings of "the wall;" the minibus stopped at 4 spots in Hamburg.

Oda Projesi & Nadin Reschke have worked together before in Istanbul on a project by Oda Projesi. (www.odaprojesi.org) The closing event marked the official opening of the exhibition on the first of September with surprises on and around the wall.

Oda Projesi: The project, *15x75m Hingucken-Weggucken*, shaped itself with the recognition of the unrecognized wall in Hamburg-Wilhemsburg; the search for new meanings of the "wall" was facilitated by the mobile nature of the minibus. One of the main tools in the project were the posters. How do you think the poster idea affected and shaped the project from the beginning to the end? What was the role of the poster?

Nadin: From the beginning I saw the posters as a tool for exchange. Because we agreed on simple material, design and a copy-shop size it was easy to produce and reproduce the posters.

    The pre-existing posters made it easier for people to join as they could refer to the texts and images from the posters that were displayed. With the children I remember that we discussed their ideas while making an audio recording for reference. The next day when they came back to our van, we had their printed posters and they started trying to read what they had said. The change from their spoken to printed words was surprising for them and defined authorship. The poster transformed something temporary like words and spoken arguments to a permanent form. At the same time they only conveyed quotes or parts of what was said. The posters were a driving force for the project.

    We started the project by asking questions to people whom we met in Hamburg-Wilhelmsburg like: *"How do you see your neighborhood change over the next 10 years?"* While remaining aware of the fact that we, ourselves were only temporary neighbors. What kind of question would you ask now, if you were back in Hamburg-Wilhelmsburg?

Günes: *What is your favorite place to be when you go out? Is there any place that you go for a picnic, for example? Any movie theatre that you regularly visit? Or a specific garden-seat where you like to sit idle and look around? Do you feel at ease when you're outside in the streets?*

    The question is a bit long. But I would like to go again to those neighborhoods that we worked with when we were in Hamburg and ask these questions. I am curious about where these people frequent, to which places they go in the Hamburg city center or in their own district. The neighborhoods that we visited to produce our posters all seemed to me isolated, as if they had turned their backs on each other at the boundaries where they actually touch each other. These borders are so sharp that no one ever gets close to the neighborhood of another.

The habitants of these self-absorbed districts spend time only in their own houses and gardens, and seem to barely have any relationship with the downtown or their environment. They all seem to have very solid explicit reasons to live in some particular neighborhood. These reasons, whatever they are, keep them from getting into a relationship with their environment. I might be totally wrong on these thoughts and it is indeed possible that the answers I'll get to my questions may change them.

Seçil: After having done the project and being back there again; I would be curious to find the same people and ask them what they remember about the project. From the neighbourhood experience we had for 8 years in Galata-Istanbul, I was always curious to see or feel the remains or the reflections of the project. Also as "the wall" started the project, I would continue asking the questions about "the wall" to more people.

Özge: Yes we had many questions at that time, we could ask more and different questions. But the questions were chosen as tools for the poster, as tools to reflect people's ideas about their neighbourhood. These were displayed on the posters, which were an easy way to distribute the different opinions.

First, when I look back towards that period and from Istanbul to Hamburg, it is urgent that we ask today, "what does *'local people'* mean, and what is displacement?" Because right now many areas of the big cities are sold for macro-economy and the people living there have to move somewhere else. For example, Istanbul Municipality is destroying the reason why Istanbul was chosen for the cultural capital in 2010, by beautifying Istanbul for 2010. The very distinct neighborhoods made unique by their inhabitants are part of this destruction.

But I would also ask Wilhelmsburgers, "what is a home?" Maybe this will enable them to look at the issue from a different perspective, from inside to the outside.

My first question above is my question to you too: "what does 'local people' mean and what is displacement?"

Nadin: I have been thinking and working on this question for the last few years. Surely my interest correlates with personal experiences of displacement after the political changes in East-Germany after 1989.

I believe that the growth and development of the capitalist system has destroyed a lot of the distinctions of local differences and cultures. Places become homogenized, equalized and commodified like you described in Istanbul. I could see it happening in Hamburg-Wilhelmsburg as well. These processes generate or push a sense of placelessness. The question is: how do we situate ourselves and what kind of strategies can we find to deal with this alienation.

Some people argue, that the importance of a particular place has been transcended;[1] it does not matter where we are living anymore as long as we have a mobile phone and internet. Cem, a German-Turkish architect whom I met as part of a project I did in Istanbul, said: "*I feel more like a potted plant, which can be placed everywhere. Everywhere where there is light, air and water the plant can grow. Roots are something I don't know and I like it this way. I mean roots in the sense of belonging to one place.*"[2]

Seçil: In reference to this question, I recall our need to re-think the people that have been moved from their houses with the gentrification process in Istanbul. As in all situations it differs according to the place and the people. Imagine the gypsy people that live for hundreds of years at the heart of the city, Sulukule. Now they are being moved to the edges of the city, near the Black Sea coast, into buildings designed to hold thousands of people. Or the immigrants generally from the east side of Turkey, whose villages have been burned down for political reasons. The people who have long lived in Tarlabaşı-Istanbul and are now being moved. Gentrification requires no local people and displacement is its rule. You need the displaced to be the actors of the city, according to the new rules.

And regarding Nadin's answer, quoting Cem, I remembered the idea of the 'rhizome' as articulated by Deleuze and Guattari: "The rhizome itself assumes very diverse forms, from ramified surface extension in all directions to concretion into bulbs and tubers. When rats swarm over each other. The rhizome includes the best and the worst: potato and couchgrass, or the weed. Animal and plant, couchgrass is crabgrass. We get the distinct feeling that we will convince no one unless we enumerate certain approximate characteristics of the rhizome. . . . Principles of connection and heterogeneity: any point of a rhizome can be connected to anything other, and must be. This is very different from the tree or root, which plots a point, fixes an order."[3]

For more information on the project, visit:
http://15x75m-hinguckenweggucken.blogspot.com

---

1 Hanno Rauterberg, *Worauf wir bauen* (Munich: Prestel 2008)

2 Nadin Reschke, *Kalinti, or What is Left Over* (Istanbul: Artist Book 2006-7)

3 Deleuze and Guattari, *A Thousand Plateaus: Capitalism and Schizophrenia* (St. Paul: University of Minnesota Press 1987)

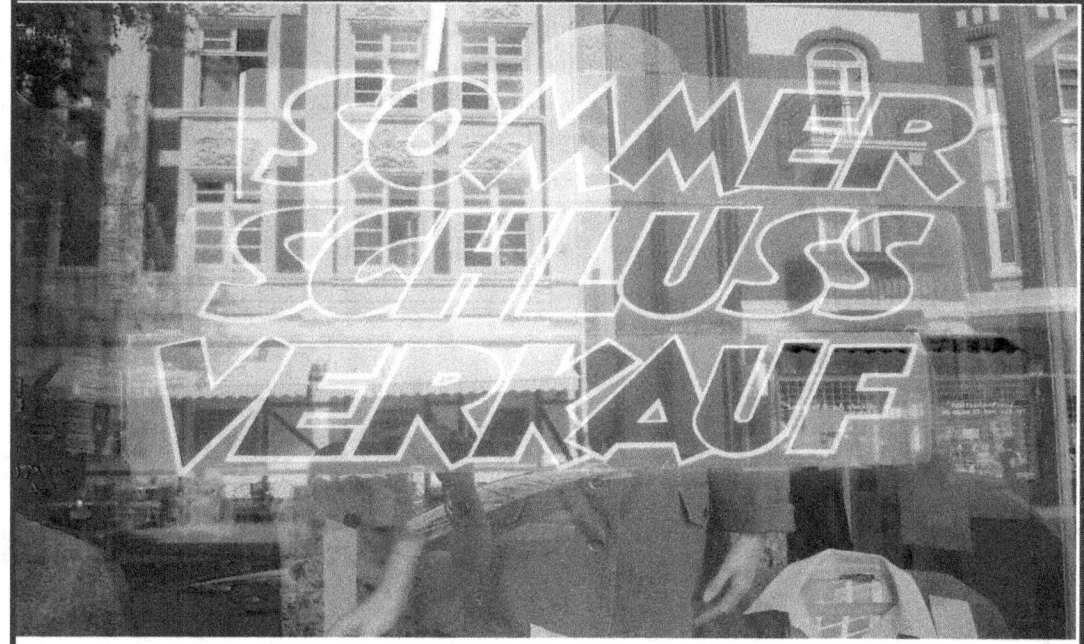

Es ist hier nicht so wie der Rest von Hamburg. Das kann man nicht vergleichen.
Hier ist die Atmosphäre wie in einer Kleinstadt. Hier trifft man immer die gleichen Leute auf der Strasse. Es ist abgegrenzter, in sich geschlossener. Es kommen nicht so viele Fremde hierher.

hingucken.weggucken@gmail.com -15x75m-hinguckenweggucken.blogspot.com

august-september 2007

"Here it is not like the rest of Hamburg. You can´t compare. Here the atmosphere is like in a small town, here you always meet the same people on the street. It is more segregated, more closed. Not many strangers come here."

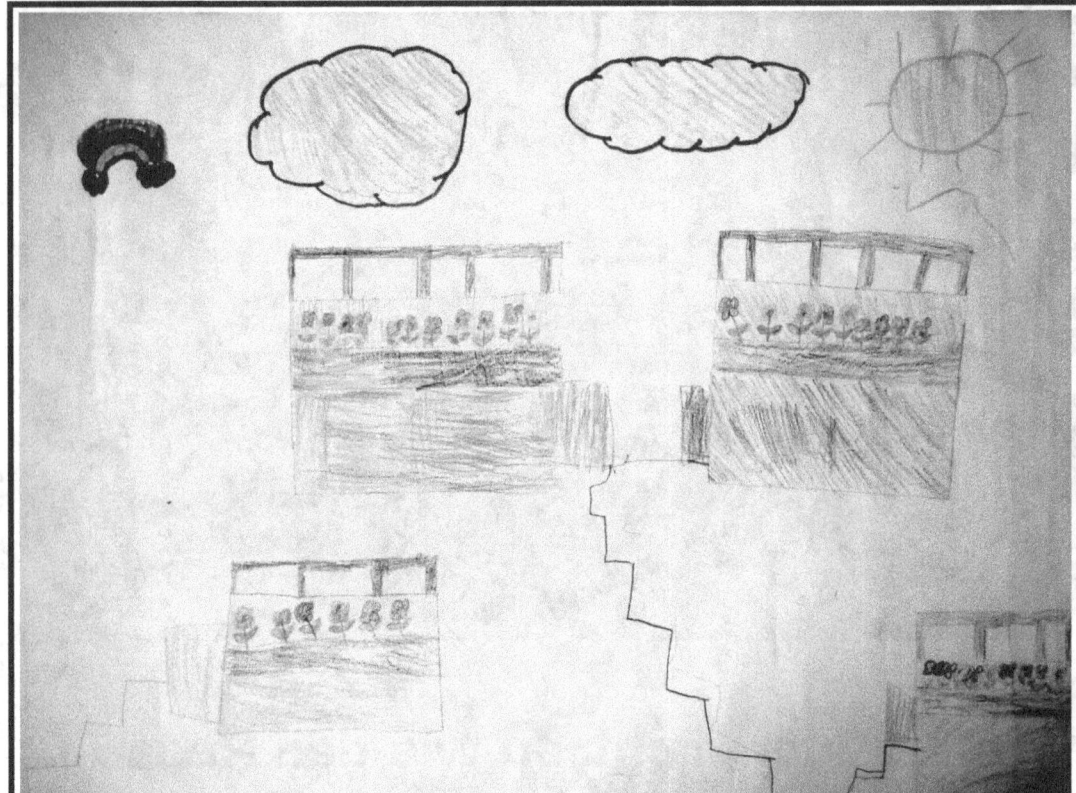

Auf der Mauer können Balkone gebaut werden. Dann können die Anwohner darauf gehen, sich hinsetzen und ausruhen. Es gibt eine Treppe, das man hochkommt. Unten habe ich auch noch einen Balkon gemacht, weil manche haben auch Höhenangst.

hingucken.weggucken@gmail.com -15x75m-hinguckenweggucken.blogspot.com

august-september 2007

"On the wall, you could build balconies. Then the residents could go there, sit and relax. There are stairs, so you can get up there. Underneath I made another balcony, because some people are afraid of heights."

15x75m/Hingucken - Weggucken

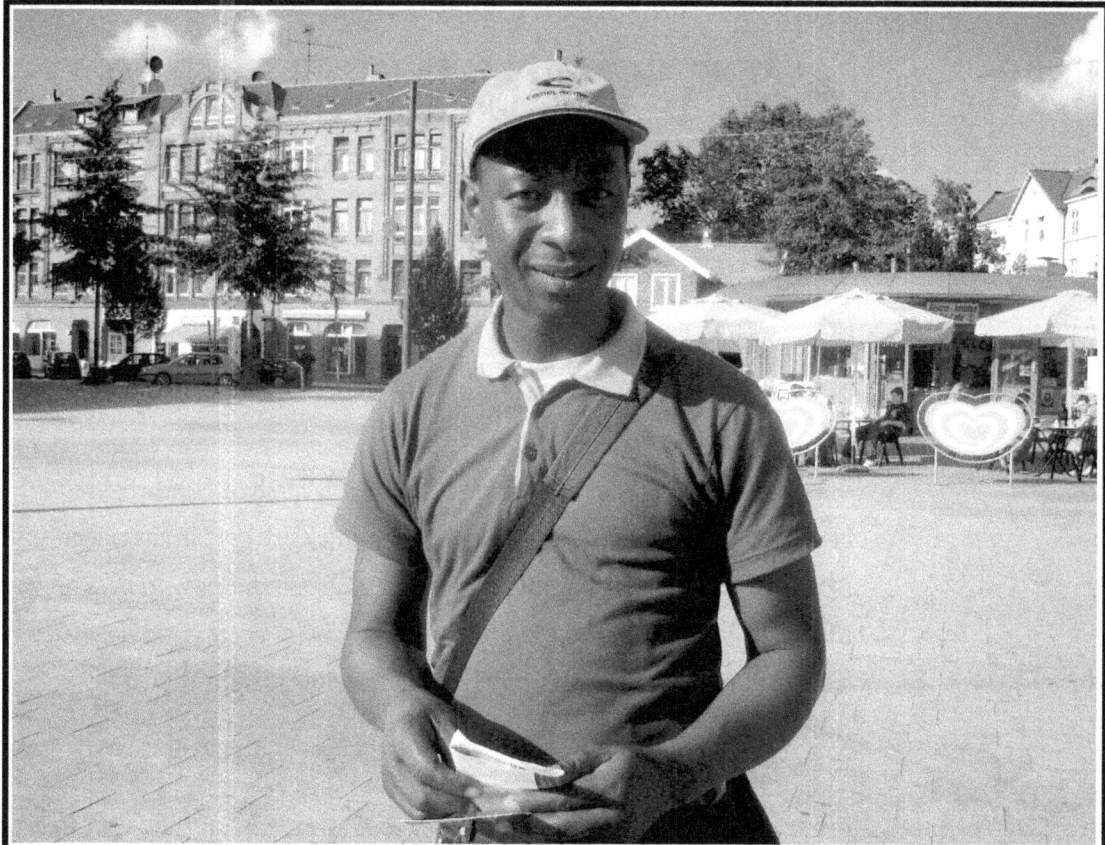

hingucken.weggucken@gmail.com -15x75m-hinguckenweggucken.blogspot.com

Eine Mauer ist eine willkürlich gezogene Linie, wo man etwas festsetzt und damit eine Grenze zieht. Eine Mauer hat etwas politisch gewalttätiges.

august-september 2007

"A wall is a randomly drawn line, where you determine something and thereby put a border. A wall is something political and violent."

It's Like a Living Room:
At Home with marksearch

Matthew David Rana

marksearch is Sue Mark and Bruce Douglas, a husband and wife team based in Oakland, California whose community projects invite people to reflect on their local communities and increase their awareness of the natural environment within the urban fabric. Their ecologically and socially-based projects rely on an accessible format rooted in conversation and daily life.

I first became aware of marksearch in 2008 while researching volunteer groups in Oakland parks. During one of my conversations with a local park steward, I was told about two artists collaborating on a project related to volunteerism and was referred to the project website: www.10000stepsoakland.org

Starting in 2006, 10,000 Steps Oakland, is a creative stewardship project taking place in four historic squares in downtown Oakland. In addition to organizing community events in the parks such as cleanings and plantings, marksearch has also conducted interviews and collected oral histories for inclusion in a series of sidewalk medallions and a walking tour. The following interview took place at their home in Oakland on February 14, 2009.

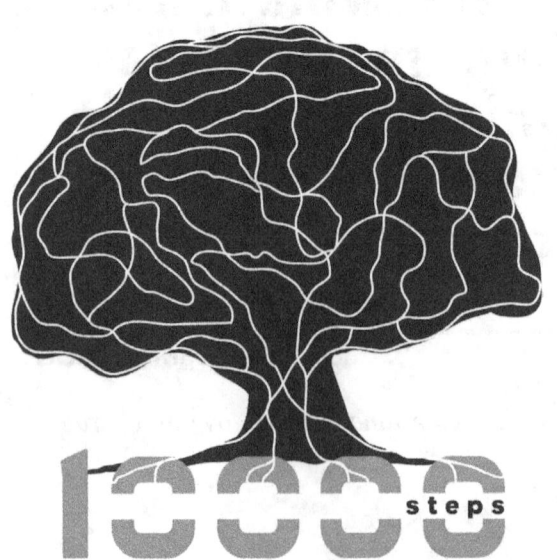

10000 steps

Matthew David Rana: What is marksearch and how did it begin?

Sue Mark: marksearch really began when I finished graduate school and I was trying to figure out what I was doing and how to understand the work I was doing. When I was in graduate school I tossed everything up in the air and started working in a completely new way and really tying things back to my original studies, which were linguistics and phenomenology. I figured out that what I'm doing is researching and searching. So it became an easy way to talk about myself.

The name is an official moniker and a way to encapsulate what we do. People don't really question what it is; they don't need further qualifications or descriptions. If I were to say "My name is Sue Mark and I'm an artist," then people will ask, "What kind of art do you do?" When I try to describe it and say I work with conversation; I work with places; I try to understand people's relationship to different places; it gets really confusing. People tend to get really confused because in their minds, art is about sculpture and art is about drawing and art is about painting and I don't do any of those things.

MDR: How did it evolve in to its current form as a collaboration?

Bruce Douglas: Well, we met while collaborating on a project outside of marksearch. It was a neighborhood project that was building a mini-park next to the post-office on Shattuck Avenue. That was in 2000. We worked together for several years, meeting and planning to create this mini-park. And then Sue managed to ask me out and we started dating. By the end of the project we were married.

SM: We missed the unveiling of the project because we were away on our honeymoon.

MDR: And the decision to work together happened organically?

SM: We already knew we could work together and I was working on stuff and I would ask Bruce, "Hey, can you help me out with this," or "Could you help me out with that?" because Bruce can pretty much build anything. marksearch has taken many different forms. But Bruce and I were in this relationship and it seemed like a natural progression to work together because we have very different but integrating skill sets and it expands the possibilities for both of us. The work that we do together neither of us can do individually. And it's continued. It's not a strategic plan it's just building on one experience and one project to the next.

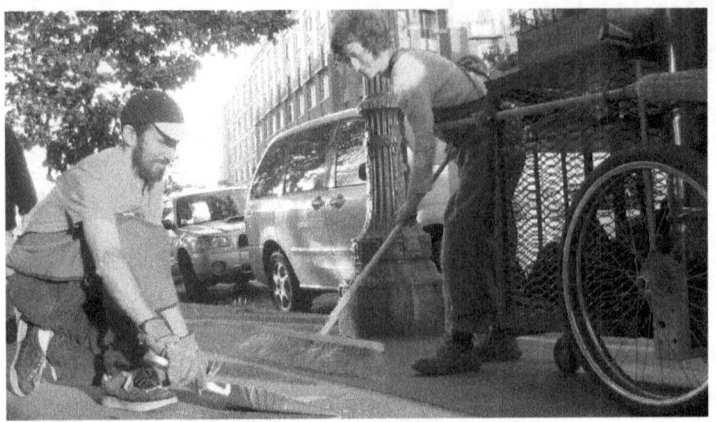

Bruce Douglas and Sue Mark sweeping in park vicinity.

. . . we thought we would spend a lot of time in parks, because we wanted to talk to people. So we started off visiting parks but by and large we didn't really find anybody there.

MDR: How did you become interested in working in parks?

BD: We worked on a project called *WE Riders* where we rode our tandem bike with a trailer around Oakland and asked people the questions, where is East Oakland and where is West Oakland. With *WE Riders* we circulated through the whole city. When we were strategizing how we were going to circulate through the city, we thought we would spend a lot of time in parks, because we wanted to talk to people. So we started off visiting parks but by and large we didn't really find anybody there. We ended up talking to people, especially in farmer's markets and especially in shopping-zone places that were semi-public but actually private spaces. With that, we really got interested in figuring out something with parks. We had recently been on a visit to New York where the parks are at all times just brimming full of people. We would be riding around and a park would be completely empty on a beautiful day on a weekend. So it's like, why? What's going on? That was our question.

MDR: Can you talk a little bit more about your project 10,000 Steps? What it is and how it evolved from that initial question?

SM: We spent time looking at different clusters of parks and we were trying to figure out, what would our focus be, what would our niche be? Because there are so many parks in Oakland;

we really have a lot of open green space. We were trying to figure out who we would align ourselves with because we wanted to work with a non-profit. We have a Creative Work Fund grant to do the project and a stipulation of the grant is to work with a non-profit to help that non-profit achieve their mission in a creative way and for the artist team to be able to develop new work that they necessarily wouldn't be able to do otherwise. I started just doing a lot of research about Oakland and I came across a study done by two professors from UC and they were talking about urban planning and urban renovation using Oakland as their model example. They started off with a historical perspective of the city and showed the plan from 1852 which was just the downtown area. There were originally seven squares that were the green cornerstones of the city and formed its perimeter. We thought it would be interesting to look at those squares and look at their context today and see how they're being used now. Our partner, the Friends of Oakland Parks and Recreation (FOPR) was very interested in looking at those downtown parks as well.

BD: They're all really at the junctures of diverse communities, more so than many other parks. Downtown is also an area that's in huge transition with former mayor Jerry Brown's goal of adding 10,000 new residences to the city. That was one of the cues for the name.

SM: And also you're supposed to walk 10,000 steps a day for good health which, depending on your pace is anywhere

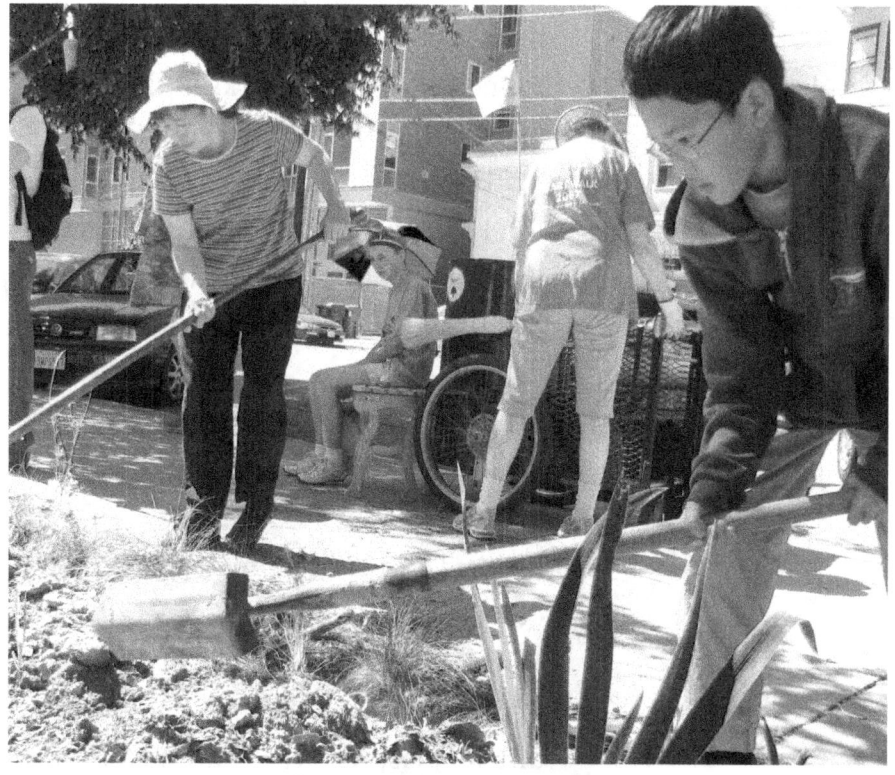

Summer solstice planting in Lafayette Square Park community gardens.

What we're really interested in is parks as our commons. This is our space, this is where everybody can be together no matter what your background is.

between three to five miles. There are 5 parks left from the original squares. We chose four of them, Jefferson, Lafayette, Lincoln and Madison. We didn't choose Harrison.

BD: Right now it's called the Chinese Garden. It's basically a senior center.

SM: It's not so very public. What we're really interested in is parks as our commons. This is our space, this is where everybody can be together no matter what your background is. It seems like it should be the most egalitarian and the most free and open space in which to be. And my fear is that if we don't use it, maybe we'll lose it.

MDR: How did you start to engage those communities and those spaces once you decided what parks you were going to focus on?

SM: In doing a lot of community work, we've learned that getting a buy-in is really, really important. We spent the first 6 or 7 months just finding out who we needed to talk to. That's one of the reasons why we wanted to work with FOPR because they're connected to all the parks in the city and they know all the neighborhood groups in the city.

BD: FOPR's job is to be fiscal sponsors for neighborhood groups who want to get grants to do projects. So they're connected to all the activities in the city that have anything to do with parks.

SM: We spent a lot of time talking to the key people and arranging different meetings.

BD: And *attending* different group meetings, introducing ourselves. The way things generally happen is people ask "Oh, why didn't we know about this?" Because there is a real lack of cross-communication with different neighborhood groups, different city departments and different activist groups. If somebody has money and funding for one thing that doesn't mean that everybody's going to be up to speed on it.

MDR: I was just curious what it had been like working in collaboration with different groups and I'm curious if you experienced any differences between constituencies and groups and if there was any conflict or resistance to the project?

SM: To answer the second question about conflict and resistance, I think we anticipated having more. People sometimes thought that our goal was to renovate the parks. So we would go to a community meeting and describe our project and someone would say, "We need barbecue pits! We need more bathrooms!" We would respond by saying that we would let the city staff know but we were not the ones who could make those kind of changes happen.

We started working three years ago when people were on a high with all the building and all the changes in downtown, so, people were really excited. I think what confused people was how we talked about it as art. So we stopped talking about the project as art in community meetings. But when we were talking with City Council people, they wanted to

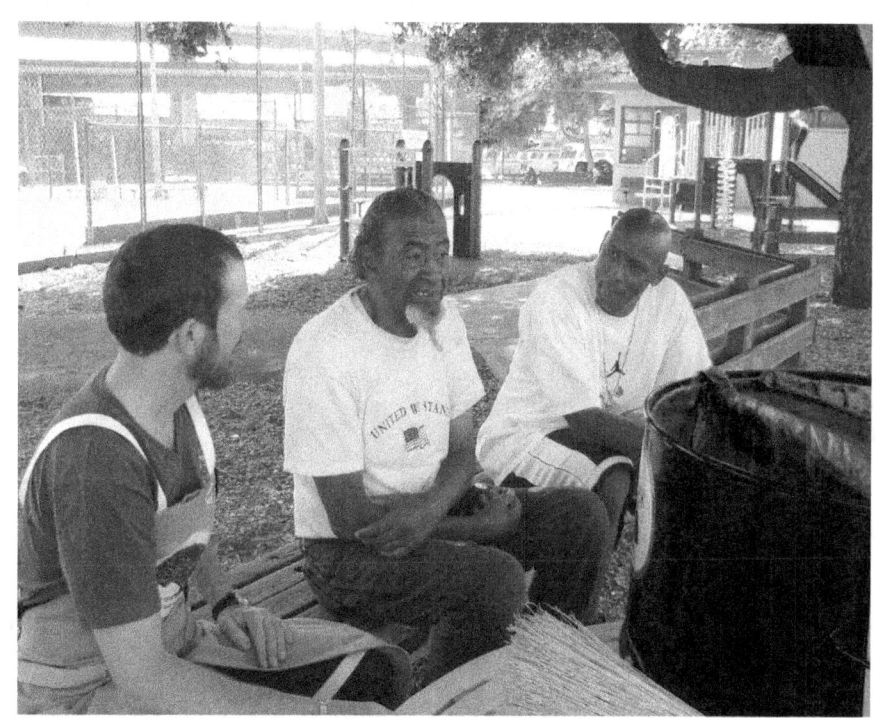

Bruce Douglas in conversation with local basketball legends at Jefferson Square Park.

I think that's the real challenge of doing this kind of work. It's really important to respect what people are already doing and that takes time to understand. We've learned that the hard way in past projects.

know about our funding and what we had done. We're kind of this hybrid entity. People see us in our uniform and people see us at different events and think that we're official. We are official, but we're not official for the city and we're not a non-profit, but we take what we're doing seriously and we respect people's needs. We spent a lot of time explaining the fact that we were not trying to take over anybody's territory. We just wanted to fill in some gaps. You know, the city staff really doesn't have the ability to go out and interview people who work in the park, that's what we've been doing. We've been collecting all these needs assessments, what people like, what people don't like, what they want to see in the parks, and that's very valuable for them.

Community groups don't have access to a lot of funds, but we have money and the ability to rove around so we can draw connections that they might not be able to do. We didn't come in and say we're going to do X, Y and Z. We came and said, "this is our project idea, to raise awareness about these parks. Can you help us know what we should do?" So we were very open at meetings when people wanted to make suggestions. It was about networking and taking time; not trying to do anything really fast. In our experience, the faster you try and do something in a community, the more trouble you get in because you don't have the time to learn the complexity of what all the interrelationships are. I think that's the real challenge of doing this kind of work. It's really important to respect what people are already doing and that takes time to understand. We've learned that the hard way in past projects.

MDR: How do you negotiate the social and political relationships that influence the use and development of the parks? For example, I'm thinking of the underlying social and economic factors that impact how the parks are regulated and maintained.

SM: Maintenance is one of the key issues that people want. In talking to a lot of different people from the director of the Lincoln Rec Center to park users and business people, they've all said, "well, we want to see the kids more involved in stewardship and taking care of the parks." So maybe that will be the next project we do because there are more than a dozen charter schools in this particular area downtown area. The other issue is who is allowed to use the parks. There is a lot of fear surrounding the parks, especially Lafayette Square Park. I think a lot of it comes from fear of the unknown. We spent a lot of time with people who hang around in the parks and they realize that people might be afraid of them and they've told us "if you're doing anything in the park, let us know because we want to help, we want to do stuff." I think there is this invisible barrier that people create in their minds. They don't want to cross the line.

MDR: Have you been able to facilitate a dialogue among groups that have different interests in the parks?

BD: That's something that we really want to do. We have a plan but it's something that we haven't really done so much yet.

SM: One thing we want to do is--and this is a key political issue--because there's basically no more money in the city--you have these four parks that are used in very different ways and in each area there are people who are really quite powerful in their communities and they don't know each other. So the next step in our project is to link the key players together so that they can pool their resources and work together so there isn't redundancy.

But as far as overcoming people's difficulties with certain kinds of park users, we've made suggestions like, come as a group or come more regularly. But there are some people who move from San Francisco and they're scared of Oakland; Oakland has a bad reputation so they might not even try.

MDR: In relation to your project, you've discussed the importance of "vital use." I was wondering if you talk a bit more about that distinction?

SM: Between use and vital use?

BD: Well, it speaks to the parks being part of a community's functioning. People don't just happen to go to the park because they're walking by and want to rest their feet. People use it as part of their life. They meet other people there or they take their meals there, do barbecuing there. They take their kids to play in the

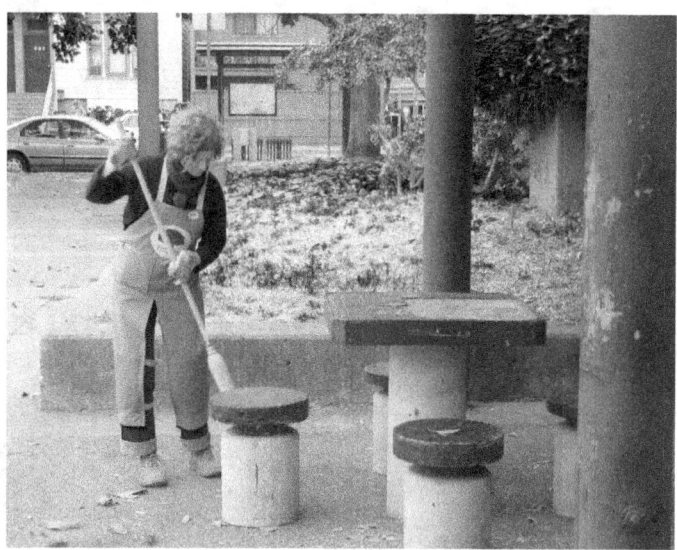

Sue Mark sweeping in Madison Square Park.

People don't just happen to go to the park because they're walking by and want to rest their feet. People use it as part of their life.

play structures or things like that.

SM: It could be a central place where people come to meet each other. It could happen on a daily basis. I think that there's a lot of transience in this area and in this region and people don't necessarily know their neighbors. There are going to be a lot of new people moving into these new downtown residential buildings and it's a place where you can casually meet people with similar interests whether it's working in a community garden or practicing tai-chi. As one of the businesswomen who works across from the park, and other users have said, "this is like a living room and it *should* be like a living room." I think for some people it's disturbing that it's a living room. But it should be a place where people can be comfortable and hang out and use it in different ways that make everyone feel good and help each other.

MDR: So it's very much about people taking ownership.

BD: Right, that's really important.

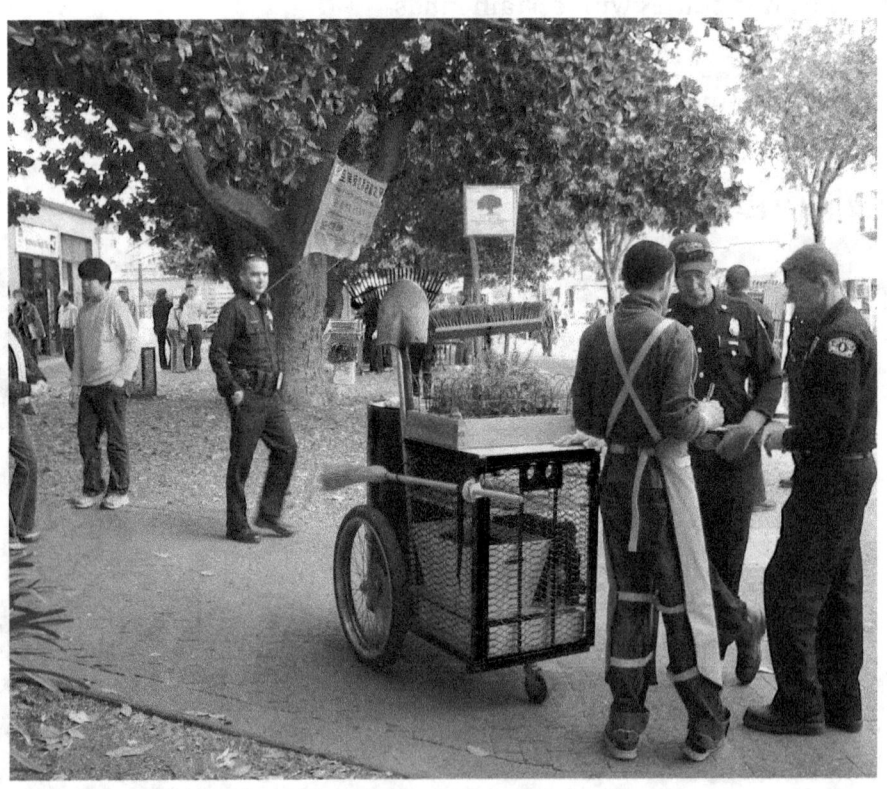

Bruce Douglas talks with Oakland police during National Night Out.

We're kind of like a multi-directional public service project. But because we're artists we can take a creative approach to something that if we worked for the city would have to be bureaucratic

MDR: Do you think that raising awareness increases a sense of people's ownership over a space?

BD: I think it's a first step. I don't think it increases in itself. It gives people an opportunity to think about plugging in somehow.

SM: We're hoping that the self-guided walking tours will make the parks more visible. From all of the park stories and histories that we have collected so far, we're going to corroboratively create a walking tour marked with permanent sidewalk medallions leading people to these four parks. Once the parks are more visible then people may want to use them and if they want to use them then they may want to take care of them and if they take care of them they may meet each other and then there's this greater integration because we can't rely on the municipality to take care of us. It's just not in the cards.

MDR: That's another thing I was curious about because you've written that your "urban investigations push the boundaries of how community-based art can influence public policy." Given what's happened with Oakland and their budget crisis, I was wondering how that's playing out.

BD: We have yet to see how that will play out with the ability to influence public policy...assuming there will still be people who work for the city of Oakland that are able to be influenced. Because our plan is being ears and eyes for the city. Collecting information about what people see as needs for the park, is something the city wasn't prepared to do before and certainly aren't now.

SM: On a more fundamental level, in terms of all the work we're doing, aesthetics are important to us in terms of having an official presence so that people will take us seriously, and can see we're doing something we believe in and that it's not a frivolous play. We want people to know that their experience matters and that their stories matter. I think we want to give all the voices equal opportunity. We're not out to change the city and we're not out to change the public but we'd like to hear from everybody and have more dialogue.

We're kind of like a multi-directional public service project. But because we're artists we can take a creative approach to something that if we worked for the city would have to be bureaucratic; if we were acting as citizens we might feel like we're fighting all the time. So even though that's our community but but it's not our neighborhood, we want to help but we don't feel indignation. We're not neutral either. If we weren't connected to

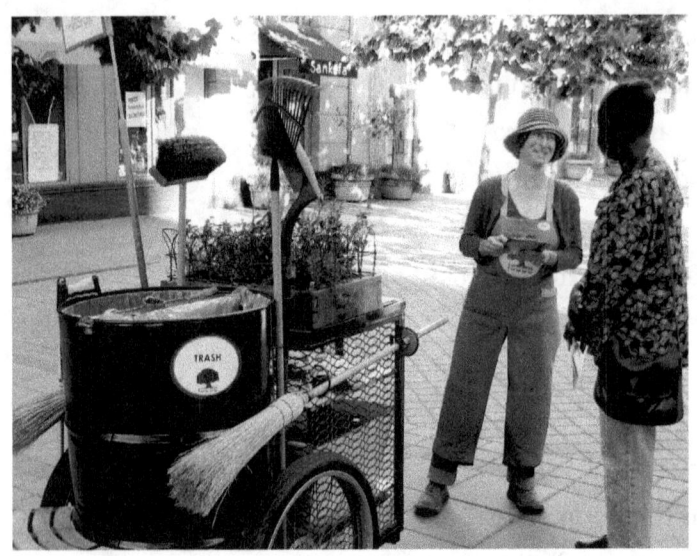

the city, what we do wouldn't really have an impact on it. Will we be able to change anything in the city? I don't know. But people are certainly excited by the fact that we are able to do something for the city that's not funded by it because the city doesn't have the funds to do it.

MDR: In a way it seems like it's almost providing a model for a consulting agency.

Sue Mark in conversation, downtown Oakland.

When you put it out there in public space, you don't own it.   **BD:** Yeah, you could think of it that way.

MDR: You're in the process of using stories about parks that you've collected from neighbors and visitors to create these self-guided walking tours and sidewalk medallions. Who is your audience, who are
you trying to speak to?

BD: The most obvious audience is pedestrians or anybody who's on the sidewalk. The important goal for our audience is the people who haven't come to see our work but they're going about their daily life. That's a really key element. That's why we wanted to use sidewalk medallions because the sidewalk is the most utilized public space in downtown. In addition to that we've been thinking of different subgroups of people. Each park has different people who frequent it now or have in the past.

SM: Our ideal is that this would be a way to link all the parks together and for everyone to see what an incredible diversity there is in a very small space and the neighborhoods are really distinct. I think that our ideal requires more money than we have. But we're hoping that the audience will be very widespread, from people who will already be there walking around downtown to people who want to seek it out because it's something interesting to do. We want to encourage people to be local tourists of their own city.

MDR: I'm curious about any challenges you've had trying to represent the communities you've been working with back to themselves in some way.

SM: It's going to be difficult because ideally we'd like to have 30-40 medallions and right now we have the funding to do 15. At this point, we want to outline the whole walking tour and have that done so that hopefully people will be so excited that they'll want to donate money or have a medallion outside their business that speaks to their community. We may not be able to please everybody and not everybody's story will be represented, but there's a lot of invisible history and daily actualities that you wouldn't know otherwise. We don't feel like we're the owners of this process, just that we're opening a channel of possibility. It's kind of open for a lot of different possibilities, which is exciting because when you put it out there in public space, you don't own it. And we don't see the walking tour as making a sculpture and putting it somewhere: it's not static. We want to see it used as part of the urban fabric and functioning as a way to bring people back to the parks. The process of making the walking tour is not us making it and putting it in. We're going to take the designs to the community groups and toss around ideas with them about what should be on the medallions. We'll work on developing the medallion content and go back to the community and ask, "Is this accurate?" We don't want to be the definitive mirror. We want to work on something and it's a really tricky position to be in, to be outside the specific community; but on the other hand we can act as facilitators because we don't represent just one community. We don't have to be one thing or the other. We can be many different things. I see that as being the root of the creative possibility.

121

Let us imagine we are actors standing on a stage. When we are on this stage we know it is not real, but we choose to trade our reality for possibility. In this frame we find liberty within our fantasies, our desires, imaginations and fictions. Here there is freedom; it just needs a little spark, some conjuring, a performance and some intonation. Here we create our world how we want it to be.

Or, let us imagine we are the audience sitting and facing the stage. In our space we say, we are grounded; our space is the space of the real, the common, and the everyday. Here we cannot place freedom above our physical needs and responsibilities. Without a stage we need rules, order and parameters, to frame and control liberty. Here freedom can be won but only by negotiation.

Now, let us imagine that the stage begins to move. It moves out slowly and meets with the space of the audience and the everyday. Perhaps it continues to expand, moving past the audience, infinitely, until we are all standing on the same stage. Or maybe it stops, level with the audience, a flat space where we are given the choice to step forward or backwards onto or off of the stage.

Or, let us imagine the reverse happens. The stage doesn't move. Instead the audience rises up to meet the stage. Maybe the audience cuts the supports and the stage collapses, crashing down onto a single plane. Or perhaps we never had the materials, the time or the patience in the first place to build the stage.

Whatever the reason, we perform anyway, forgetting who is in and who is out of the performance. We are confused and a little scared by this experience but the play is good, so good, so we keep performing. The script is real and imaginative. The set remarkable, the props are seamless and yet clearly fabricated. And our performances are strong so strong, that we don't stop.

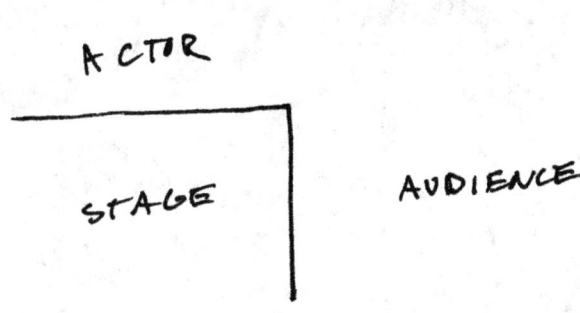

ACTOR

STAGE   AUDIENCE

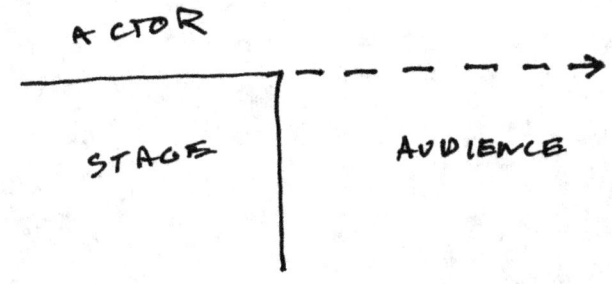

ACTOR

STAGE   AUDIENCE

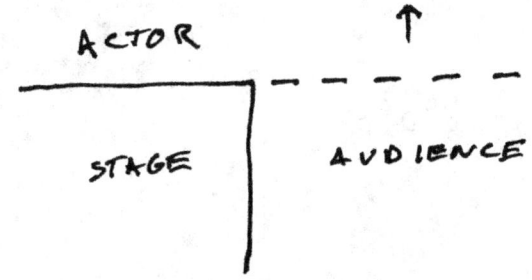

ACTOR

STAGE   AUDIENCE

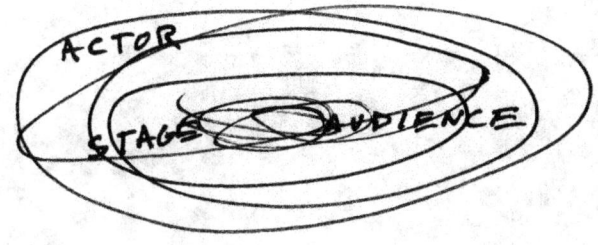

ACTOR

STAGE   AUDIENCE

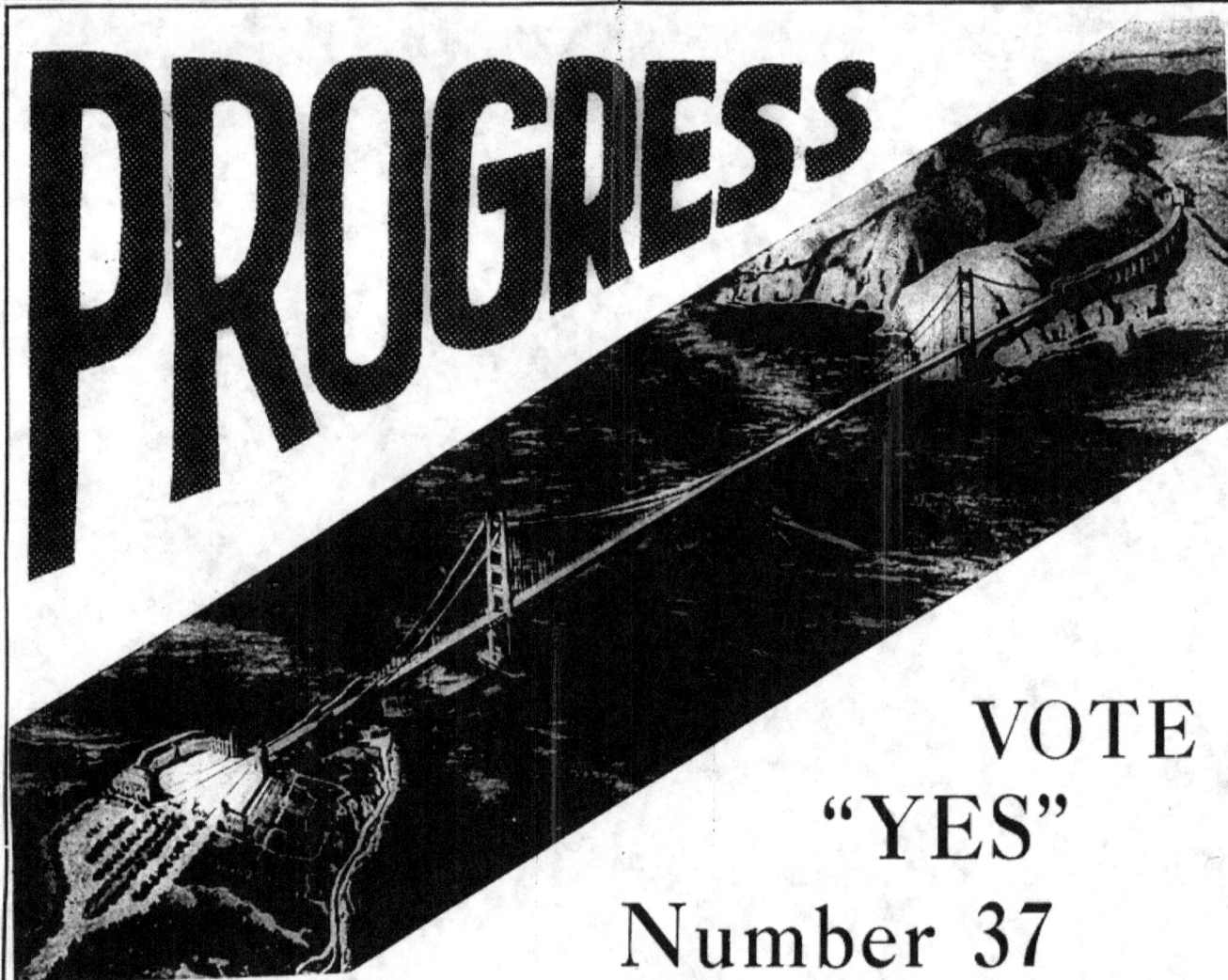

PROGRESS

VOTE "YES" Number 37

Great bridges are milestones of progress. They are the signposts of civilization. The bridge, since the days of Caesar, has been identified with the development of the human race. In the United States the bridge has become a part of our national life. Destroy the Nation's bridges and the Nation's industry will be paralyzed. San Francisco today occupies a unique position among American cities. Since the days when the sturdy Argonauts founded the little village of Yerba Buena, she has been hemmed in on three sides by water. Travelers to and from San Francisco by land must cross the water. This is the penalty she pays for possessing what has justly been termed the world's greatest natural harbor. For years she has struggled to expand with the handicap of inadequate water transportation. With the spectacular development of automotive transportation during the past 25 years, this handicap has made itself felt ever the more keenly. Today the point has been reached when the ferries, groaning under their burdens, are no longer sufficient to take care of San Francisco's transportation needs. A means of rapid and continuous transportation must be provided, if San Francisco is to keep pace with her sister cities of the West. The Golden Gate Bridge offers the first real relief for a situation that has become intolerable. Its construction will once and for all time smash the barrier that hems in San Francisco on the north. It will open up the vast hinterland known as the Redwood Empire, furnishing safe and swift transportation to this newest national playground, at the same time joining the severed ends of the California peninsula and placing San Francisco on what is destined to become a great international highway, extending from Buenos Aires to the Arctic.

Issued by the **INFORMATION BUREAU, GOLDEN GATE BRIDGE** *and* **HIGHWAY DISTRICT** *at 95-A Market Street, San Francisco, where full information relating to the Golden Gate Bridge is available to the Public.*

The GOLDEN GATE BRIDGE is Number 37 on the Ballot

Manifeast Destiny

Lynne McCabe

The car groans, its black paint already scalding in the early morning sun. And trying to squeeze one more thing into the all ready overflowing trunk I burn my hand. "Everyone in?" he asks, "mmm..yessh" I say, hand stuck in mouth, sucking the pain, "right then, we're off".

The road is parched. Its taut line, seemingly endless, strains to hold the ground. The heat peels it from its delineated course giving the impression that it has, floating heaven wards, left us for a better place. Looking out of the windows on either side, the landscape as it passes, is unwavering in its sameness. And the man beside me driving, my husband, turns and brightly says, "Only ten more hours and we're out of Texas." I feel his words sit with me, 't e n h o u r s,' time and distance move at their own speed here. Before moving to Texas I understood ten hours as

Building a bridge is a war
with the forces of nature
- Joseph Strauss[1]

From the moment John C. Freemont had named the bay "Chrysopylae,"[2] an homage to the golden horn in Constantinople, which was quickly anglicized to 'The Golden Gate', the people of San Francisco had dreamed of connecting the two headlands, of 'mending the continent'[3] and in the 1920's it seemed a bridge was an idea whose time had come. One man, Joseph B. Strauss, with the help of the people of San Francisco would be instrumental in transforming this fanciful dream into a stunning reality. It was to prove a long and difficult journey not without significant cost to both Strauss and the people of San Francisco.

On August 18th 1886 the self-proclaimed emperor of the United States and protector of Mexico, Norton 1[4] issued a decree that ordered the construction of a suspension bridge to be built connecting San Francisco to Sausalito.[5] However it would be another forty years until the city's chief engineer Michael O'Shaughnessy, under instruction from the San Francisco board of supervisors,[6] would invited Strauss and other engineers to investigate if a bridge could be built.

a long haul flight. But today, sitting in this hot black car, I know that ten hours will barely be enough time to leave 'Tejas' and enter 'Nuevo Mexico', barely. I tell myself I am prepared; I have enough water for all of us for three days, just incase. I have fruit, I have nuts, I have water, just in case.

I slowly succumb to the sameness. As it moves and stays where it is, my eyelids falter and close. There, in the bruised darkness waits John Ford and his searchers[1] and his dark murderous sky. I don't really remember the film but they are all here now, Natalie Wood and her feral grunts and John Wayne, his largeness etched across the landscape. A car careens around the corner just missing the quiet man. I recognize it as Ellen and Clark's car. I know this because of the dead grandmother strapped to the roof.[2] Mr. Ford and Mr. Wayne do not approve, what kind of manifest destiny is this they ask. I can't answer, my mouth is full of sand and fear. Joan Didion is there, sitting in the shade, watching me, writing everything down. "Only eight more hours and we're out of Texas" his voice reaches me from the long line he has cast into my depths, "What?" I answer from the deep

The ensuing discussions firmly grounded the building of the Bridge as an extension of Californians' 'manifest destiny.'[7] While also putting forth the argument that the bridge would secure San Francisco as the economic center of Northern California and allow the surrounding counties to the north to take advantage of the economic boons' brought about by an increasingly automobile dominated society.

Undercutting a bid of $100,000,000 Strauss claimed the bridge could be built for much less and so he undertook the initial design of the project and by August of 1921 had handed to O'Shaughnessy a blueprint for a $17,000,000 Bridge.[8] The initial design was so ugly and ungainly however that it quickly provoked protest from San Francisco esthetes, which was compounded by environmentalists. As the design languished on O'Shaughnessy's desk for two years, Strauss ever diligent and bent on making his plan a reality used this time to charge his engineers, in particular Charles Ellis and Clifford Paine,[9] with designing a more elegant bridge. He also went about drumming up supporters who lobbied on his behalf against the protestors and with whom in 1923, he gained permission from the state assembly to form a district having the power to levy taxes, issue bonds and build a bridge. And so the Golden Gate Bridge and Highway District was formed.[10]

The District was comprised of San Francisco, Marin, Sonoma, and Del Norte counties plus portions of Napa and Mendocino counties and had the power to levy taxes on property owners in all these areas. If the bridge construction dragged on or halted altogether, every property owner under its govern would be financially liable.[11] The plan was to only levy taxes until the bonds would be ready to be sold however with the growing voices of opposition claiming

"Only eight more hours?" "mmm...
Yessh" I say, " I suppose..." surfacing,
"where's the map?"

His eyes are inscrutable behind
his glasses, just like Roy Orbison.
"Water"? "What"? "DO YOU WANT
WATER?" "Oh no, I'm fine". "I brought
enough, just incase", "what?" He
looks confused and irritated; it is
beyond him why I weighted down the
car with all this water. There are plenty
of gas stations, I can hear him think,
we are not going into the desert.
Except that we are and I brought it
just in case. If the road had more
turns we would hear the glug of it all
as it sloshed backwards and forwards
churning in its plastic containers.
But the road is straight so it just sits
back there taking up valuable room,
waiting to be drunk.

At frequent intervals the road will
offer up some victim to its relentless
repetition. I quickly take note;
Two deer, one prairie dog, one
unconfirmed hawk/ golden eagle, four
squished armadillos, A million bugs,
one whole opossum and too many
random opossums parts, melting
into the tar becoming one with its
linear propulsion, to count. In his text
"Meditations on Deer head nation,"3
Mark Wallace details the disembodied

that the bridge would cost more like
$112,000,000, and the ever increasing
financial depression the idea of selling
the taxpayers on a huge indebtedness,
did not look like an easy task to Strauss
and his district. However it was to be
the depression that would prove to be
Strauss's greatest ally in the battle for
the public's vote. [12]

The general manager of the
District, Alan McDonald was reported as
claiming that the "Golden Gate Bridge
will cost the tax payer his vote and
that is all."[13] The district estimated
that $35,000,000 in construction would
translate into about $750,000 a year in
wages. The president of the San Francisco
Chamber of Commerce himself declared
that, "it's the job of every voter in the
city to create jobs by voting for the bond
issue."[14] And the media savvy Strauss
enlisted the papers in his campaign to
convince the people of san Francisco of
the bridges merits. The Examiner claimed,
"The mightiest suspension bridge in
the world will soon span the Golden
Gate" and The Chronicle simply stated,
" the bridge when built will be worth so
much to San Francisco and its whole
district that it will be worth even a
considerable deficit for some time"[15]
never one to shy from the lime light
Strauss was quoted as saying:

> San Francisco has often done the
> impossible. Now it only remains
> for her to connect up with the
> contiguous territory to make her the
> great city she is destined to be.[16]

The public began to warm to his bold and
ambitious plan.

However as the ballot day drew
closer opposition raged. There were
those who believed that a bridge was just
the wrong idea and proposed a 'better'
one themselves. In his 1929 pamphlet,

nature of American culture using the 'deer head' as metaphor. It is compelling but not as compelling to me as the statistics he cites that that buck Texas' 'huntin' n killin' image. Apparently in 1998 the hunting stats on deer kills put Texas, coming in at a measly 645,000 way behind other states such as Pennsylvania who racked 1,299,372 kills. These facts make me feel sad about leaving.

The landscape is scattered with horses and cows, pastoral tableaus that simply repeat, rewind and repeat. Pick-ups coast by us ferrying gormless dogs, heads and tongues hanging out of the windows, grinning at us, accusing us of not being no fun. At some point, I'm not sure when, we stop for to pee and I hear what I could have sworn was a rattlesnake. Urine stopped short, pants down we scramble back to the car. In the distant, but not so distant, past travelers going west like us had to deal with similar dangers like being trapped by snow or eaten by their companions. On February 9th 1874 Alferd Packer[4] set out with five other men to try and make it through the Rocky Mountains for Gunnison to lay claim to land, gold and a prosperous future. The story goes that finding themselves trapped by bad weather and with not enough

"Dam-Bridge, Which?" Cyrus C Walker proposed to, "make a great fresh water lake of all the interior of the San Francisco Bay," by constructing a dam/barrier that could hold a road and railroad if need be.[17] Unfortunately Mr. Walker's plan seems to have sunk without a trace from the public machinations. Even an early backer of the project Michael O' Shaughnessy began to publicly questioned the building of a bridge during the depression.

> Mr. O'Shaughnessy to Strauss,
> " How long will your bridge last?"
> Strauss: " Forever"
> Mr. O'Shaughnessy: " And how long is forever?"
> Strauss: "That I don't know!" [18]

Despite the opposition, the people of San Francisco threw themselves behind Strauss and his grand plan and on Nov 4th 1930 the Bridge Bond, (Proposition 37) was carried overwhelmingly, with a 'YES' vote of 109,919, to a 'NO' vote of 34,966. [19]

Strauss's district asked for bids on June 17 1931[20] and with financing seemingly secure had surveys conducted, but a new round of litigations would hold up construction for the rest of the year. The district had received a genuine offer from the bank of America to buy the $6,000,000 worth of bonds prepared for market, however this was dependant on a court test to determine the legality of the taxing powers of the district.

Bridge opponents, especially a group of anonymous, 'taxpayers' seized the opportunity to try once more to scupper the bridge altogether. Attorney Warren Olney entered a petition charging that the bridge district had been illegally formed. This was based on the unfortunate error on the part of the office of voters, whereby they had miscalculated the number of signatures on the San

provisions to last until spring Packer resorted to eating his companions. Manifeast destiny.

Chasing the sunset, we pull into the 'Cactus Restaurant' for dinner. The word 'restaurant' being played a little fast and lose here. It is a truck stop apparently fitted out for children or the inhabitants of a David lynch dream sequences, both of whom make an appearance while we sit awkwardly at the shrunken counter, folding our legs and bodies up under us as the waitress who address us as "Sugar" and has very little of her own teeth brings us patty melts that reveal their mistaken intention. Paying the bill and unfolding our cramped legs we start to leave. Just by the door is an incongruous and dusty revolving display case for two lonely crystal animals, a bear and a deer. I have to peel G's feverish little body away from it and he looks up at me eyes questioning but I have no explanation for him. I don't know. Getting back in the car I slip and bang my head and my knee. They sing together in dull throbbing unison. Wounded, huge treacherous sobs escape me, crying all the salt my body desperately needs into the sleeve of his shirt. The tears come and they don't stop, not one of Roosevelt's public

Francisco petition for the formation of the District, making more than 75% of its taxable assets illegitimate.[21]

When pressed on who these "anonymous taxpayers" were, Olney finally admitted that he represented ninety one taxpayers and the Southern Pacific – Golden Gate Ferries Ltd, a company which was owned by the hugely influential Sothern Pacific Railroad and whose business would be directly threatened by the opening of the bridge; a huge public outcry ensued.[22]

However, even though the courts had voted in favor of the district the court ruling came after the deadline from the Bank of America offer ran out, leaving the district cash strapped and hemorrhaging money. If something miraculous didn't happen soon Strauss and his backers dream would be over before it really began. Again the people of San Francisco stepped in, they refused to have a huge corporation like Sothern Pacific Railroad stand in the way of a project that had become an emblem of unemployment relief. The district and its advocates mustered every resource they had to bring down their adversaries. The newspapers, motor dealers of San Francisco, civic groups organized boycotts and the president of the local Labor Council organized the support of the labor unions behind the bridge.[23]

In the face of such obvious public contempt the ferry company slowly withdrew their opposition, they still maintained the bridge would be a financial and civic disaster but decided that they would no longer oppose the construction.[24] Strauss seeing that the district was financially exhausted and $250,000 in debt went once again to the Bank of America who agreed for a second time to buy all $6,000,000 worth works could dam them. I sense my husband watching me, watching me cry. And its good because that's what we do, we bear witness. My son, now strapped into his car seat in the back of our hot black car. Surrounded by water, watches us both, seemingly unperturbed.

The day is cooling. The hotel is not far and we have succeeded in almost getting out of Texas. And the thought crosses my mind that maybe we won't or shouldn't. This is not a redemptive narrative the journey does not end, the water doesn't cleanse anything, and there are no fresh starts. There is love, there is commitment, and there is the decision made anew each day to stay and be with the people in our lives. To stay in our lives. There are children and their wants, their playdoh, their plastic dinosaurs, their juice boxes and their cries from the back of the car of, "are we there yet". There is reading 'The runaway bunny' over and over and over and there is all this everyday, this is 'The Everyday'. I look down at the map as we lumber into the car park of the Hampton inn, Fort Stockton, Texas, and see the space between 'there and here and their' still so large, almost unthinkable and impossible.

of bonds and advanced the limping project $200,000 immediately. After winning the election and staring down the Southern Pacific Railroad it looked like the Bank of America offer would be sunk by a technicality in some ten-year-old legislation. Just when it seemed the bridge would be forever wrapped up in beauracratic red tape and never come into being, the Chairman of the Bank of America, Amadeus P. Giannini stepped in.

When he found out that the Golden Gate Bridge was going into the red he saw immediately the civic necessity of funding the project, "I know" he is reported to have said, " San Francisco needs that bridge. We will take the bonds"[25] Construction commenced on January 1933 and ran without halt until completion in May of 1937. As Strauss himself said, "It took two decades and two million words to convince the people the bridge was feasible."[26] During the long arduous struggle to begin construction Strauss's marriage had dissolved and he suffered a nervous breakdown. As construction finaly got underway, strauss would not be there to see it. Under his doctor's instructions, he had retired to the Adirondacks for six months to recover from the immense physical, psychological, and emotional strain years of fighting for his dream had cost him. Leaving Clifford Paine, his assistant, to begin building the bridge without him. [27]

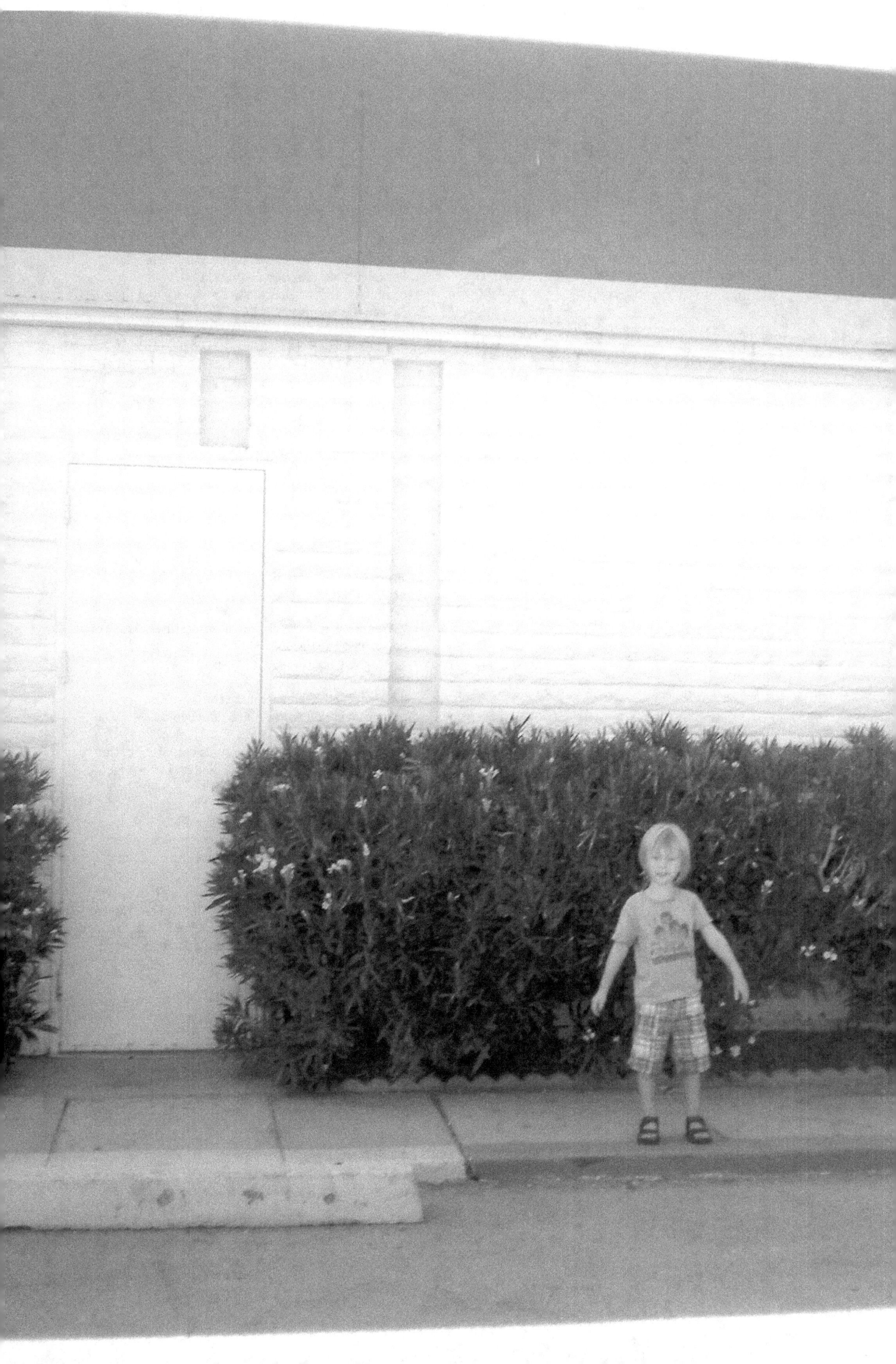

1 The Searchers. By Frank S. Nugent and Alan Le May. Dir. John Ford. C.V. Whitney Pictures . Warner Bros. Pictures, n.d.

2 Vacation by John Huges. Dir. Harold Ramis. Warner Bros. Pictures

3 Wallace, Mark. "Meditations on Deer Head Nation." Fold Magazine, n.d.

4 Banks, James E. Alferd Packer's Wilderness Cookbook . Vol. 2nd edition . Filter Press, 1998.

1 Cassady, Stephen, Spanning the Gate, The Golden Gate Bridge, Mill Valley, CA: Squarebooks, 1986. p10

2 Donald MacDonald and Ira Nadel, Golden Gate Bridge: history and design of an icon, San Francisco: Chronicle Books, 2008. p 5

3 Lampson, Robin. The mending of a continent, Berkeley, Calif.: Archetype Press, 1937. Poem commissioned to celebrate the completion of the Golden Gate Bridge in 1937.

4 Dillon, Richard H. High steel: building the bridges across San Francisco Bay, Millbrae, CA.: Celestial Arts, 1979 p.8. Norton the first was a speculator who had lost his mind and fortune trying to corner the rice market. He was beloved as a scruffy city mascot and issued many decrees his most famous being the demand for a bridge to be built across the Golden Gate.

5 Dillon, Richard H. High steel: building the bridges across San Francisco Bay, Millbrae, CA.: Celestial Arts, 1979. p. 8

6 Dillon, Richard H. High steel: building the bridges across San Francisco Bay, Millbrae, CA.: Celestial Arts, 1979. p.10

7 Weinberg, Albert Katz. Manifest destiny; a study of nationalist expansionism in American history. Chicago: Quadrangle Books, 1963, c1935 p.10

8 Cassady, Stephen, Spanning the Gate, The Golden Gate Bridge, Mill Valley, CA: Squarebooks, 1986. p.20

9 Van der Zee, John. The gate: the true story of the design and construction of the Golden Gate Bridge. New York: Simon and Schuster, 1986. p. 120. There is still controversy over who actually came up with the elegant engineering marvel that eh bridge design evolved into. In many documents the bridge design is accredited to the Strauss Engineering Company, i.e. Joseph Strauss but at the first conference of the National Academy of Sciences ever held on the pacific coast Mr. Ellis after eloquently outlining the bridges many engineering feats quietly asserted, "and then Mr. Strauss gave me some pencils and a pad of paper and told me to go to work".

10 Dyble, Amy Louise Nelson. Paying the toll: a political history of the Golden Gate Bridge and Highway District, 1923-1971. 2003. p. 14

11 Cassady, Stephen, Spanning the Gate, The Golden Gate Bridge, Mill Valley, CA: Squarebooks, 1986. p.24

12 Cassady, Stephen, Spanning the Gate, The Golden Gate Bridge, Mill Valley, CA: Squarebooks, 1986. p.32

13 Cassady, Stephen, Spanning the Gate, The Golden Gate Bridge, Mill Valley, CA: Squarebooks, 1986. p.32

14 Cassady, Stephen, Spanning the Gate, The Golden Gate Bridge, Mill Valley, CA: Squarebooks, 1986. p.32

15 Cassady, Stephen, Spanning the Gate, The Golden Gate Bridge, Mill Valley, CA: Squarebooks, 1986. p.32

16 Cassady, Stephen, Spanning the Gate, The Golden Gate Bridge, Mill Valley, CA: Squarebooks, 1986 p.23 17 Walker, C. C. (Cyrus C.) Dam - bridge, which? San Francisco, CA: C.C. Walker, Wale Printing Co, 1929 p. 4

18 E.J. Knapp. The great Golden Gate trivia book. San Francisco: Chronicle Books, 1987 p 96.

19 Summary of the Statements of the votes, General election, November 4th 1930. San Francisco p24.

20 Dillon, Richard H. High steel: building the bridges across San Francisco Bay, Millbrae, CA.: Celestial Arts, 1979 p 11

21 Cassady, Stephen, Spanning the Gate, The Golden Gate Bridge, Mill Valley, CA: Squarebooks, 1986 p 33

22 Van der Zee, John. The gate: the true story of the design and construction of the Golden Gate Bridge. New York: Simon and Schuster, 1986. p 139

23 Cassady, Stephen, Spanning the Gate, The Golden Gate Bridge, Mill Valley, CA: Squarebooks, 1986 p 34

24 Van der Zee, John. The gate: the true story of the design and construction of the Golden Gate Bridge. New York: Simon and Schuster, 1986. p 147

25 Van der Zee, John. The gate: the true story of the design and construction of the Golden Gate Bridge. New York: Simon and Schuster, 1986. p 160

26 Cassady, Stephen, Spanning the Gate, The Golden Gate Bridge, Mill Valley, CA: Squarebooks, 1986 p 12

27 Van der Zee, John. The gate: the true story of the design and construction of the Golden Gate Bridge. New York: Simon and Schuster, 1986 p 178-9

Bibliography: Manifeast Destiny

Golden Gate Bridge . Dir. Laura, and Ben Loeterman Longsworth. PBS Home Video, 2004.

Adams, Charles F. Heroes of the Golden Gate. Palo Alto: Pacific Books, 1987.

Arnold, Caroline. The Golden Gate Bridge. New York : F. Watts, 1986.

Banks, James E. Alferd Packer's Wilderness Cookbook . Vol. 2nd edition . Filter Press, 1998.

Cassady, Stephen. Spanning the Gate : the Golden Gate Bridge . Mill Valley: Squarebooks, 1986.

Chester, Michael and George R. Stewart. Joseph Strauss, builder of the Golden Gate Bridge. New York: Putnam, 1965.

de Andrade, Oswald. The Cannibal Manifesto . Trans. Stephen Berg. Vols. Number 1,. Cannibalist Review , 1928.

Dillon, Richard H. High Steel : building the bridges across San Francisco Bay. Millbrae,: Celestial Arts, 1979.

Donner, Gene. The Beautiful Bridge of Death : accounts of those who died, or nearly died, in falls from the Golden Gate Bridge. San Francisco: The author, 1995.

Dyble, Amy Louise Nelson. Paying the toll : a political history of the Golden Gate Bridge and Highway District. 1923-1971. Berkeley , 2003.

"Golden Gate Bridge fiesta edition." The Call Bulletin. San Francisco: Hearst Publications, 1937.

Horton, Tom and photography by Baron Wolman. Superspan : the Golden Gate Bridge. Santa Rosa: Squarebooks, 1997.

Knapp, E.J. The Great Golden Gate Bridge Trivia Book . San Francisco: Chronicle Books, 1987.

Koestenbaum, Wayne. Hotel Theory. Soft Skull Press, 2007.

Lampson, Robin. The Mending of a Continent. Berkeley: Archetype Press, 1937.

Lewis, J. Patrick. Monumental Verses. Washington,: National Geographic, 2005.

Lewis, Karen. Building the Golden Gate Bridge : a directory to historical sources. San Francisco: Labor Archives and Research Center, San Francisco State University, 1989.

MacDonald, Donald, and Ira Nadel. <u>Golden Gate Bridge History and Design of an Icon</u>. San Fransisco, 2008.

Pelta, Kathy. <u>Bridging the Golden Gate</u> . Minneapolis: Lerner Publications Co, 1987.

San Francisco Synthesizer Ensemble. "50th anniversary suite for the Golden Gate Bridge." Scott Singer Productions, 1987.

Stahl, Frank L. <u>The Golden Gate Bridge : report of the chief engineer, volume II.</u> San Francisco: Golden Gate Bridge, Highway and Transportation District, 2007.

Straka, Marilyn. <u>Golden Gate Bridge, Fort Point : self-guided walks</u> . San Francisco: On the Level Excursions, 2002.

Strauss, Joseph B. and Clifford E. Paine. <u>The Golden Gate Bridge; report of the chief engineer to the Board of directors of the Golden Gate Br.</u> Golden Gate Bridge and Highway District. San Francisco: Golden Gate Bridge and Highway District, 1938.

<u>The Golden Gate Bridge</u> . Jaffe Productions in association with Hearst Entertainment. A&E Home Video, 1995.

<u>The Joy of Life</u> . By Jenni Olson. Dir. Jenni. Olson. Frameline. 2005.

<u>The Searchers</u>. By Frank S. and Alan Le May (novel) Nugent. Dir. John Ford. C.V. Whitney Pictures . Warner Bros. Pictures, n.d.

Van der Zee, John. <u>The Gate : the true story of the design and construction of the Golden Gate Bridge</u>. New York: Simon and Schuster, 1986.

Walker, C. C. <u>Dam - Bridge, Which?</u> . San Francisco: Wale Printing Co, 1929.

Walker, C. C. <u>The Barrier Dam: why? where? and how?</u> San Fransisco: Walker, C. C., 1930.

Wallace, Mark. "Meditations on Deer Head Nation." <u>Fold Magazine</u> (n.d.).

Wojnarowicz, David. <u>Close to the Knives: A Memoir of Disintegration.</u> . New York: Vintage Books, 1991 .

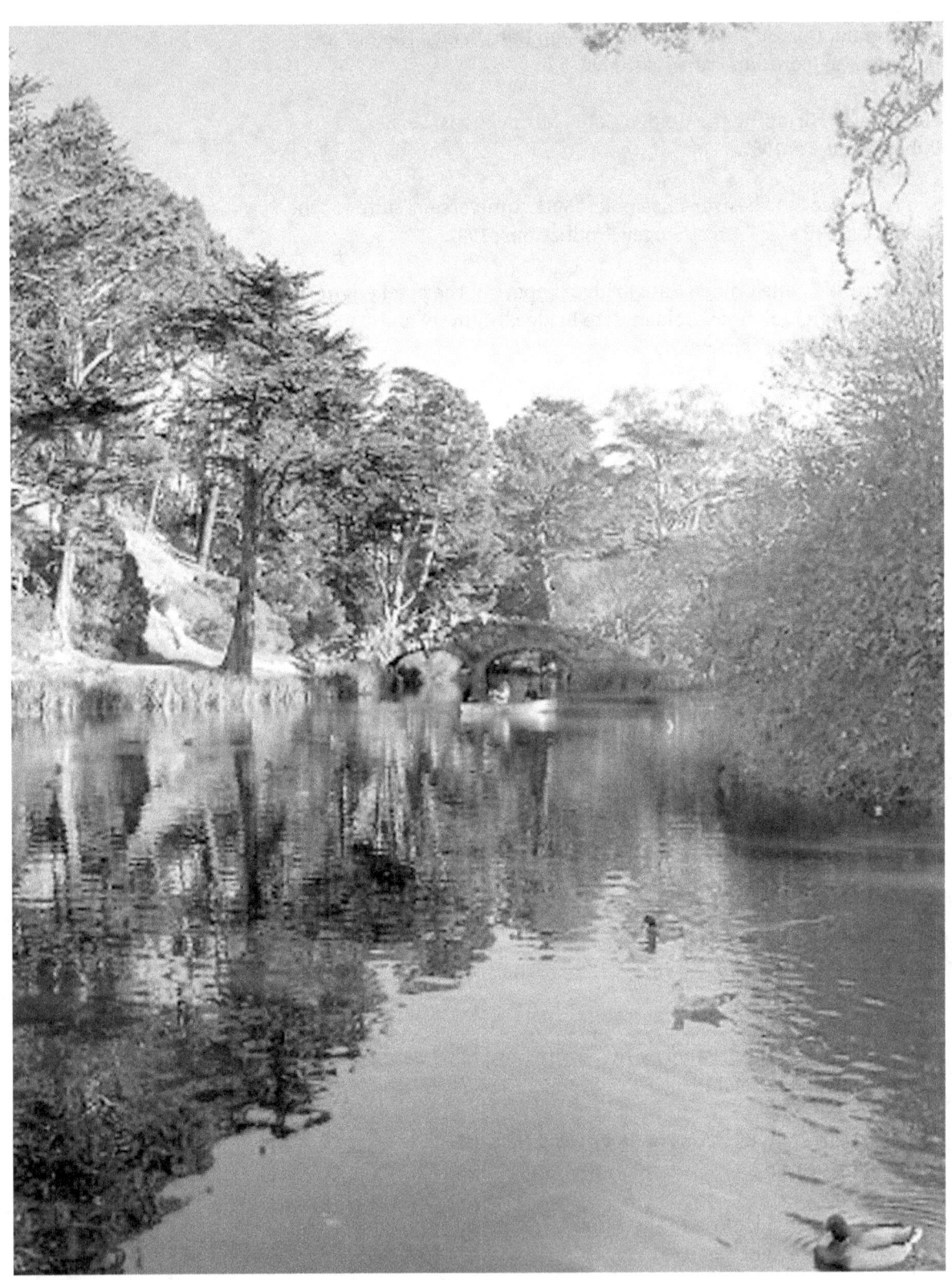

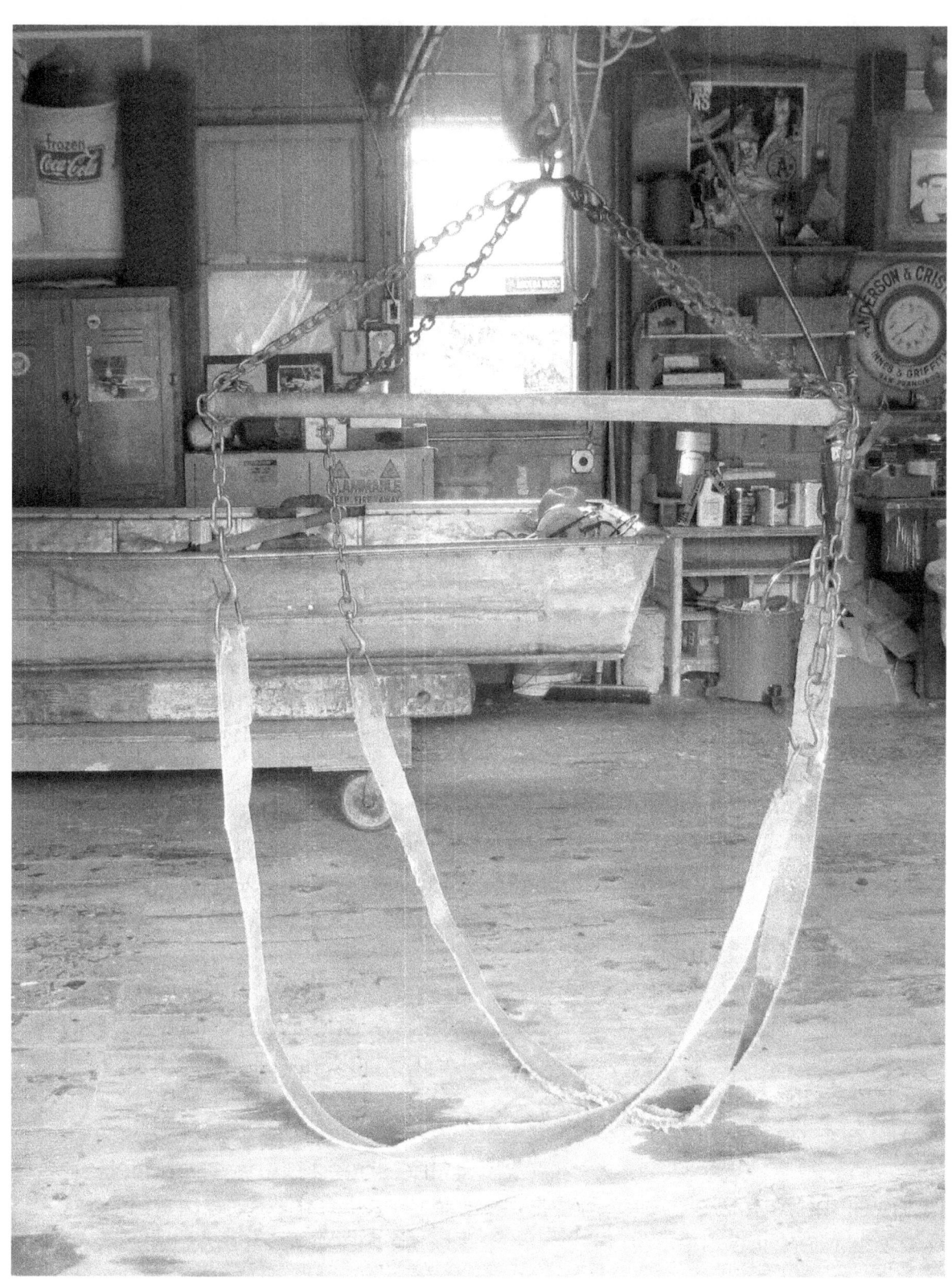

THE CREATURE OF STOWE LAKE
A SUBPLOT TO THE NARRATIVE WRITTEN IN GOLDEN GATE PARK

It was announced on a black and
white poster.

There was a photocopy of a
photo and a description written
in permanent marker that
explained what to look for.

"On the hottest days the
water will part."

"Do not feed."

This act of public service
was tacked next to colored
pictures of native birds.

You could learn their Latin
names and read how they
build nests and procreate.

You could also see them
pulled down abruptly and
hear their shrill gargle.

But information like this
would not be laminated.

None of the regulars could
explain where it came from.

Not the Chinese in the morning
or the French at lunch.

Not even the Russians
in the afternoon.

The old people.

They weren't here for that sort
of thing.

They knew it existed, but at this
point in their lives they were dealing
with a different set of fears.

"Focus on something positive."

The Mayor wouldn't acknowledge,
let alone offer to comment on it.

As long as there was country music,
he could believe that it was 1950.

The teens, naive to its impact,
giggled and shrugged saying
that they hadn't seen it in
a year. "I don't know."

It may have been hidden by the
scent of eucalyptus and masked
by the flickering light off the
water, but you could see it.

In the speed of the swimming
birds and in the eyes of the boat
house manager, it was with us.

Resting under five feet
of diluted algae.

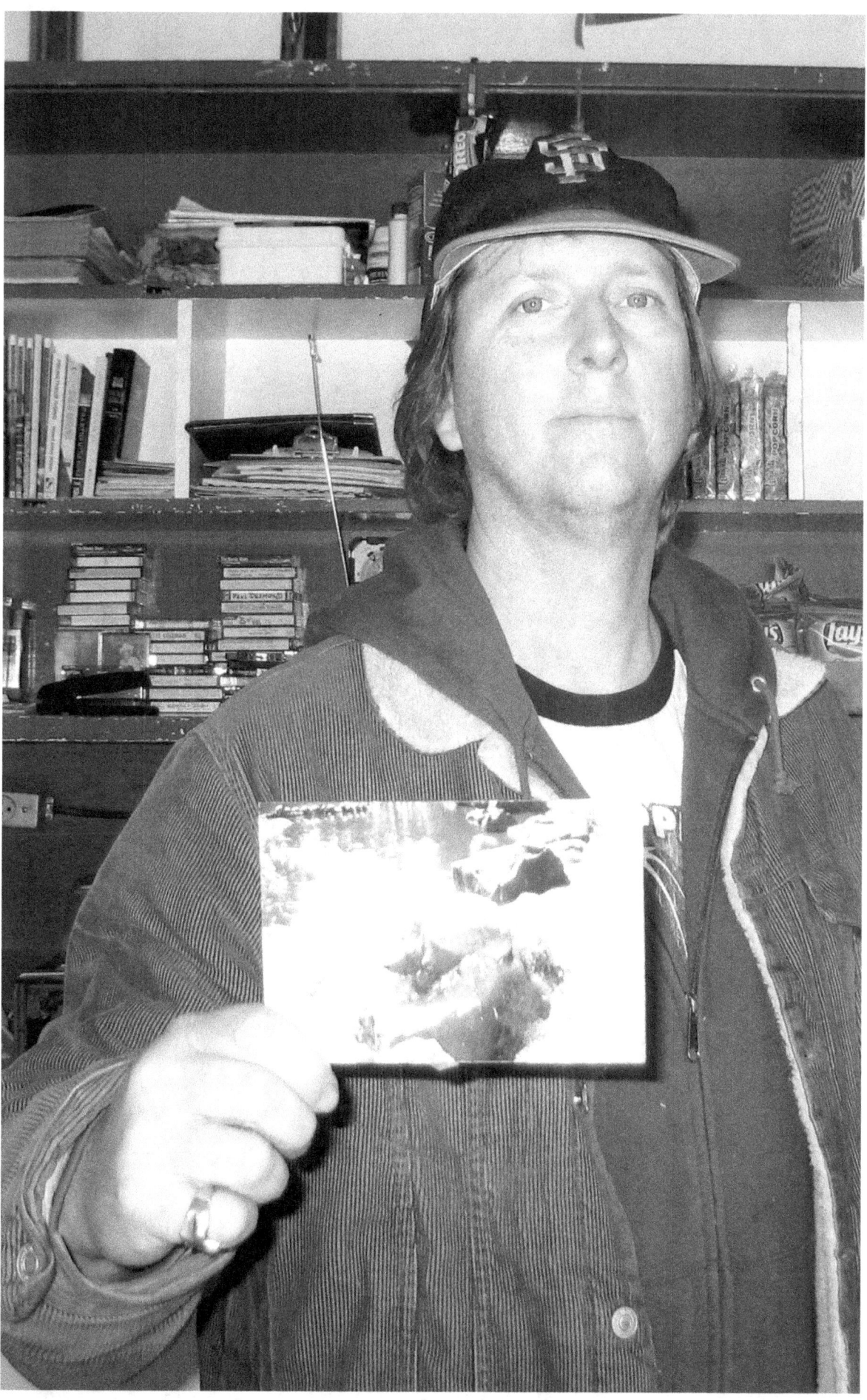

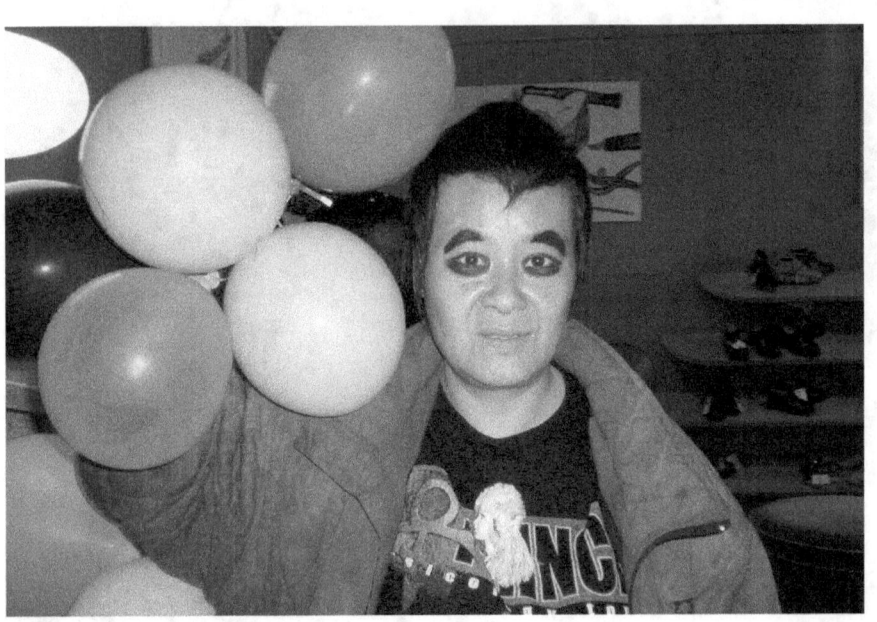

About Lillian
Rebecca Ora

Jim

How do I identify with her?

I don't think I Identify with her very much.

But in some ways, I feel envious of her.

Because its obvious that it doesn't take very much to make

her happy, and when I see her she usually is very happy,

and she obviously doesn't have a lot of material things.

It takes very little for her to get by.

And, although I don't want to be picking food out of the

garbage and stuff, still there's this sort of—I don't know

how to say it—this sort of envy I have about her.

She just kind of keeps rolling along.

The time she disappeared... I don't really know.

I could be making stuff up in my head, but it seems

that, adding to the fantasy I already have in my head

of her (which is nonsexual; absolutely nonsexual),

I would say I think that she had some

problems with her medication.

I don't know if she was hospitalized, or something.

But I don't even know what medication she's on.

So I think she said something like that in

passing that she couldn't sleep, or...

I really don't know.

Monika

I would say at least six years. I think five or
six years—that seems about right.
Yeah, she creeped me out.
She just kind of wandered in, and knowing where we
are and how many homeless people we have around
here, we were like "Who the hell is this?"
And she would come by, and at first I was
like "Keep her away from me."
She was creepy to me. Just kind of wandered in.

I think Denny kind of egged her on. He kept being like "So, c'mon!
What's your story? Where are you from? What are you doing?"
And I was like "Eeew, eeew eew!"
Part of it is that she's very attracted to women, so
she puts up a very different energy to women than
she does to men. But the longer she kept coming
in, the more I was just like "Put up with her."
And I still put up with her.
There are some parts of her that are really interesting,
then parts of me, I'm like "What is with this woman?"
But I think she's been invited in.   No one's
really said, "You have to not come in."

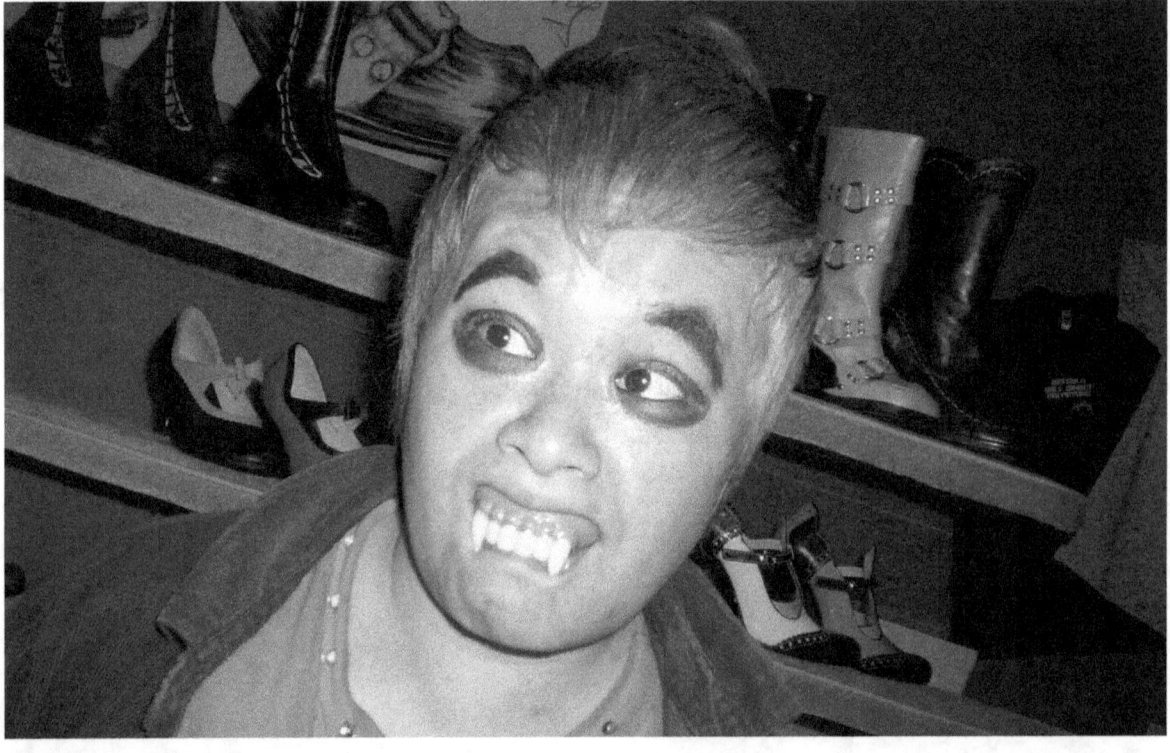

And she's, for the most part, harmless. She's not asking
for money or accosting people or coming across as
aggressive. That would be terms for... "No more."

I think a part of it is that we've somewhat, to
her mind, have become her friends.
And I think Lillian's life revolves around a lot of time spent
in a social situation where she gets to interact with people.
When she wanders the streets, she's made acquaintances.
And if you go anyplace often enough people get
to know you, whether they like you or not.

Jim
Lillian kind of rides that line sometimes.
When nothing's going on, its great to have
that interaction with somebody.
Especially with someone like her, who's very interesting.
But when it's busy, she can be kind of annoying.
Because she has no boundaries.
And that's something that I kind of admire
about her is her place in society.
She doesn't really give a shit about anything.
And it's very obvious.
When she comes in, I'll be with a customer,
or ringing somebody up.
And she'll come right up to me and she'll say, "Hello,
Honey! Do you have any food for me today?"
And I just say "Lillian, I'm with a customer!"
And I've told her over and over and over, but she doesn't care.
She's just in her own....
Sometimes it's humorous.
Sometimes it can be very annoying.
And customers obviously look at her, and they just don't
understand who this person is. Especially on Haight street.
They probably think she's just some wacko that walked in.
 And who knows?
I think some people might be afraid of her.
But...
She's her own person.

Denny

I don't think Lillian is schizophrenic, I don't, I really
don't. I think that medication she had is—I know she
takes Ambien for a sleep disorder, she says she has trouble
sleeping at night, and basically she's up a lot at night.
But she's present, she's not spaced out, she's certainly
not mentally retarded, I mean, there's something going
on there—I don't know exactly—but she doesn't lash
out, she doesn't have Tourette's or whatever.
She has her moments where I feel like she crosses the line, but
I think when you look like Lillian and you are so used to being
criticized by the rest of the world that she can kind of throw it
back once in a while. You know, people are staring at her, and

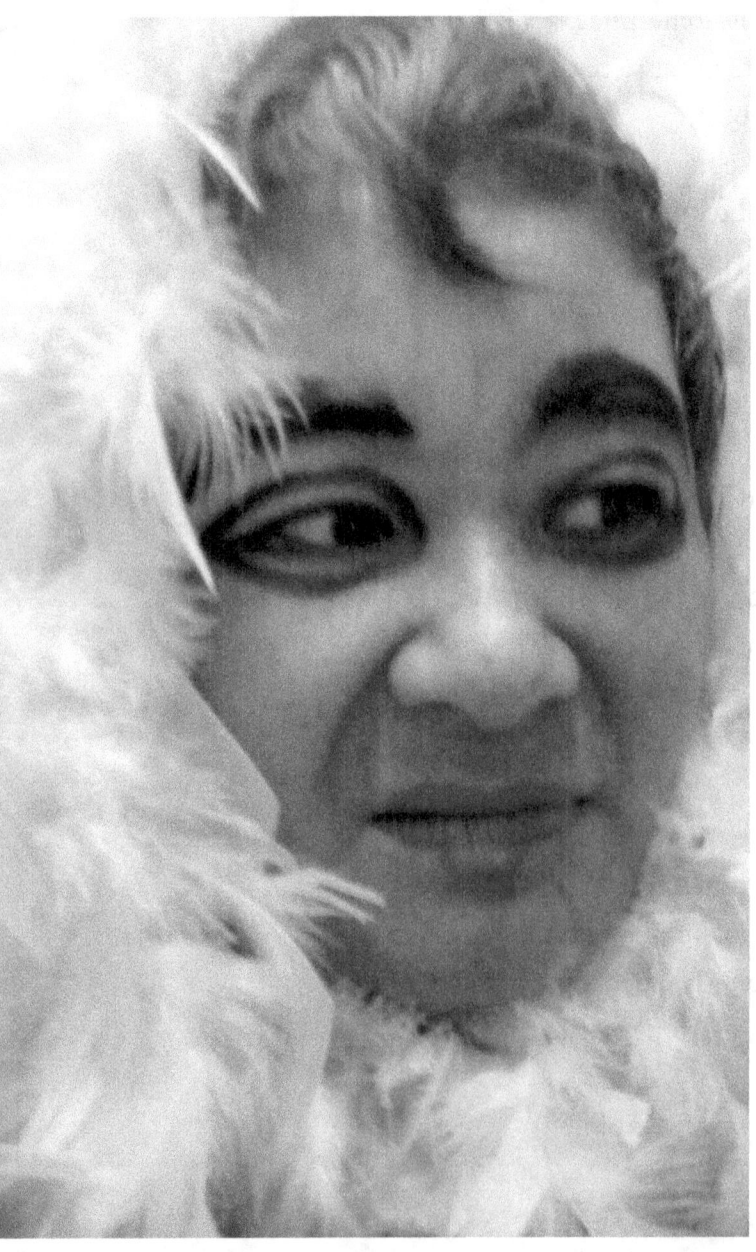

saying that she's ugly,
she'll tell people that
they're ugly and fat
too, I think its kind
of funny, actually.
But I do have to
keep her in check,
because, y'know....
I just think that Lillian
is someone who fell
through the cracks.

You know, it's funny
because I can't really
speak for what Lillian
thinks about herself,
but she does look
in the mirror a lot,
and she says "ugly"
a lot, and it's funny,
though, because she
doesn't look disgusted
when she says it, she
almost looks humored
by it. I really am
curious about how she

feels when she looks at herself in the mirror, because most
of us get up and look at ourselves in the mirror and go,
"Oh, I look terrible today! Look at my hair," or "I haven't
shaved" or this and that, or "I'm fat," whatever, y'know?
Lillian looks at herself in the mirror more than
anyone I've ever known in my entire life.
She styles her hair probably at least ten times while I'm
in her presence. She's always looking in the mirror and
she's always re-doing her makeup, making sure.
You know she works hard to look this way.
She doesn't just roll out of bed, she actually takes time to do
this sort of stuff, to pick out her outfit and to do it like this.
So it's funny. When I look at her saying that she's ugly in
the mirror I don't feel like, "Oh, poor Lillian, she thinks
she's so ugly," because she's not. I think she just looks
at herself and thinks, "Oh, I'm just such a freak."
I don't think that she has a negative self-image. I
don't think that anyone would make herself look
like that if she thought she looked ugly.
I mean, she knows she's got no teeth, but you know
what? She's always smiling and relatively happy. I rarely
see her ever sad. She's happy in her own world.
I've seen her progressively lose more and more teeth as I've
known her through the years. I'm not sure how her teeth got
so terrible. But y'know there's other famous people with bad
teeth, too. You know Edith Massey, from the John Waters movies,
she had horrible teeth, and the guy from The Pogues, he had
terrible teeth, so I just look at it and kind of have to shrug my
shoulders, because it's kind of hard to figure out how she sort
of, like, got to this point. There's only one Lillian, and there's no
doubt about it. She's a pretty recognizable face around town.

Jim

When I've seen her outside she has this... almost
very defiant body language about her.
When she smokes, it's very strong and powerful.
It's not just this casual thing that she's doing.
It's like she's getting the most out of it.
And I don't know if it's because of where she lives,

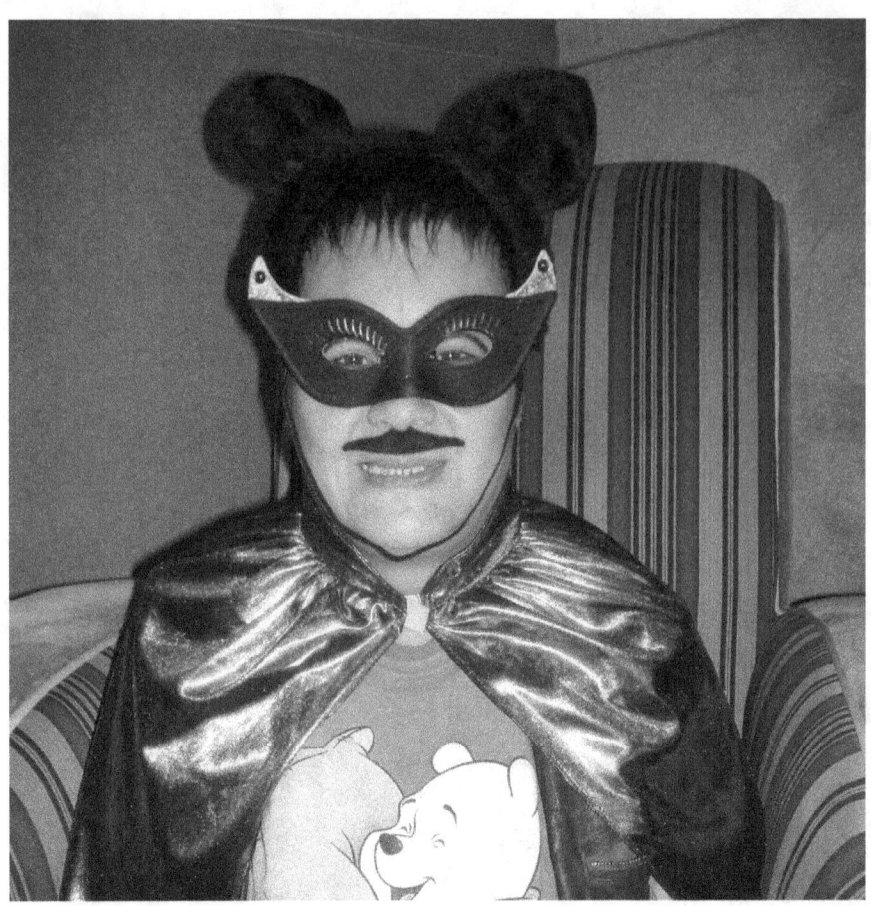

but she seems to have this defiant personality
when she's walking around outside.
But then I've seen her dancing on the corner,
or interacting with people she knows.
I've seen her when I'm coming back to the store.
And I'll pass by her.
She's definitely in her own little world.
She has a sort of tunnel vision where she's very focused.
And if she has a cigarette, and she's stomping
toward where she needs to go.
And I'll be walking toward her, and she won't see me.
And I'll say, "Lillian!"
And she'll see me.
And she'll say "Hi honey!"
 And she'll dance, or do her other thing.
The other thing is this pelvic thrust, which
is a very Lillian kind of thing.
But as soon as she sees me, her whole demeanor, it just cracks.
The ice falls, and she's happy and whatnot.

Monika

It's been an interesting journey.

I think she's not illusionary about her own life. I don't think she's painted herself into some, "This is my life, It's wonderful!" But I think she kind of wanders. She's totally an urban nomad. She goes from different parts of the city, and it's amazing how many people know her. I was at a makeup counter downtown and they knew Lillian (and they hide their makeup every time Lillian comes their way).

I think her story would be "Child, raised I believe in China, came here, her illness developed and she became separate from her family."

I mean, she's educated! She can read, she can write, she can speak two dialects of Chinese. She's not some drug-doing hippie on the street who has no life. She, in her own way, has created this life of going store-to-store and talking with people and hanging out with them as her daily routine. And I think she seems fairly happy. I've never heard Lillian be like, "I want to move," or "I want to change," or "I want to die." For her, the social scenario makes her life complete.

Denny

I think most people would look at Lillian and just be like "Get away! You're a freak, you smell, you're weird." But there's something about her that just to me is really just not magical— she just really, like, pulled me into her world. It's like I said, it's like a John Waters movie, it's like sometimes you can't look away, sometimes its so fascinating and its like a bad B-movie or something. She's funny, and you know, she's a normal person, she's not a freak. She's no threat to me, or anything, I'm never worried about her stealing from me or anything like that. You know, there's some homeless people on the street—Lillian's not homeless, too. She has a home, she eats, she's not like somebody that I'm threatened by. Although at first glance, you'd look at her and feel like "Oh my god, get this person away from me," or "Get her away from my child," or whatever. But she's always sweet and funny, and maybe she kind of has her moments where she makes you a bit crazy, but for the most part she's entertaining, you know? And I think people like her are so used to being ignored.

On the Outskirts

Amy Franceschini
and Michael Swaine

Policy, Thoughts and Proposals Having to Do With Outdoor Advertising.

1. In 1965, the Highway Beautification Act (HBA) initiated by First Lady "Lady Bird" Johnson and signed by her husband, President Lyndon B. Johnson, called for "control of outdoor advertising, including removal of certain types of signs, along the Nation's growing Interstate System. It required junkyards along Interstate or primary highways to be removed or screened and encouraged scenic enhancement and roadside development." Signs not subject to meeting the HBA criteria are limited to directional and official signs, signs advertising products for sale on the property on which they are located and those advertising the distribution by nonprofit organizations of free coffee to individuals traveling on the Interstates.

-Scenic America

*Along the highway on Interstate 5 in California are a series of
decaying signposts calling out crop names. These brown and white
signs are very nondescript and can easily be overlooked. I have
driven on this route between Los Angeles and Sacramento for
over 35 years and never noticed the signs until my father pointed
them out to me last year. As we passed through America's Bread
Basket, between two rotting fence posts, I spotted a sign that read
"Cotton", but the crop behind the fence was an almond orchard.
A little further down the road another barely legible sign—white
paint flaking off-read "Sugar Beet", but behind this sign were herds
of cattle. These interpretative signposts, once placed by Lady B.
Johnson's Highway Beautification Act, are now historical markers of
a faded era of industrial agriculture.*

proposal #1

all billboards
should be changed into
pegboards
and then the large pegboards
would have tools hanging
large lending libraries of tools
ladders to get to the tools
and librarians to check-out
and check in-tools
i guess the librarians should have a sun hat and sun screen
like life-guards at the beach
but still the glasses that make librarians librarians

2. "Billboard control and removal under the Highway
   Beautification Act has largely been a failure, achieving
   little toward the accomplishment of stated Congressional
   goals. Crippling amendments, " loop-holes" in the
   designation of commercial and industrial zones, the
   exemption of on-premise signs, a lack of national
   standards, reliance upon the use of eminent domain
   rather than the police power to remove non-conforming
   signs, inadequate appropriations for the program and
   general indifference among former supporters have been
   the main causes of the Act's ineffectiveness. Extensive
   amendment and vigorous administration are essential
   if the Act is ever to be effective. At one site [in 1983 in
   Louisiana] over 2,000 feet of vegetation and trees were
   cut and cleared to enhance the visibility of two signs"
   — leaving behind more than 900 stumps.
   -US General Accounting Office (1985 report).

I imagine approaching a billboard late at night during a road trip
through Louisiana. The light from the sign pours across the road
highlighting a field of stumps- seating for an outdoor cinema or a
monument to a former forest?

proposal #2

or should billboards be places to put unpaid bills, eviction
notices a public display of capitalism going wrong

3. In January 2007, Sao Paolo's mayor, Gilberto Kassab,
    enacted a ban on billboards which extended to all
    "outdoor advertising". Since then billboard armature,
    banners and walls have been removed. With this removal
    came some unexpected results. People were seeing long-
    standing favelas, or slum-like neighborhoods, for the first
    time because they had previously been blocked from
    view by billboards. And people passing by certain shops,
    whose windows were once covered by ads, now looked
    in to see poorly treated immigrant laborers, who had
    once worked and slept in the shops unnoticed. As the ads
    come down and more of the city is revealed— including its
    impressive urban architecture—citizens are adjusting
    to their new landscape.

    *Maybe the city will hire local muralists to paint scenes of
    jungles or mansions to cover up what had been previously
    hidden by advertisers.*

proposal #3

students who don't want to be in school could paint new
lesson plans to people about what is going wrong with the
education model and their solution like...

"Tom said to himself that it was not such a hollow world, after
all. He had discovered a great law of human action, without
knowing it — namely, that in order to make a man or a boy
covet a thing, it is only necessary to make the thing difficult
to attain. If he had been a great and wise philosopher, like the
writer of this book, he would now have comprehended that
Work consists of whatever a body is obliged to do, and that
Play consists of whatever a body is not obliged to do. And this
would help him to understand why constructing artificial
flowers or performing on a tread-mill is work, while rolling
ten-pins or climbing Mont Blanc is only amusement. "

-Mark Twain, *Tom Sawyer*, chapter two, 1876.

4. In 1968, Vermont prohibited new billboards and provided
    an amortization period of five years to remove existing
    billboards. By 1974, Vermont felled its last billboard.

    Ted Riehle, moved to Vermont from New York City in
    search of a slower, quality life. As a Republican Vermont
    legislator in 1968, he put forth a ban on billboards. This
    made Vermont the first state in the U.S. to make billboards
    illegal. His success in passing the bill is rooted in Riehle
    winning over the garden clubs of Vermont. He visited every
    garden club in the state to generate support.

Definitions of "outdoor advertising devices" as stated in 1968 Vermont legislation against billboards:

(A) A writing, picture, painting, light, model, display, emblem, sign, or similar device situated outdoors, which is so designed that it draws the attention of persons in any public highway, park, or other public place to any property, services, entertainment, or amusement, bought, sold, rented, hired, offered, or otherwise traded in by any person, or to the place or person where or by whom such buying, selling, renting, hiring, offering, or other trading is carried on.

(B) A sign, poster, notice, bill, or word or words, in writing situated outdoors and so designed that it draws the attention of and is read by persons in any public highway, park, or other public place.

(C) A sign, writing, symbol, or emblem made of lights, or a device or design made of lights so designed that its primary function is not giving light, which is situated outdoors and draws the attention of persons in any public highway, park or other public place. According to the Committee's report, "Our scenic resources... have contributed much to our economic development by attracting tourists,...residents, and new industries and cultural facilities. ...[T]he scattering of outdoor advertising throughout the state is detrimental to the preservation of these resources, and consequently to the economic base of the state."

The Universe as Understood from Within the Confines of My Body, 2009

Ruth Robbins

RECONSTRUCTING THE UNIVERSE: 12/3/08-4/26/09

Everyday I will complete a drawing of the night sky. I will begin with the North Star and add a new star each day for 144 days— the interval in between my mother's diagnosis with terminal cancer (December 3, 2007) and her death (April 26, 2008). My mother's illness and death have left me feeling out of sync with the current moment. I will use this daily practice as way to reorient myself, utilizing the stars as a calendar. Today is February 25th. I have completed 84 star charts. I will complete sixty-one more.

TIME

Time: the indefinite continued progress of existence and events in the past, present, and future, regarded as a whole

Cosmic time: the time covered by the physical formation and development of the universe currently set at 13 billion years (+/- 2 billion)

Solar time: Sun time. **Apparent solar time** is based on the daily motion of the true sun, in other words, the actual position of the sun in the sky. This is the version of solar time that a sundial shows. It varies throughout the year due to earth's axial tilt and elliptical orbit. **Mean solar time** is used for accurate timekeeping, including all civil timekeeping and is based on how the sun would move in the sky if there were no irregularities in Earth's motion. A mean solar day is 24 hours measured from midnight to midnight.

Sidereal time: Star time. Time based on the rotation of the Earth with respect to the background of fixed stars. A sidereal day is the time required for one complete rotation of the Earth on its axis with respect to a fixed star. It is an unvarying unit equal to 23 hours, 56 minutes, 4.09 seconds of solar time. 144 star days is seven hours shorter than 144 sun days.

DEATH IN THE PARK

November 2, 2008

San Francisco, Treat Park

In the park there are altars to mothers, fathers, infants, husbands, *offrendas* to those who died with AIDS, in wars and on the border. Together they form a heterogeneous everybody. Individuals publicly invoke their own dead trusting the attendees to find their own resonance. Together they form a field of memory with infinite moments of access. Most altars have a space for offerings from strangers who are moved to celebrate their dead, and people bring photos, flowers, candy, cakes, fruit, keys or candles. Or they don't. Or they confuse celebrating the dead with mourning the dead and decide that since they are not in mourning this festival doesn't apply to them. They come to watch and once there, plain-faced and carrying no mementos of their beloved dead, want to participate. Tonight there are no spectators. We all know death.

RECONSTRUCTING THE UNIVERSE: 12/3/08-4/26/09
I am working from a star chart containing 144 stars arranged in constellations. I make this drawing outside, under the sky. Orient the star chart as a reflection of the stars as they are at the moment. The stars are in continual motion in the night sky. The reflection is true for about an hour.

The best time is just around dusk. At this hour, I rule the universe. In the sky the stars come out one at a time as I'm painting. I also feel safer working alone in the parking lot. I'm pacing out the stars. Marking their relative positions in relation to my body. At this scale the little dipper is about the size of a bus. I am painting with chalk. I mix it with water to make white paint. In the rain the chalk lasts about an hour. It's been raining for weeks. The last thing I do is take a photograph. The street lamps blur in the long exposure.

PLUS OR MINUS 2 BILLION
Astronomical scale is vast. I am unable to visualize such enormous numbers with a brain that is designed to think on bodily scale. I can only have these thoughts inside of my body, on earth. For humans, the body is the standard of measure. We measure distance in feet, time with breath. It hurts to think a billion.

1 million seconds is 12 days.
1 billion seconds ago was 1978.
1 trillion seconds ago was 31,688 years ago.
One trillion seconds ago Neanderthals and Homo sapiens coexisted on earth.

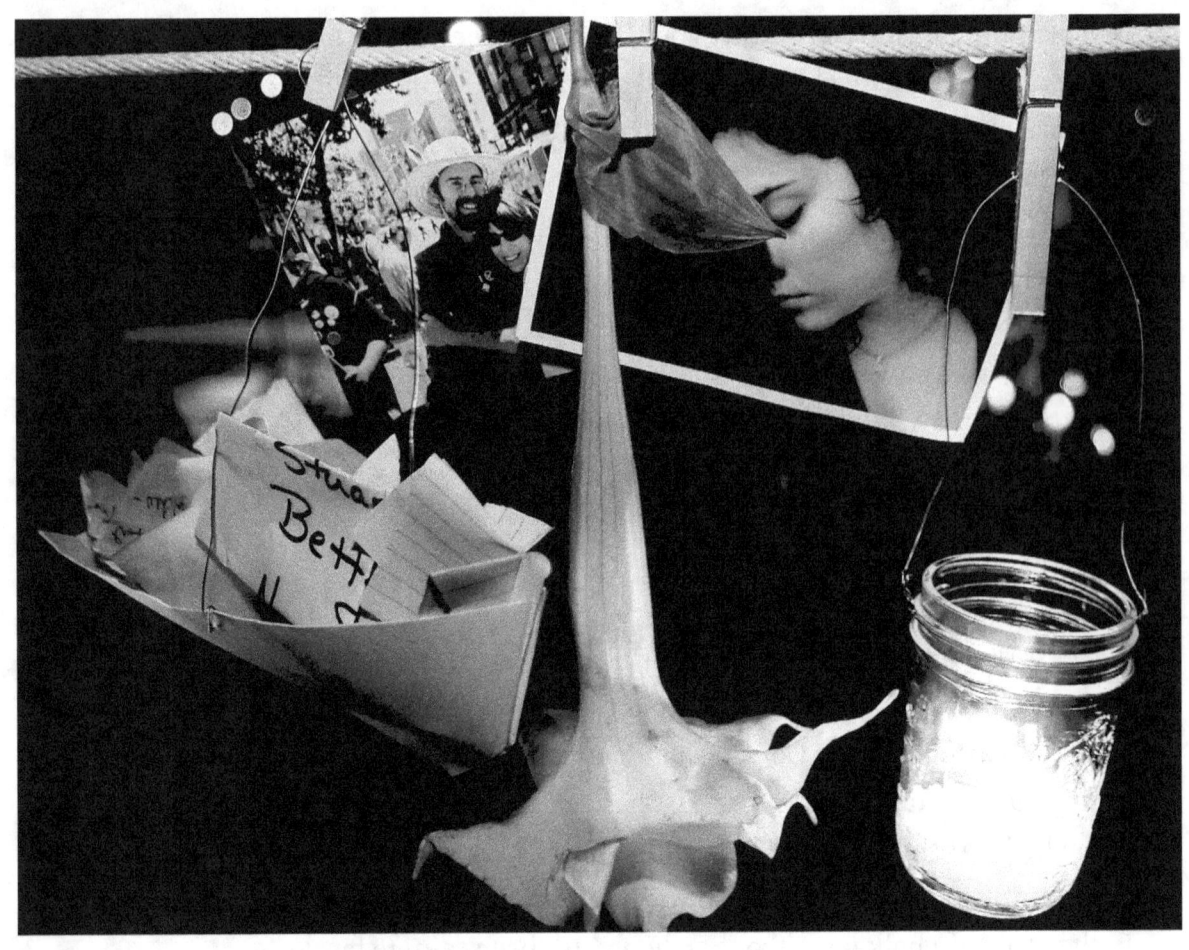

DEATH IN THE PARK

Two months after my arrival in California and six months after
my mother's death, I built an altar for the San Francisco Day
of the Dead festival. My altar was in service to the unprepared
celebrant. I prepared 30 paper rowboats, each about a foot long, 4
inches wide and 3 inches deep. Each rowboat had several benches
and an oarsman rowing in the back. I strung a clothesline on a
pulley stretching from a five foot stand on the grass to a street
lamp on the sidewalk, about 25 feet up the pole. I hung the boats
alternately with candles in jars; both elements were strung on
wire and attached to the line with clothespins. Attached to the
stand were small clipboards stocked with rice paper and pencils.
Celebrants wrote messages to the dead on the paper and tucked
them into the boats, others left mementos on the benches or hung
photos or flowers from the line. As the area closest to the ground
filled with notes and offerings, I pulled the pulley and the boats
begin their ascent – a progression of boats carrying messages and
love to the beloved dead. I prepared 2,000 sheets of paper and

they were gone in ninety minutes. For the rest of the night we improvised. Celebrants wrote on receipts, money, notebooks were gutted to restock the clipboards. After the festival I dismantled the altar, abandoning the pulley on the streetlamp and packing the overflowing boats away.

LIGHTSPEED

Light-years are the standard astronomical unit of measurement. A light-year measures distance, not time. One light-year is the distance that light travels in one year. The speed of light is 186,000 miles a second or 11 million miles a minute or six million million miles a year. Six million million miles is a six with twelve zeros after it. I can't hold this number in my head.

There is no way to look at the stars as they appear now. The stars vary in their distance from our planet; the farthest objects we can see with our naked eyes are about 2,000 light-years away. The closest star is the sun. The sun is ninety-three million miles away, that's eight light minutes. The next closest star is four light-years away. Four years ago my mother's existence was a fact, part of the fabric of my universe.

DEATH IN THE PARK

North of the border, death is a traveler. He arrives hooded and grinning, and we are not smiling. South of the border, they live with death. If you live with death long enough, you have to look him in the face. Feed him, and it won't be long before the jokes start. There's lot of joking tonight. We are celebrating the dead and teasing death. With our ancestors around us, death isn't so scary. Half the people here tonight have been there and back.

LOOKING UP

The movements of the celestial sphere form the superstructure to our most elemental understanding of where and when we are here and now. The where and the when are structurally linked, they are two expressions of our planet rotating around the sun. Units of years, months, days and hours, defined by the mass of the earth and its axial rotation and its distance from the sun. If these physical facts were different, we would have a different time scale. Latitude is best understood in the sky. Travel north or south, and the days get longer or shorter, new stars appear and familiar ones fail to emerge at dusk. It's human nature to travel past our horizons. Once familiar landmarks disappear, travelers must look up to determine their location and direction.   At sea, there are no landmarks. The Pacific Ocean was navigated before it was mapped, without a compass.

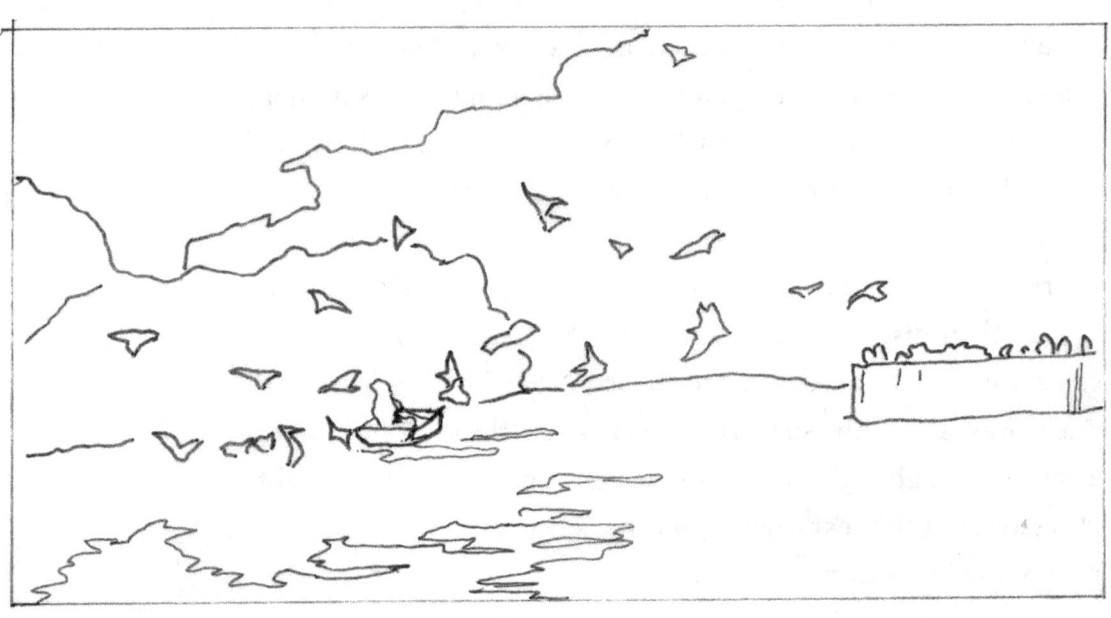

DEATH IN THE PARK
Golden Gate Park, Stowe Lake

I rented a rowboat from the man selling popcorn by the lake. Carrying the boats from the Day of the Dead altar, I rowed away from the dock. I filled the small boats with breadcrumbs and launched the boats and messages into the lake. They floated until the seagulls arrived. The birds filled the air, devouring the breadcrumbs and sinking the boats. The birds accelerated the soaking of the boats and their contents, returning them to wood pulp at the bottom of the lake. Four old women watched from their bench. I told them about the altar and the festival. They said they were Chinese. They said the Chinese know about death. They said I was a good girl.

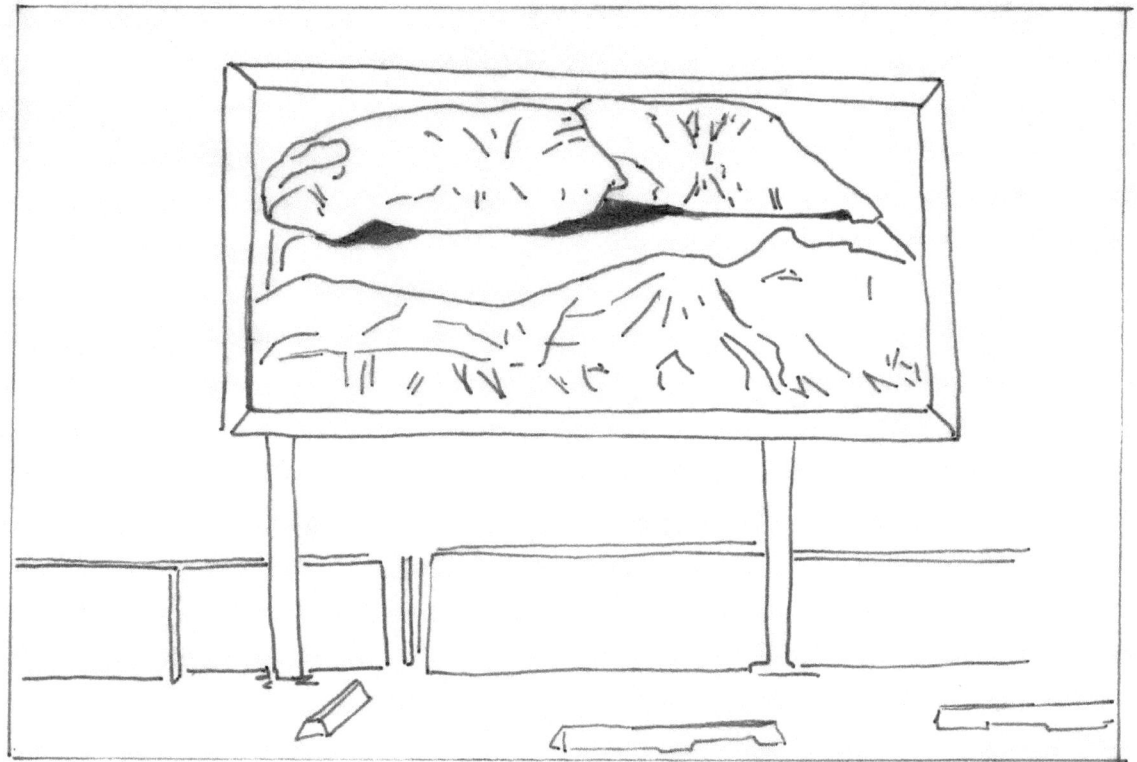

WITHOUT EXPLANATORY TEXT

"Untitled", 1991
Felix Gonzales-Torres

Displayed on twenty-four New York City billboards,
without explanatory text. The nature of loss is that the
thing/feeling/person you are missing isn't there. There is
nothing to see. It's invisible.

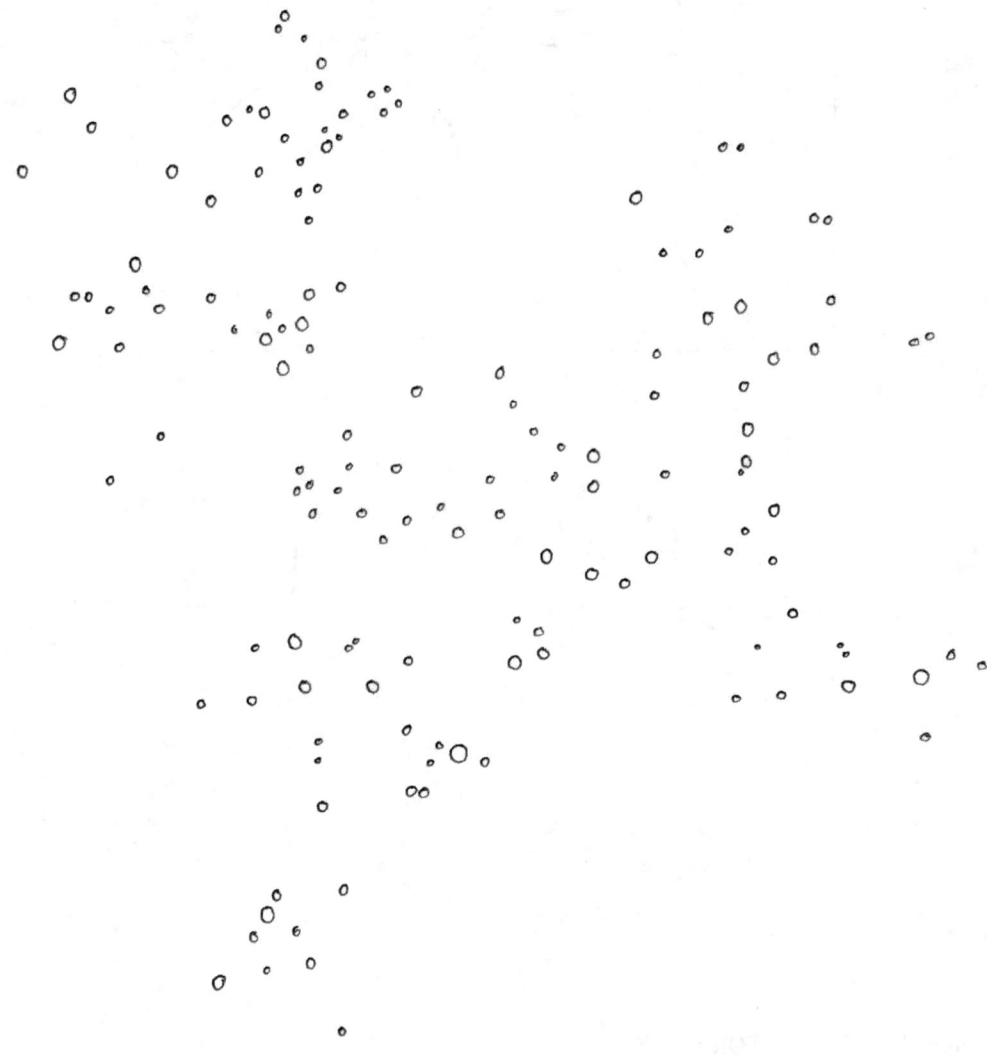

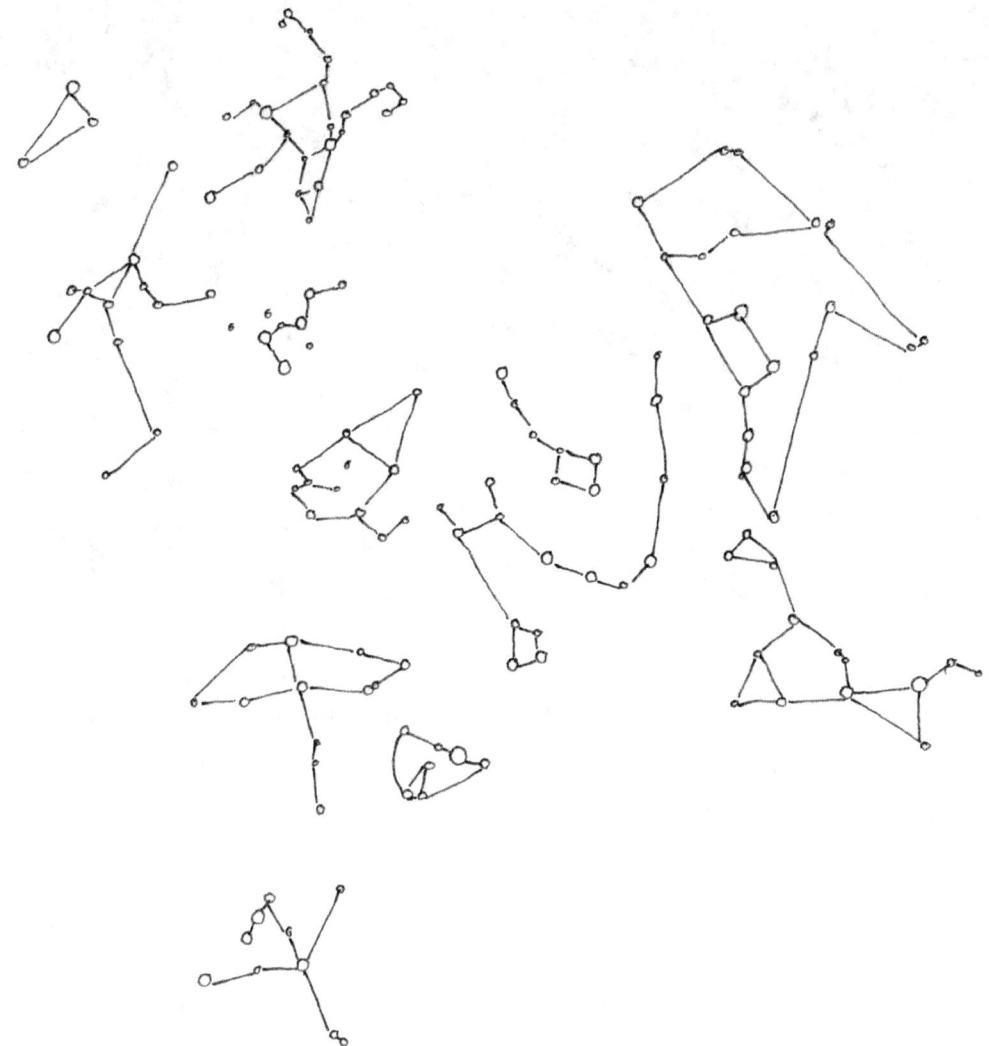

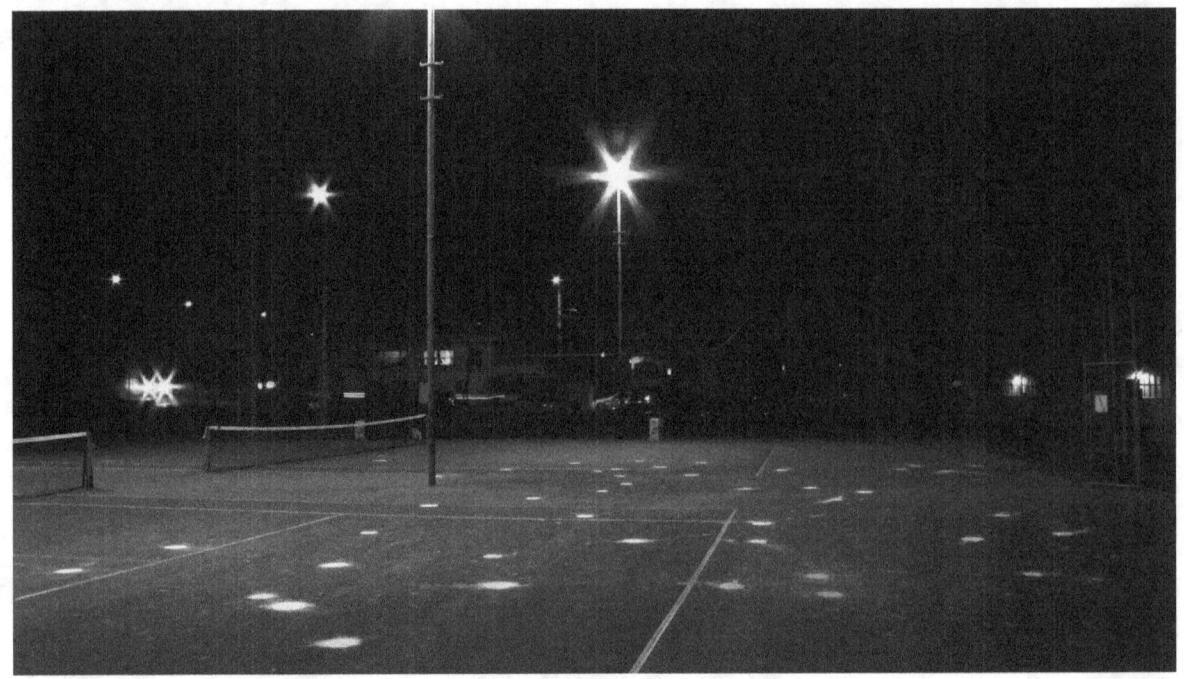

RECONSTRUCTING THE UNIVERSE: 12/3/08-4/26/09

I chose 144 stars that never set.   They are up there in the day too.
If you're reading this in the northern hemisphere, they are above
you right now.   My 144 stars form twelve constellations, among
them two lovers, two bears, a harp, dragon and swan. Every
culture has created a map of the sky, seeing images of themselves
between the bright points.   The stars that form the constellations
aren't really close together; they're just off in the same direction.
The shapes they form are relative and tell us more about our
location then theirs.   The constellations are the language that
makes the night sky legible.   It is not possible to learn the stars
one at a time. We group them together and tell ourselves a
story about those groups. This narrative is what transforms the
meaningless vastness into a navigable field.

We don't understand our lives as a series of individual events.
Families group events and people together and tell stories about
those groups.   This is the first story of who we are.   When my
mother got sick, the story my family was telling failed.   We
didn't have the narrative structure in place for a sudden ending.
We are rewriting the myth now, trying out different ways to
arrange our pasts so that the story makes sense in the present.
In the meantime, I am borrowing some stories that have been
told for a very long time.

LOOKING UP

Objective Cosmos: The physical universe and all its laws. Every
star, comet, galaxy, comet, quasar, nebula, and gamma ray
burst and all the rules, forces, and mysteries that govern their
existence. This cosmos is best understood by abandoning your
body and mentally escaping the earth's gravity. This universe is
measured in light-years and is rich in the magic of being a small
part of something vast and ordered and terrifying and beautiful.

Subjective Cosmos: The night sky and its entire splendor. A
breath interrupted by a shooting star and the exhalation
that follows, the cold grass soaking your shoulders. This is a
personal relationship conducted on earth, decoded by myths.
This universe is measured in lives and breaths and is rich in the
magic of being a small part of something vast and ordered and
terrifying and beautiful.

RECONSTRUCTING THE UNIVERSE: 12/3/08-4/26/09

During the 144 days that I knew my mother was dying, I felt
myself in orbit around this truth: this is supposed to happen.
Those of us who witness a parent's death are the lucky ones. This
is part of what it means to be human. This is the way time works.
One year later, for a 144-day interval, I am attempting to embody
both the cosmic and the human scale. I am mapping a new myth
that can hold the cold beauty of a world without my mother. I am
in a place that I do not recognize, and I am looking up.

The Moral Economy of the Land-Animal

Matthew David Rana

The first prayer, as I've heard it called subsequently, was loud and full of the large animals who, as they moved, stamped a river of mud through the acorns and the little fallen leaves that covered the land-animal. The drey was warm and my belly was close to full in the mottled mauve haze of evening. It had been a long day. But there, scampering up the tree in a state of mortal dread was Jimothy, bringing warning of the live creatures: "They are coming."

From my vantage point, I was able to sense their arrival well in advance of Jim's alarm. Not only could we hear their low collective murmur (so unlike our own), but we saw the tiny fires that they brought with them. Strangely, they were without food. Navigating past the threshold and onto the body of the land-animal, they converged at once, from all directions in a pungent co-mingling. We had seen things like this before. But those were typically festive occasions, equal in their loudness but with the large animals lumbering along directionless, vocalizing at random: the aroma coming not from the sheer number of bodies, but from their massive cargo of food.

That night, however, their lumbering was significantly more decisive, more intentional. They demonstrated affection on each other as they plunged their shovels and spades into the land-animal. Their vocalizations, garbled from their empty guts, carried with them a desperation, a solemnity typically absent. We knew, implicitly, that nothing would be the same after this. No more motionless beseeching, no more intent gazing--as though I were in fact the vulnerable one in my relative smallness-- into the curiously deep eyes of the large animals. From now on, they would save their bread. This is how we were ushered back from the time of plenty; so goes the cornucopia of my life, I thought.

"We must defend ourselves," Jim chirped. My sense of duty tends to prevent me from such convenient and impulsive maneuvering. What, Jim, was there to defend? "Our young! Our very right to life! Are we not creatures of the good? The thou of the oaks and the stewards of the land-animal?"

Indeed, was not the land-animal, in its present configuration and boundaries a creation of the large animals in the first instance? How would we even begin to defend those boundaries as you so call them? Furthermore, was it not they who overflow the super-abundance of our soft boxes? What do we have to fear?

"Everything, Theopold. Everything."

Now, I have always maintained that conflict in whatever form, whether it be with cats, crows, dogs, hawks, owls, raccoons, or every now and again the large-animals, is a part of our stream of existence, and, to a greater or lesser extent, punctuates it. If Jimothy or I were to be borne aloft in the grip of an owl's talons, so be it. Which is not to say that I am not pleased that we've avoided it thus far. I am pleased. This is to say that, for all its unusual qualities, the prayer seemed natural.

Survival, it must be understood, is being part of a system: I am a live-animal occupying a small but necessary niche within a broader ecology of live-animals. We play our role, that is, we each contribute in our own way to the natural. To that end, it is no great secret that we are seekers of pleasure. I, for one, dig. I seek out food and bury it in order to generate a surplus, a cache. I derive a peculiar satisfaction from putting my claws into the body of the land-animal: from scratching away at the top layer to the cool, damp soil. Which is to say nothing of how it feels when it clumps around my paws, its distinctive scent. It is a full, sensuous experience. It is a secret knowledge that I treasure within my fluff: a personal geography of the land-animal that is my gift. That a crow should, from its perch on hot wires, steal my cache, is natural. Whatever value the cache may possess in and of itself and inasmuch as it has a value as food, it may attain an even greater value in the belly of a crow than in my own. Because that is not always the case, the secret is knowing when to eat and when to bury. And, I should hasten to add, where to bury. I am not overly-precious with my surplus. I can live with less.

There have been times of disease and rain and famine. Those times were natural. There was a time before the time of plenty. That time was natural. Our lot has been to be adaptive, to scamper swiftly, abruptly: to attentively perch on our haunches. We are industrious. Generally speaking, we move with, never against. It is in our nature to be content, merrily going about our business... satisfying our endless curiosity on the body of the land-animal, in whatever configuration it presents itself. On this, we chattered deep into the night because, unfortunately for me, Jimothy did not see it this way. According to him, our purpose alone was the purpose.

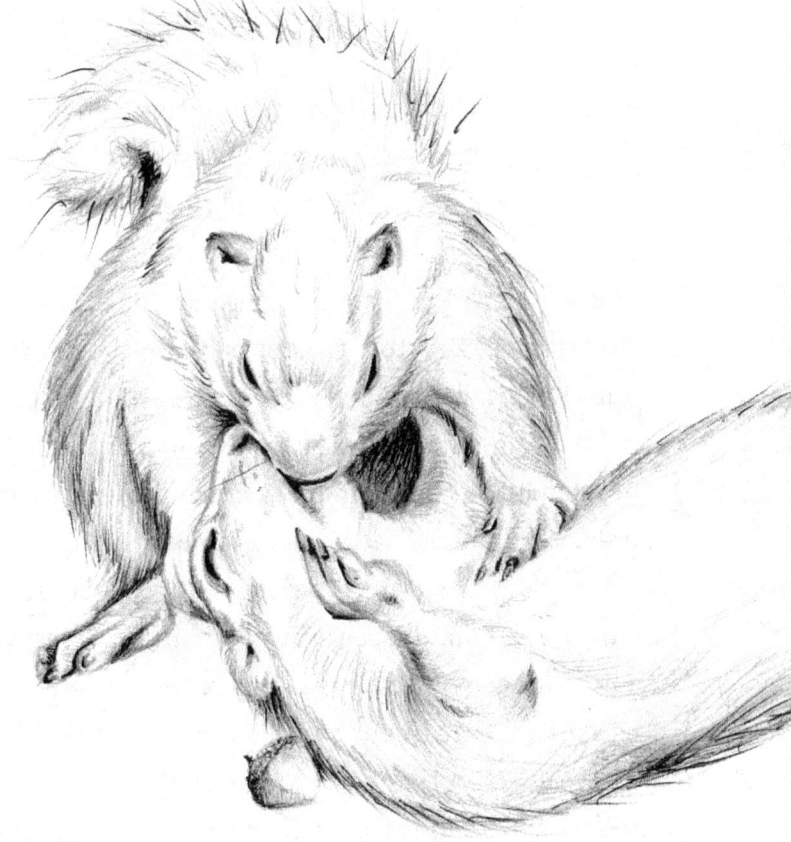

...

The land-animal has four corners, each of which is delineated more or less sharply by the threshold that connects them. It is subdivided into administrations: sand, hot-top, slick-top, top-top, creek, trees and dogs. These are further subdivided into parts which are then subdivided into individual sectors which, in turn, fall under tender. I should hasten to add that there is a subdivision boxes of which there are two sub-categories: soft and hard. The soft boxes contain food and are not fenced. Within them I can find many kinds of food: offerings from the large animals. The hard boxes are an extension of the land-animal itself and are fenced. They contain food which is an offering from the land animal. This food is the gift: the white root, the tasty leafy and the sliver seed. Though they grow on the old magnolia, I have never eaten a mushroom.

I am the soft box tender of sector g-2, which was a lovely little patch (and superabundant) adjacent to the hard boxes near the creek and opposite the sand. There are different administrations, different subdivisions of the land-animal beyond the threshold. I cannot pretend that I take no notice of the world beyond my boxes.

...

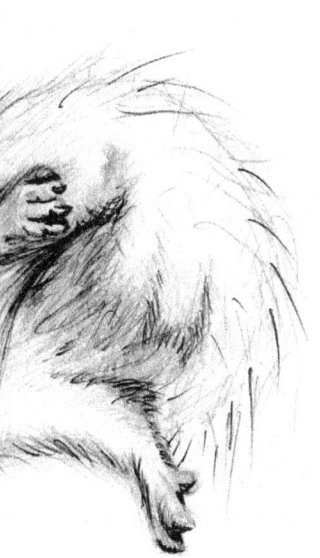

The first prayer was perhaps the first and only demonstration of pure love that I had, up to that point, witnessed between the large animals. Mostly I've borne witness to several demonstrations of displeasure and conflict between them. Of course, I have seen them demonstrate affection--in a manner of speaking. I had seen them on occasion laying beside each other, basking in our day and warming their smooth skin and expressing their love with their mouths, arms, legs and hands. I had even seen them attempt to demonstrate affection on their dogs. I should hasten to add, I have no love for dogs because they chase me and think I am food. It has happened that I once bit a dog on its back. It was a small thing, without fur and easy to make an example of. I remember the way it vocalized its pain. I remember scurrying down the fence and lying in wait.

Make no mistake, the first and, I might add, unambiguous sign of danger is a dog. A correction: either a dog or a raccoon... emerging, oily and rank from the orifice at the threshold of the land animal to prowl our boxes for food. They are, indeed, rabid and masked like thieves. The raccoon spirit is a dark spirit: a nightmare. Dogs are not dark spirits; they are stupid.

...

The second prayer was far from optimal and based on a logic of maximal extraction. I say "far from optimal" in that it seemed to be without purpose. I say "maximal extraction" because they never put anything in the land-animal to be reburied. There was surplus, but no cache.

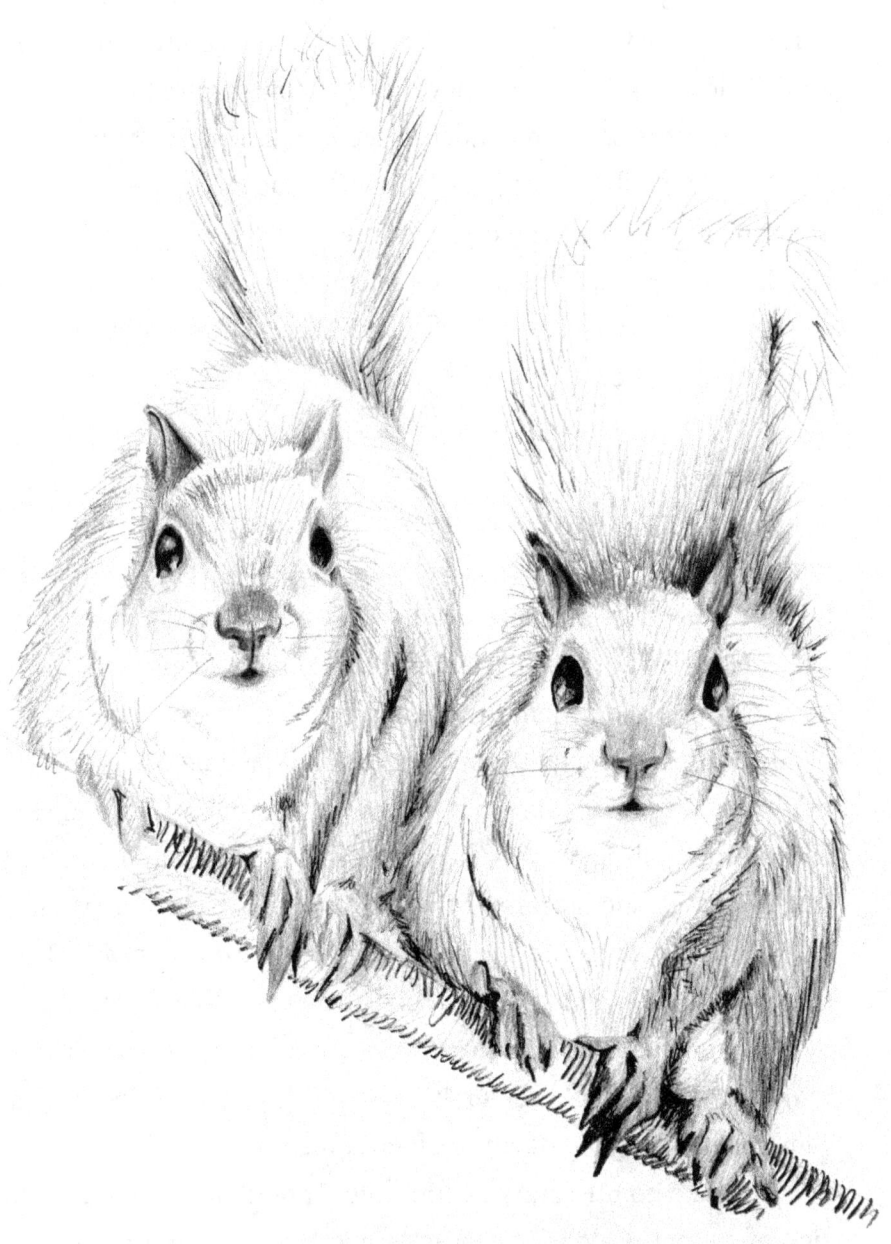

It happened early in the day, just as I was foraging in
my boxes for any remaining food that had not been scavenged
by dark spirits. I am somewhat embarrassed to admit that,
at the time, I was so involved that I hardly smelled them as
they approached. The large animals congregated on the creek.
Increasingly pungent as they toiled, they drove their shovels and
spades deep into the land animal, re-contouring the creek bed
into tiny mountains. They put things in large noisy sacks as they
moved along the water. They cut the brambles and picked the sour
berries, putting hand to mouth as they dug into evening. The bays
arched over the dogwoods.

Pleased with what they had done, they scampered out of the creek, flinging aside their spades and shedding their adornments. The large animals rolled in the mud that they had made, demonstrating their affection on each other, and washing themselves in the creek. It was strange how they danced, alternately grouped in rows and without any discernible purpose. Some danced slowly, arms extended, legs bent slightly at the knee, balancing, rotating. Some danced with abandon and immoderation. Some curled in to a ball and sustained vocalizations. Jimothy looked on in silence. "What do they make?"

The air grew cool around us as we sat watching the large animals dancing into exhaustion. It was already night before we returned to the drey. I have very few regrets. May they make what they make forever. This cannot be good.

...

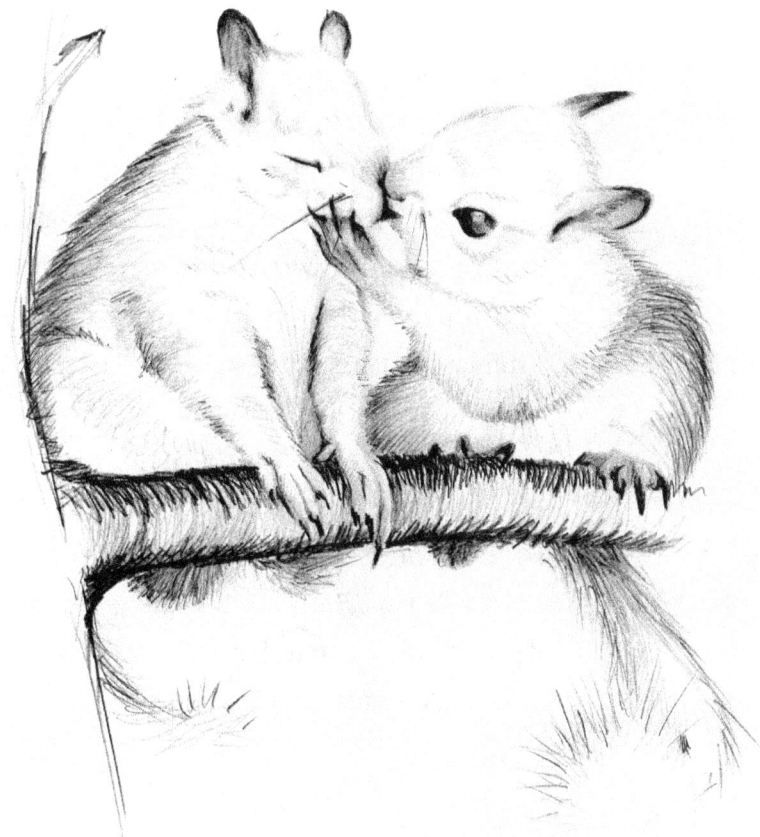

Ride the Elephant

Ted Purves

"Can a public really exist apart from the rhetoric through which it is imagined?"

- Michael Warner, Publics and Counterpublics, 2005

I recently spent a day with my son at an amusement park, being thrown around by high-tensile steel machines, propelled by roller-coaster cars down 90 ft. plunges, and spun through the air with my feet dangling below. I enjoyed it more than I ever would have imagined.

Towards the end of our day, we wandered past a sign offering elephant rides. How could we not get on? After a day of being strapped into the ergonomic vehicles that both convey you through and protect you from the intense physics of thrill rides, the process of learning how to sit on an elephants back presented an alternate challenge. I remember the rigidity of its spine, the impossible rough density of its skin, the power of its swaying gait. It was the only ride offered to us that we could have actually fallen off of.

After spending much of the fall tramping through Golden Gate Park with the Social Practice Workshop, I found myself most enthralled with its incoherence rather than its beauty. It is usually more enjoyable to go to parks than to write about them, so it seems best to keep this brief. I want to thank all the participants in the workshop for the patience and curiosity they brought to the year. It is difficult to become a public together. Thinking back to the amusement park, I recall it mainly as a series of offers. Over here, you can see this. Come here, and you may ride this. Between the roller-coaster and the elephant are two lessons. I learn them again and again. It takes courage to get on. It takes balance to stay on.

-Ted Purves, Oakland, 2009

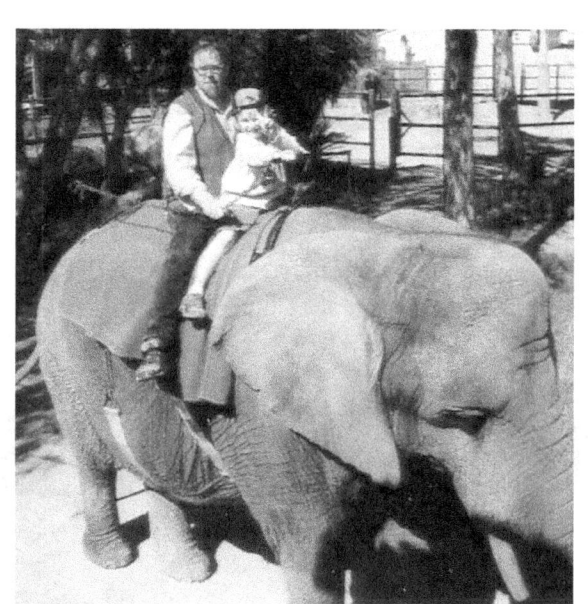

Biographical Information

Iain Boal is an Irish social historian of technics and the commons, a member of the Retort collective, a group of writers, artisans and artists based in the San Francisco Bay Area. He is one of the authors of Retort's *Afflicted Powers: Capital and Spectacle in a New Age of War* (London, Verso, 2006) and co-editor with James Brook of *Resisting the Virtual Life: The Culture and Politics of Information* (San Francisco: City Lights 1995)

Amy Franceschini is a pollinator working in various media trying to understand the cultural perception of conflict between humans and nature. Her projects encourage formats of engagement and production. Often taking form as long-term collaborations, her projects reveal ways that local politics are affected by globalization. Amy founded Futurefarmers in 1995, and Free Soil in 2004. Her solo and collaborative work have been included in exhibitions internationally including ZKM, Whitney Museum, the New York Museum of Modern Art and Yerba Buena Center for the Arts, San Francisco. She received her BFA from San Francisco State University and her MFA from Stanford University. She is currently a professor of Art + Architecture at University of San Francisco and a visiting faculty at California College of the Arts.

Malak Helmy is an artist working in Cairo and San Francisco. She is currently an MFA candidate in Social Practice at the California College of Art in San Francisco. She earned her BA in Performing and Visual Arts and Islamic Art and Architecture from the American University in Cairo and the University of Washington, Seattle. Helmy co-founded Pericentre Projects in October 2008 who recently curated the Kharita Symposium on Urban Trajectories in Cairo. www.pericentreprojects.org

Forrest Lewinger is an artist and musician living and working in San Francisco. He has just recently graduated from the California College of the Arts in the Social Practice area of concentration. Look for him everywhere.

Anthony Marcellini's practice is focused on generating spaces to consider how to have a world. He is driven by moments when moves are made towards greater expressions of freedom or realizing utopian dreams. These moments maybe fleeting and precarious but they liberate how we live and perform in our everyday lives. His aim is to use art, writing and curating as tools to, not simply demonstrate how we might make things better, but to make a better world, a reality. From 2000-2004 Anthony co-founded and directed the artists collaborative, *It Can Change*, a collective which produced art, interventions, and performances in public and private sites. From 2004-2007 Anthony was the Curatorial Assistant at the non-profit gallery Art in General. He will complete his MFA in Social Practice at California College of the Arts in spring 2009.

marksearch, an Oakland wife-husband team, has been creating community art projects since 2000. In their unique brand of interdisciplinary art, marksearch creates interactive projects inviting people to reflect upon their communities and increase their awareness of the natural environment within the urban fabric. These ecologically and socially-based projects rely on daily life experience, weaving the needs and views of local agencies and the public with the specific qualities of local history, the built environment, and the ecosystem. Using kinetic vehicles, traveling signage, unconventional surveys, and official logos, they craft a conversational commons, pushing the boundaries of how community-based art can influence public policy.

Lauren Marsden is part of the East Vancouver diaspora and is currently pursuing her love of trains, freeway greenery, and other people's homes. Recently, she was a board member of the non-profit art space, the *fifty fifty arts collective* in Victoria, BC and the Public Art Committee for the City of Vancouver. She was a recipient of the Helen Pitt Fund award for visual arts as well as the British Columbia Arts Council Scholarship. Her art practice is based on local research and public installations, which explore tensions between civic, corporate, and personal spaces. Some themes and materials include signage, archives, stories, and urban mythology. She is currently living and working in the Excelsior district of San Francisco.

Lynne McCabe is a multi- disciplinary artist who's interactive works focus on a process led and collaborative practice, creating work that is the product of social engagement and negotiation. McCabe designs environments whereby she can manipulate socially constructed notions of authority and trust. By referencing cultural indicators of safety, intimacy, and authority McCabe actively and cooperatively investigates the subtle negotiations of power and truth within a social context. McCabe is currently pursuing an MFA at California College of the Arts and is the founder of SHE WORKS FLEXIBLE NOW, a critical artistic exploration centered in Berkeley, CA. Largely dematerialized, which houses' a variety of artistic endeavors from child rearing to occasional performances to project research and development. It houses a library, an exhibition and performance space, and a fireside discussion forum.

Originally from Scotland McCabe received her B.A with honors from The Glasgow School of Art in 1999 and held a residency at The School of the Art Institute, Chicago in 1996. She was a recipient of a 2008 Artadia Award and when asked her son and frequent collaborator describes her as 61 years old, 8ft tall and most like Batgirl than any other cartoon character.

myvillages.org is an international artist initiative, founded in 2003 by Kathrin Böhm (D/UK), Wapke Feenstra (NL) and Antje Schiffers (D). Our interest is the rural as a space for and of cultural production. Myvillages.org activities range from small scale informal presentations to long term collaborative research projects, from work in private spaces to public conferences, from exhibitions to publications and from personal questions to public debate.
Ongoing projects include:
- *Bibliobox*, a travelling archive. The box contains information about art projects in the rural context and can be folded out to reveal a small presentation.
- *I like being a farmer and I would like to stay one*, a project with European farmers. Oil paintings of farms are bartered for videos made by farmers.
- *International village shop*, an initiative to trade and exchange rural produce across rural networks. In cooperation with locals and institutions we constantly develop new produce for our shop.
- *Former Farmland.* While you are standing on their former farmland farmers change their knowledge with you via mobile phone.

Find more at www.myvillages.org

Piero Passacantando is an artist and teacher currently based in the Bay Area. He explores the possibilities of an artistic practice rooted in curiosity, play and experimentation. Starting from the perspective that life is ultimately a mystery to be explored without a preconceived destination, Piero moves across genres, medias and themes. He then constructs heterogeneous installations from discreet works, aiming at representing the non-linearity of his creative process.

Oda Projesi is an artist collective based in Istanbul composed of Özge Açıkkol, Güneş Savaş and Seçil Yersel. In 2000, they begun running a multi-purpose 45 square-meters space in Galata, which functioned as a non-profit space with zero budget, hosting nearly 30 projects. They focused on shifting the usual role of the audience and notions of public space in the contemporary art scene. In 2005, they were evicted due to the neighborhood's process of gentrification. Since then Oda Projesi has a mobile status and continues to raise questions on space and place with relationship models by using different mediums and different spaces like radio stations, books, postcards, newspapers or giving form to different meeting points. Exhibitions include: Documentaries in 5533 art space and *17' Necati Bey* in Hafriyat in İstanbul; *Don't Step on The Green* in Yerba Buena Art Center, San Francisco; *conglomeration map* in the 3rd Guangzhou Triennial, China; *15x75m Hingucken-Weggucken* in Wilhelmsburger Freitag in Hamburg.
For further info: http://www.odaprojesi.org

Ted Purves is a writer and artist based in Oakland. His public projects and curatorial works are centered on investigating the practice of art in the world, particularly as it addresses issues of localism, democratic participation, and innovative shifts in the position of the audience. He produces socially-based projects in collaboration with Susanne Cockrell under the umbrella name of Fieldfaring (www.fieldfaring. org). Their recent project The Meadow Network, was initiated as a part of the exhibition *The Gatherers, Greening our Urban Spheres*, at the Yerba Buena Center for the Arts in San Francisco. He was the founder of the MFA concentration in Social Practice at California College of the Arts in 2005, and is currently the Chair of the MFA Fine Arts Program. Purves's book, What We Want is Free: Generosity and Exchange in Recent Art, was published by SUNY Press in 2005.

Rebecca Ora, intrigued by skewed and warped relationships, works in cinematic, photographic, and theatrical media. Her current oeuvre explores the phenomena of the eccentric in everyday life. Addressing ambiguous ethics and the spectacular, Rora has attended artist-in-residency programs in Arad, Israel; Johnson, Vermont; and New Delhi, India. She now works toward her MFA through California College of the Arts.

Matthew David Rana is an artist and writer based in Oakland, California. His recent projects are a form of social documentary and reportage. Part of a broader investigation into the construction of counter-narratives, his comics, newspapers and zines foster person to person exchange while exploring the conflicts and desires that are part of our everyday experience. These projects are unified by an interest in the relationships between text and image, theory and practice, and issues surrounding economic participation and involvement in public life.
Matthew's work has been shown nationally including Los Angeles and New York, and internationally in Sweden and Italy. He is currently pursuing a dual MFA/MA in Social Practice and Visual & Critical Studies at the California College of the Arts. He holds a BFA in Art Studio from the University of New Mexico.

Ruth Robbins is a nomadic artist and ceremonialist currently based in Oakland. She is happiest when working outdoors and inhabiting the intersections of lighting, installation, science and ritual. She works in a variety of media to create spaces of mental and emotional promiscuity that order to excite the collective social imaginary. While working Ruth is guided by pleasure, delight and desire and considers these sensations to be a meaningful forms of participation for her audiences. She is currently leading a clandestine star gazing society dedicated to re-uniting subjective and objective experiences of the night sky.

Michael Swaine is an artist and inventor. His projects include *Reap What You Sew: Generosity Project* for which he pushed an old-fashioned ice cream-style cart with a sewing machine on it through San Francisco, sewing and repairing clothes for anyone who requested it. His work has been exhibited at Yerba Buena Center for the Arts, Southern Exposure gallery, and Headlands Center for the Arts. Swaine studied advanced ceramics and sculpture at the School of the Art Institute of Chicago. Since 1999, he has worked as part of the artists collective Futurefarmers.

Nick Tobier is a public performer whose work is rooted in the social lives of public places. He studied landscape architecture at Harvard's Graduate School of Design and subsequently worked as a landscape architect in private practice and with the NYC Parks Department, Bronx Division. Tobier's interest in the potential of public places has manifested itself in built public projects and actions in San Francisco, Detroit and New York, internationally from Toronto to Tokyo.

Brindalyn Webster is an MFA (Social Practice) candidate at CCA. Whether it is between Webster and a the person she is interviewing, or the audience and the resulting work of art, providing space and attention in the act of listening is an essential act in her work. Her project SUPERMARKETS (a collection of songs that help vendors at Bay Area Farmers' Market work) is currently traveling through Europe in the media archive Bibliobox. In 2008, she organized and conducted a multi-lingual sing along in Bergsjon, a suburb made up of immigrants and refugees in Sweden. Traditionally, Swedish 'All Sangs' are composed of folk songs promoting nationalism through group singing. BERGSJON PUBLIC ALL SANG was a collection of childrens songs sung by the refugees in their mother language. Songbooks were provided to encourage singing along. Her work can be viewed at www.brindalyn.com

Anna Whitehead makes videos, music, and performances exploring the formation and presentaiton of oppositional racial, sexual and gender identities through dance, masquerade, minstrelsy, and collaboration. Often, these oppositional identities tend to speak a language of wandering freedom – or homelessness, depending on one's perspective. Having lived or spent significant time in the United States, France, England, Burkina Faso, and Jamaica – as well as in a multitude of gendered and racial skins – she has found that what is oppositional shifts according to ones' spatial context. Thus it is that her interests reside in the spaces (like the space of urban gentrification) that create a perfect storm of loss, restlessness, wandering, and new definitions of home. She frequently performs as Jailbird Thunderheart or as one half of the bicoastal multimedia performance troupe Eating the Other.

Image Credits

About the publisher

Practice & Practice publishes and distributes digital and physical books featuring art projects that engage in systems or economies that extend beyond or outside of a gallery context. These curated publications are constructed as a vehicle for the discussion and dissemination of projects that, because of their chosen form, may have previously been excluded from a larger dialog.

A note on the type

I'm a Park and You're a Deer was set in Gentium, a typeface designed by Victor Gaultney and opened to world-wide contribution and collaboration in 2005. It is available for use, modification, and redistribution under the SIL Open Font License. The type takes its name from the Latin word meaning *of the nations*. This choice reflects its primary goal of encouraging international publication through the offering of an extended family of glyphs. The ever broadening family of typefaces called Gentium offer high readability, economy of space, and an efficient, yet delicate letterform.